"This book provides an overview of the magnitude and measurement of gambling-related harms as well as the various prevention and treatment approaches available to minimize these harms. This book is exceptionally comprehensive, timely, and written by many of the leaders in the field. An essential resource for policy makers, clinicians, and researchers. Highly recommended."

– **Professor Robert Williams**, Faculty of Health Sciences and
Coordinator, Alberta Gambling Research Institute, Canada

"For most primary care professionals, this book transports us to a new field of addictive disorder. Comprehensive and insightful, it gives an excellent example of the application of public health to the field of gambling. After reading this book, healthcare professionals and those concerned by addictions will have a clear understanding of a modern public health approach, which is based on the latest knowledge and human rights."

– **Professor Idris Guessous**, Head of the Division of Primary
Care Medicine, Geneva University Hospitals, Switzerland

HARM REDUCTION FOR GAMBLING

This edited volume aims to facilitate the evolution of the new public health approach towards gambling. Bringing together the work of international experts, it gives a current overview of the field, highlighting the need for a coordinated framework of prevention and harm reduction measures to replace current "player protection" measures.

Chapters begin by exploring the impact of problem gambling, looking at its effects on several levels, ranging from the individual to the family and society. Subsequently, an overview of prevention and harm reduction models is presented, bringing the reader to an in-depth understanding of what a public health approach to gambling would entail. Later chapters focus on potential challenges to monitoring and evaluation, inviting the reader to envisage possible barriers towards implementation and ways of overcoming these. The book concludes with recommendations on how to take a harm reduction approach, from a political and human rights perspective.

This work gives a rare synopsis of the present-day issues when considering the implementation of a harm reduction strategy for gambling. Recent work by key professionals is presented in order to encourage further developments in this ever-changing domain. Such issues will be relevant to all those with an interest in the field of problem gambling, from clinicians, students and healthcare professionals, to politicians.

Henrietta Bowden-Jones is a Medical Doctor specialising in Addiction Psychiatry. She is the Founder and Director of the National Problem Gambling Clinic, UK, and President of the Medical Women's Federation. She is an Honorary Clinical Senior Lecturer at the Faculty of Medicine, Imperial College, UK.

Cheryl Dickson has a Doctoral Degree in Clinical Psychology. She specialised post-qualification in the field of problem gambling and has worked since 2009 for the Centre du jeu excessif (Centre for Excessive Gambling), Lausanne University Hospital, Switzerland.

Caroline Dunand is a Psychologist who has worked for over ten years as a Research Fellow at the Centre du jeu excessif (Centre for Excessive Gambling), Lausanne University Hospital, Switzerland.

Olivier Simon is a Psychiatrist with a Master of Public Health Degree. He is Head of the Centre du jeu excessif (Centre for Excessive Gambling), Lausanne University Hospital, and Senior Lecturer at the Faculty of Biology and Medicine at University of Lausanne, Switzerland.

HARM REDUCTION FOR GAMBLING

A Public Health Approach

Edited by Henrietta Bowden-Jones, Cheryl Dickson, Caroline Dunand and Olivier Simon

LONDON AND NEW YORK

First published 2020
by Routledge
2 Park Square, Milton Park, Abingdon, Oxon OX14 4RN

and by Routledge
52 Vanderbilt Avenue, New York, NY 10017

Routledge is an imprint of the Taylor & Francis Group, an informa business

© 2020 selection and editorial matter, Henrietta Bowden-Jones, Cheryl Dickson, Caroline Dunand and Olivier Simon; individual chapters, the contributors

The right of Henrietta Bowden-Jones, Cheryl Dickson, Caroline Dunand and Olivier Simon to be identified as the authors of the editorial material, and of the authors for their individual chapters, has been asserted in accordance with sections 77 and 78 of the Copyright, Designs and Patents Act 1988.

All rights reserved. No part of this book may be reprinted or reproduced or utilised in any form or by any electronic, mechanical, or other means, now known or hereafter invented, including photocopying and recording, or in any information storage or retrieval system, without permission in writing from the publishers.

Trademark notice: Product or corporate names may be trademarks or registered trademarks, and are used only for identification and explanation without intent to infringe.

British Library Cataloguing-in-Publication Data
A catalogue record for this book is available from the British Library

Library of Congress Cataloging-in-Publication Data
A catalog record for this book has been requested

ISBN: 978-1-138-59093-9 (hbk)
ISBN: 978-1-138-59095-3 (pbk)
ISBN: 978-0-429-49075-0 (ebk)

Typeset in Bembo
by Apex CoVantage, LLC

CONTENTS

Contributor biographies	*x*
Preface	*xvii*
Nady el-Guebaly	
Acknowledgements	*xx*

Introduction	1
Cheryl Dickson, Caroline Dunand, Olivier Simon and	
Henrietta Bowden-Jones	

SECTION I
Impact and current understanding of gambling disorder — 3

1 Gambling and democracy *Peter J. Adams*	5
2 Measuring harm from gambling and estimating its distribution in the population *Matthew Browne*	14
3 The social cost of excessive gambling *Claude Jeanrenaud, Mélanie Gay, Dimitri Kohler, Jacques Besson and Olivier Simon*	23
4 The normalisation of dangerous gambling: an ethical issue *Jim Orford*	36

viii Contents

5 Family members affected by excessive gambling 45
   Jim Orford

6 Neurocognitive components of gambling disorder:
   implications for assessment, treatment and policy 54
   *Juan F. Navas, Joël Billieux, Antonio Verdejo-García and
   José C. Perales*

SECTION II
Harm reduction models and initiatives 69

7 Defining harm reduction as part of a public health
   approach towards gambling 71
   *Olivier Simon, Jean-Félix Savary, Gabriel Guarrasi and
   Cheryl Dickson*

8 Effective harm minimisation practices: public health
   implications 78
   Darren R. Christensen

9 Harm prevention and reduction efforts in gambling
   disorder: an international perspective 91
   Charles Livingstone

10 The role of treatment in reducing gambling-related harm 102
   David C. Hodgins and Magdalen Schluter

11 Public health and gambling: the potential of *nudge* policies 112
   Magaly Brodeur

12 Early detection of at-risk gambling to reduce harm 120
   Suzanne Lischer

13 Behavioural tracking in gambling: the use and efficacy
   of online responsible gambling tools 128
   Mark D. Griffiths

SECTION III
Challenges to evaluation and monitoring 141

14 A logical framework for the evaluation of a harm reduction
   policy for gambling 143
   Jean-Michel Costes

Contents **ix**

15 Is income derived from problem gambling a good
assessment indicator of a responsible gambling strategy?   153
Jean-Michel Costes

16 Challenges of online gambling for risk and harm reduction   162
Louise Nadeau, Magali Dufour, Richard Guay, Sylvia Kairouz,
Jean-Marc Ménard and Catherine Paradis

Conclusion   172
Cheryl Dickson, Caroline Dunand, Olivier Simon and
Henrietta Bowden-Jones

Index   *175*

CONTRIBUTOR BIOGRAPHIES

Peter J. Adams practiced initially for 13 years as a clinical psychologist in hospital, community and private practice settings. This led to his current role as a Professor in the School of Population Health and Associate Director of the Centre for Addiction Research at the University of Auckland. He has published widely on addictions including gambling and impacts on families. He has published five sole-authored books, three with high relevance to gambling research and services: *Gambling, Freedom and Democracy* (NY: Routledge), *Fragmented Intimacy: Addiction in a Social World* (NY: Springer) and *Moral Jeopardy: Risks of Accepting Money from the Tobacco, Alcohol and Gambling Industries* (Cambridge University Press, 2016).

Jacques Besson is Honorary Professor of Psychiatry at the University of Lausanne. He is the former Head of the Community Psychiatry service at the Lausanne University Hospital. He was the founder and leader of the Addiction units, including the Centre du jeu excessif (Centre for Excessive Gambling). He is now Invited Professor at the Institute of Humanities in Medicine at the University of Lausanne. His interests in research include the relationships between neuroscience and spirituality and between psychiatry and religion.

Joël Billieux is Associate Professor of Clinical Psychology and Psychopathology at the University of Luxembourg. He holds a PhD in Psychology from the University of Geneva, Switzerland. His main area of research concerns the psychological factors (cognitive, affective, motivational) involved in the etiology of addictive behaviours, with a particular focus on self-regulation-related processes. He is also interested in the conceptualisation and diagnosis of behavioural addictions. He is an expert in a World Health Organization workgroup related to the public health implications of behavioural addictions associated with the excessive use of information and communications technologies (ICTs), and a board member of the International Society for the Study of Behavioral Addictions (ISSBA).

Contributor biographies **xi**

Henrietta Bowden-Jones is the Founder and Director of the National Problem Gambling Clinic, the first NHS service designated to treat problem gambling in the UK, now in its eleventh year. She is the Spokesperson on Behavioural Addictions for the Royal College of Psychiatrists, Honorary Clinical Senior Lecturer in the Department of Medicine, Imperial College, and President of the Medical Women's Federation in the UK and Fellow of the Royal College of Psychiatrists. Dr Bowden-Jones is a member of the Addictions Executive Committee at the Royal College of Psychiatrists and a board member of the International Society of Addiction Medicine (ISAM). She was made an Officer of the British Empire OBE in the New Year's Honours 2019 for Services to Addiction Treatment and to Research.

Magaly Brodeur is the Resident-Doctor at the Faculty of Medicine and Health Sciences at the University of Sherbrooke (Canada). She has a PhD in the public health sector and has worked since 2004 on the subject of gambling. Her main area of expertise is the analysis and management of public policies. She is the author of one of the very few books available on the history of gambling in Quebec. She has also received numerous awards and research grants, including a prestigious scholarship from the Trudeau Foundation.

Matthew Browne is Associate Professor of Psychology and a member of the Experimental Gambling Research Laboratory at Central Queensland University. He has recently led several major research projects focusing on quantifying the social impact of gambling for statutory authorities in Australia and New Zealand. His main area of research is in health-related and addictive behaviours, as well as delusional beliefs. He is interested in all aspects of computational statistics, psychometrics and quantitative methods for the social sciences.

Darren R. Christensen received his PhD in Psychology from the University of Canterbury, New Zealand. He has previously worked at the University of Arkansas for Medical Sciences and at the University of Melbourne examining the efficacy of contingency management as a treatment for substance dependence and problem gambling. He is currently the Chair in Gambling sponsored by the Alberta Gambling Research Institute in the Faculty of Health Sciences at the University of Lethbridge. His research includes developing behavioural and pharmacological treatments for problem gambling, neuroimaging of problem gamblers and evaluations of harm minimisation measures.

Jean-Michel Costes, sociologist, demographer and epidemiologist, comes from research direction at the Ministry of Health. He was Director of the French Monitoring Centre on Drugs and Drug Addictions (OFDT) from 1995 to 2011. He is currently the Secretary-General of the French Monitoring Centre on Gambling whose mission is to study gambling patterns and gambling-related social impact in France.

xii Contributor biographies

Cheryl Dickson is a UK qualified clinical psychologist with experience in clinical work and research. She specialised, post-qualification, in the field of gambling disorders. Since 2009, she has been working in collaboration with the Centre du jeu excessif (Centre for Excessive Gambling), Lausanne University Hospital, where she has been involved in numerous publications and written presentations on the subject of gambling and substance disorder. Dr Dickson held a key role in organising the 3rd and 4th International Multidisciplinary Symposia on Excessive Gambling, as chairperson the English-speaking Committee.

Magali Dufour is a Doctor in Psychology and Professor at the University of Quebec in Montreal (UQAM). She's part of the HERMES team, at the Institut sur les dépendances and at the Charles-Lemoyne Research Centre. She is interested in behavioural addictions, including gambling disorder and Internet addiction and has published numerous articles on those subjects. She has been part of the Online Gambling Working Group and is currently a member of the Low-Risk Guidelines Working Group. She is presently conducting various clinical and research projects amongst poker players, problematic Internet users and amongst young who have at-risk behaviours.

Caroline Dunand is a psychologist and research fellow who has worked, since 2008, for the Centre du jeu excessif (Centre for Excessive Gambling), Lausanne University Hospital. She collaborated in a training project for the Certificate of Advanced Studies, working with Lausanne University Hospital and The Lausanne Federal Institute of Technology. She was involved in developing an e-learning tool to train doctors and medico-social professionals in the field of addictive disorders. She provides regular editing and reviewing support to institutions in the field of excessive gambling.

Nady el-Guebaly is Professor and Head, Division of Addiction, Department of Psychiatry at the University of Calgary, Canada. He is Past Board Chair and Past Research Director of the Alberta Gambling Research Institute. He is the Founding Past President of the International Society of Addiction Medicine. He is Editor-in-Chief of the *Canadian Journal of Addiction* and Senior Editor of *Textbook of Addiction Treatment: International Perspectives.* Dr el-Guebaly was appointed as a Member of the Order of Canada.

Mélanie Gay has a master's degree in Economics from the University of Neuchâtel. During her studies she was involved in several research projects, in collaboration with Professor Claude Jeanrenaud. The main focus of her work was the development of a new approach to estimate the productivity cost of gambling disorders. In particular, she developed a methodology that aimed to assess indirect morbidity costs. Since 2013, she has been working as an economist at the Swiss Federal Office of Energy.

Contributor biographies **xiii**

Mark D. Griffiths is a chartered psychologist and Distinguished Professor of Behavioural Addiction at the Nottingham Trent University and Director of the International Gaming Research Unit. He is internationally known for his work on gambling and gaming addictions has published over 730 refereed research papers, five books, 150+ book chapters and over 1000 other articles. Dr Griffiths has won 19 national and international awards for his work. He also does a lot of freelance journalism and has appeared on over 3000 radio and television programmes and written over 350 articles for national and international newspapers and magazines.

Gabriel Guarrasi has a master's degree in Clinical Psychology and Psychopathology from the University of Lausanne. He has been working with perpetrators of domestic violence since 2019 at the Centre Prévention de l'Ale. His interests include the psychotherapeutic effect of acting in a clinical setting and work in the addiction field. Following a placement as Research Collaborator at the Centre du jeu excessif (Centre for Excessive Gambling), Lausanne University Hospital, he is currently working on clinical research into motivational interviewing with young people with alcohol concerns at the University's Service of Addiction Medicine.

Richard Guay has had a long career with the Royal Canadian Mounted Police and the Ministry of Public Safety of Quebec. He is currently the Director of Verification and Investigation for the Office of the Quebec Commissioner of Lobbying.

David C. Hodgins is a Killam Annual Professor of Clinical Psychology at the Department of Psychology, University of Calgary, and is a research coordinator with the Alberta Gambling Research Institute. He is also a registered clinical psychologist. His research interests focus on various aspects of addictive behaviours including relapse and recovery from substance abuse and gambling disorders.

Claude Jeanrenaud is Professor Emeritus at the Faculty of Economics and Business, University of Neuchâtel (Switzerland). He holds a PhD in Economics from the University of Neuchâtel. He has been teaching public economics and public finance since 1996 and has published several articles, research papers and technical reports on the social cost of addiction (smoking, alcohol and gambling disorders, use of illicit drugs). He has undertaken consultation work with the Swiss Federal Government, several Swiss cantons, the Organisation de coopération et de développement économiques (OECD) and the World Bank Institute.

Sylvia Kairouz is Associate Professor in the Department of Sociology and Anthropology at Concordia University. She published extensively in sociology, social epidemiology and public health journals and won the Brain Star Award of the Canadian Institute of Health Research for her innovative work on the role of social contexts in addictive behaviours. Dr Kairouz is currently engaged in funded research examining comprehensive multilevel models of determinants of gambling behaviours. She has piloted six large population surveys in Quebec over the last

xiv Contributor biographies

five years and collaborates with scholars and key institutions in Quebec, Canada and internationally. She holds a Fonds de recherche du Québec – Société et culture (FQRSC) research chair on the study of gambling and is the head of the Lifestyle and Addiction Research Lab at Concordia University.

Dimitri Kohler has a PhD in Health Economics from the University of Neuchâtel. He has been involved in several social cost studies of addictive disorders (tobacco, alcohol, gambling), and particularly in estimating the health-related quality of life (HRQoL) costs associated with gambling disorder. He worked at the Swiss Health Observatory between 2012 and 2016 on projects measuring the quality of hospital services in Switzerland and bed planning for cantonal nursing homes. He currently works at the Swiss Cancer League, where his research focus is cost and reimbursement for cancer treatments.

Suzanne Lischer has worked as Lecturer and Project Manager at Lucerne University of Applied Sciences and Arts – School of Social Work (HSLU) since 2008. She has been the Head of the Competence Centre for Prevention and Health, Lucerne, Switzerland, since 2017. Her main teaching and research interests are harm-reduction in gambling and public health for addictive disorders. In recent years, she has worked on various research projects with an emphasis on early detection in the gambling sector. She has also worked, as an external professional, to develop social concepts for Swiss casinos, in accordance with the Swiss Casino Act.

Charles Livingstone is Associate Professor in the School of Public Health and Preventive Medicine, Monash University. He is also head of the Gambling and Social Determinants Unit within the School of Public Health and Preventative Medicine. He has research degrees in Economics and Social Theory. Dr Livingstone's current principal research interest is critical gambling studies, including, in particular, gambling policy reform and the politics, regulation and social impacts of electronic gambling machine (EGM) playing. He was a member of the Australian Government's Ministerial Expert Advisory Group on Gambling 2010–2012. He contributes regularly to public debate around gambling issues via media and otherwise and committed to developing research knowledge into forms that that can better inform policymaking and public debate.

Jean-Marc Ménard is a clinical psychologist, graduated from the University of Quebec at Trois-Rivières. He is a senior advisor in mental health and addiction at the Integrated University Health and Social Services Centre of Mauricie and Centre-du-Québec, Clinical Director of the Research and intervention group on psychoactive substances Quebec (RISQ), Lecturer at the University of Sherbrooke and member of the Clinical Excellence Committee on Mental Health, Dependence and Youth and Family Services at the National Institute of Health and Social Services Quebec.

Contributor biographies **xv**

Louise Nadeau, Professor Emeritus at the Department of Psychology, University of Montreal, is an Elected Fellow of the Royal Society of Canada (2015) and the Canadian Academy of Health Sciences (2016) and was awarded l'Ordre national du Québec (2017) and the Order of Canada (2018). Dr Nadeau's multicentric and transdisciplinary research focuses on the prediction of recidivism amongst high-risk drivers convicted for driving under the influence, the co-occurring disorders in addictions and behavioural addictions such as gambling and Internet addiction.

Juan F. Navas is a researcher from the Mind, Brain and Behaviour Research Centre at the University of Granada, Spain, and has authored numerous papers on affective dysregulation in gambling disorder. His interests involve the transference of basic research to applied contexts, and he currently collaborates with the Andalusian Federation of Rehabilitated Gamblers in improving treatment protocols for gambling disorder. Before beginning his academic career, he led several projects aimed at reducing risks of addictive behaviours and preventing social exclusion of juvenile delinquents and former inmates.

Jim Orford trained in clinical psychology and obtained his PhD at the Institute of Psychiatry in London and is now Emeritus Professor of Clinical and Community Psychology at Birmingham University. He has researched and written extensively about gambling and other addiction problems and was an academic advisor to the British Gambling Prevalence Surveys. In 2011, he published his book, *An Unsafe Bet? The Dangerous Rise of Gambling and the Debate We Should Be Having*, and in 2012, he founded Gambling Watch UK, which campaigns for a public health approach to gambling and against the further expansion of gambling.

Catherine Paradis is Senior Research and Policy Analyst at the Canadian Centre on Substance Use and Addiction, where she leads and participates in projects conducted in partnership with public, private and nongovernmental organisations to promote public health and public safety. She provides leadership for the Postsecondary Education Partnership – Alcohol Harms (PEP-AH) which she currently co-chairs. She is one of the experts responsible for the production of the Canadian Low-Risk Drinking Guidelines. Before joining CCSA, she was the Scientific Coordinator for the Quebec Provincial Online Gambling Working Group. Dr Paradis holds a PhD in Sociology from the University of Montreal.

José C. Perales is Associate Professor at the University of Granada, Spain. He holds a PhD in Psychology, and his main area of research involves the use of experimental methods for the understanding of neurocognitive processes involved in addictions and other risky behaviours in real-life contexts. He is Secretary of the Board of the Society for the Advancement of Judgment and Decision-Making Studies. He has been doing publicly funded, industry-independent research on gambling behaviour since 2008, and he regularly collaborates with centres affiliated with the Andalusian Federation of Rehabilitated Gamblers.

xvi Contributor biographies

Jean-Félix Savary is the General Secretary of the French speaking association of addiction professionals (GREA). In this capacity, he is deeply involved in the political process in Switzerland concerning regulation and addiction management and contributes regularly to the public debate. He specialises in public policy, coalition building and advocacy.

Magdalen Schluter is a graduate student of Clinical Psychology at the University of Calgary (Canada). She received her BA in Psychology at the University of British Columbia. Her research interests include the conceptualisation of addictive disorders and understanding the role of behavioural impulsivity in the development and maintenance of addiction.

Olivier Simon trained as a psychiatrist and holds a Master of Public Health degree. Since 2002, he has worked as Head of the Centre du jeu excessif (Centre for excessive gambling) at Lausanne University Hospital. He is a Senior Lecturer at the Faculty of Biology and Medicine at the University of Lausanne. Simon is President of the Regional French-speaking Medical Association for Addiction Medicine (Collège romand de médecine de l'addiction) and a member of the board of the Swiss Society of Addiction Medicine, with particular responsibility for its ethics/ deontological and addictive behaviours sections.

Antonio Verdejo-García is Associate Professor of Psychology and Medical Research Future Fund Fellow at the Monash Institute of Cognitive and Clinical Neurosciences (MICCN). He is also Deputy Director of the MICCN Addiction Program. His research focuses on unravelling the cognitive and neural substrates of addiction and developing novel neuroscience informed interventions to treat addictive disorders. This research has been translated to new assessment and intervention tools, clinical guidelines of the Spanish Society of Drug Dependence and policy recommendations of the Australian Academy of Science and the World Health Summit.

PREFACE

Nady el-Guebaly

Gambling and the ingredients of a public health framework

The tenets of public health have humble origins and are historically linked with recurrent pandemics of infectious diseases. The notion of "miasma" (bad air) as a major cause of communicable disease in the sixteenth century was to be replaced by the germ theory of disease in the nineteenth century, ushering the modern search for the interactive roles of variables derived from an agent, a host and the environment. Following successful models tested with alcohol, tobacco and other substances, a similar public health framework has been proposed over the last 20 years to inform the prevention and treatment of problem gambling and associated comorbid disorders (Korn & Shaffer, 1999). The framework would identify target demographics and systematic disparities in health status more susceptible to associated gambling-related harms. The model would also pay particular attention to the context and environment, now termed social determinants, in which gambling behaviour occurs.

An expanding body of research reflected in this book recognises amongst others the intertwined impacts of gambling on emotional and physical health but also financial well-being, relationships and cultural harm. These impacts are not only affecting people who gamble but their family, friends and community (Browne et al., 2016; Gambling Research Exchange Ontario, 2017). Potential harms are compounded by the fact that only 7–12% of problem gamblers ever seek treatment for their gambling behaviour (Slutske, 2006).

The traditional public health framework also identifies three levels of prevention recognising the continuum of gambling problems from potential to severe harm in the population:

- Primary prevention addresses gambling-related harms before they occur.
- Secondary prevention reduces gambling-related harms in the early stages through early identification of at-risk gamblers.

xviii Preface

- Tertiary prevention minimise the impact of gambling-related harms through increased access and availability of treatment, services and support.

(Gambling Research Exchange Ontario, 2017)

It is also recognised that a much broader segment of the population experiences mild to moderate harm, whilst a smaller proportion of individuals will be affected by severe dependence and harm; this reality has been termed the "prevention paradox".

In addition to mental health and substance use disorders, a host of social determinants shape the trajectory of gambling experience including gender, age, cultural traditions, socioeconomic status and legal jurisdictions.

Despite the recognition of problem gambling as representing a significant public health problem, research on effective gambling harm minimisation is still relatively new and lags behind similar investigations in the fields of alcohol, tobacco and illegal substances. The World Health Organisation has published guidelines on alcohol and tobacco policy. International conventions exist for illegal substances, but no corresponding document has been developed for gambling. Auspiciously, many of the related public health policies and international conventions could be adapted to address gambling related harms. Examples would include a minimum legal age for gambling participation, mandated gambling and consumer protection strategies in licensed venues and availability of brief interventions (Gainsbury, Blankers, Wilkinson, Schelleman-Offermans, & Cousijn, 2014).

However, the evidence in support of other measures, such as limits on opening hours and gambling venues' density and increased taxation, remains tentative. More recently, prevention studies confronting the world of Internet gambling are still in their infancy. Internet gambling is a particular example of the difficulty in establishing effective gambling regulation due to the difficulty in controlling access and availability of Internet gambling sites, relative anonymity of users and operators, lack of physical boundaries between jurisdictions and disparity in the physical locations of players and providers (Gainsbury & Wood, 2011).

International comparisons of current national gambling policies could be of help in identifying relatively effective harm minimisation measures. For example, the European Union restrictions on gambling are only allowed to address consumer protection, prevention of criminal activity and protection of public order. A qualitative comparison of French and Finnish national policies reports that France's restrictive policies are mainly justified in terms of preventing criminal activities whilst the Finnish legislation emphasises the charitable causes funded by gambling, a claim not accepted by the European Union. Both countries increasingly promote consumer protection (Marionneau, 2017). Quantitative comparisons of outcomes could help outline preferred strategies.

In Switzerland there are important differences in the law and policies for casinos and lotteries due to a dual system of federal regulations for casinos and cantonal regulations supervising lotteries. A more coherent regulatory strategy learning from the experience of both components of the dual system would be both advisable and possible (Billieux et al., 2016).

In summary, this book's three sections constitute a significant step in advancing the theoretical public health framework, its potential in informing effective policies to minimise gambling related harm and current challenges in evaluation and monitoring. This body of work is highly recommended to policymakers, professionals and students of the field.

References

Billieux, J., Achab, S., Savary, J. F., Simon, O., Richter, F., Zullino, D., & Khazaal, Y. (2016). Gambling and problem gambling in Switzerland. *Addiction, 111*(9), 1677–1683.

Browne, M., Langham, E., Rawat, V., Greer, N., Li, E., Rose, J., . . . Best, T. (2016). Assessing gambling-related harm in Victoria: A public health perspective. *Victorian Responsible Gambling Foundation*, 14–17, 103–104.

Gainsbury, S. M., Blankers, M., Wilkinson, C., Schelleman-Offermans, K., & Cousijn, J. (2014). Recommendations for International gambling harm-minimisation guidelines: Comparison with effective public health policy. *Journal of Gambling Studies, 30*(4), 771–788.

Gainsbury, S. M., & Wood, R. (2011). Internet gambling policy in critical comparative perspective: The effectiveness of existing regulatory frameworks. *International Gambling Studies, 11*(3), 309–323.

Gambling Research Exchange Ontario. (2017). *Applying a Public Health Perspective to Gambling Harm*. Retrieved from www.greo.ca/en/programs-services/resources/Applying-a-public-health-perspective-to-gambling-harm-October-2017.pdf

Korn, D. A., & Shaffer, H. J. (1999). Gambling and the health of the public: Adopting a public health perspective. *Journal of Gambling Studies, 15*(4), 289–365.

Marionneau, V. (2017). Justifications of national gambling policies in France and Finland. *Nordic Studies on Alcohol and Drugs, 32*(3), 295–309.

Slutske, W. S. (2006). Natural recovery and treatment-seeking in pathological gambling: Results of two U.S. national surveys. *American Journal of Psychiatry, 163*(2), 297–302.

ACKNOWLEDGEMENTS

First, we are indebted to our authors for sharing their knowledge and experience – without their hard work and commitment to the field of harm reduction, this book would not have been possible.

We also give special thanks to our conference partners for the 3rd and 4th International Multidisciplinary Congresses on Harm Reduction, namely: Addiction Neuchâtel, Addiction Suisse, Addiction Valais, Association Européenne pour la Promotion de la Santé, Association Vaudoise de Médecins Concernés par les Addictions, Azzardo e Nuove Dipendenze, Clinique Belmont, Collège national universitaire des enseignants d'addictologie, Caritas Fribourg, Citizen@Work Swiss, Collège Romand de Médecine de l'Addiction, Département de psychiatrie du CHUV, Dettes Conseils Suisse, European Association for the Study of Gambling, Fachverband Sucht, Fédération Addiction, Fondation les Oliviers, Forum Suchtmedizin Ostschweiz, Groupement Romand d'Études des Addictions, Gruppo Azzardo Ticino – Prevenzione, Infodrog, Istituto di Ricerca sul Gioco d'Azzardo, Mission interministérielle de lutte contre la drogue et les conduites addictives, Le Pélican/Bruxelles, Observatoire des jeux – Ministère français des finances, Perspektive Thurgau, Praxis Suchtmedizin Schweiz, REPER Fribourg – Promotion de la santé et prévention, Réseau fribourgeois de santé mentale, Rien ne va plus, Santé bernoise, Service d'addictologie des Hôpitaux universitaires de Genève, SOS-Spielsucht, Swiss Academy of Medical Sciences, Swiss Museum of Games, Swiss Gamers Network, Universitäre Psychiatrische Dienste Bern, Universitäre Psychiatrische Kliniken Basel, Zentrum für Spielsucht und andere Verhaltenssüchte/Zürich.

And finally, our sincere appreciation to the institutions offering financial support to the two congresses: Office fédéral de la santé publique, Fondation SANA, Fonds national suisse de la recherche scientifique, Kanton Zürich, Académie suisse des sciences médicales, Programme intercantonal de lutte contre la dépendance au jeu, Interkantonales Programm Glücksspielsuchtprävention Nordwest-, Ost-, und Innerschweiz, Réseau de coopération MedNET du Groupe Pompidou (Conseil de l'Europe), Swiss Society of Addiction Medicine.

INTRODUCTION

*Cheryl Dickson, Caroline Dunand, Olivier Simon
and Henrietta Bowden-Jones*

Gambling disorder has been medically recognised as a chronic illness for many years. However, its integration to the medical classification system, as an addictive disorder, is relatively recent (DSM-5, 2013). This change reflects a growing body of thought, which enables parallels to be drawn with other addictive disorders and effective practices from these fields more readily adapted and applied. The way has been paved for a public health approach towards gambling disorder, which aims to improve the population's health at an organisational level through the work of public services. Such an approach requires a shift from current player protection measures, which are based on gambling industry concerns, towards a focus on preventing harm to the population at large, including those at low-risk and relatives affected by gambling. The effectiveness of this approach relies on structural and behavioural prevention measures being applied, alongside more general socioenvironmental determinants, as part of a comprehensive framework and the necessary underpinning of these efforts through public policy.

In order to contribute towards the evolution of a public health approach, this book aims to provide a current overview of the field and propose alternatives to the global approach towards gambling-related harm. The book begins with an overview of gambling disorder, as we currently understand it, and its impact on both the population at large and most vulnerable individuals. First, we look at how gambling has proliferated in our society and the need for a unified approach in assessing gambling-related harm. Issues such as the social cost of gambling and its normalisation are also explored. Further chapters highlight the negative impact of problem gambling on family members and significant others, and we end the first section with consideration of recent neurocognitive evidence and its implications for policy, prevention and treatment.

The second section focuses on harm reduction initiatives with suggestions for practical application. We begin with a chapter on defining risk and harm reduction as a public health approach, followed by an international overview of current efforts and a review into the effectiveness of prevention strategies. A range of practical interventions are considered including the role of treatment in reducing gambling-related harm, potential of *nudge* approaches within public health initiatives and the instruments available for early detection. This section finishes with a chapter outlining the potential use of online gambling tools for behavioural tracking.

In the last section of this book we highlight major challenges to evaluation and monitoring efforts faced by the gambling-related harm field. A comprehensive framework for prevention and harm-reduction is considered, and the need for effective indicators and independent monitoring bodies is highlighted.

The issues considered in this collective work are key topics at the forefront of the field. Many of these were presented and discussed at the 3rd and 4th International Multidisciplinary Symposia on Gambling Disorder (January 2014 in Neuchatel, and July 2018 in Fribourg, Switzerland). It is hoped that more detailed consideration of the current issues presented in this work will inspire further development of effective harm reduction policies and practices.

SECTION I

Impact and current understanding of gambling disorder

1

GAMBLING AND DEMOCRACY

Peter J. Adams

In most modern economies, in the short period of two to three decades, gambling has moved from a dispersed cottage industry to a high-volume consumer enterprise – an industrial revolution on a worldwide scale. As a cottage industry, it took the form of relatively low consumption occurring in specific social venues such as racetracks or bingo halls. Then, at the forefront of this industrialisation, eight million gambling machines have been distributed into various locations throughout the world: in the US onto riverboats, reservations and casinos, in Australia into bars and sports clubs, in Europe into bars and state casinos – and now bookie shops in the UK – and in Asian nations into the rising number of large casinos – including the pachinko and the pashikura parlours of Japan. This epidemic of machines has deepened, with the steady improvements and refinements of electronic and psychological technologies. The dominance of gambling machines has swept aside the social and cultural aspects of gambling in favour of individualised consumption with social engagement and cultural dimensions reduced to a minimum (Schull, 2012). And yet, in many people's minds, gambling is still associated with the virtues of a cottage industry: moderate, fun-oriented consumption, social involvement and community fundraising. But the realities of mass consumption are very different. Where machines are present, rates of problem gambling average around 2% of populations with a range of other serious impacts in terms of people's finances, family relationships, employment, mental health and involvement in crime (Australian Productivity Commission, 2010; Williams, Volberg, & Stevens, 2012).

In *Gambling, Freedom and Democracy* (Adams, 2007), I present the case for viewing the global expansion of commercial gambling as mimicking the expansion of other extractive industries such as native forestry or intensive mining. The book describes how the key drivers for both expansions are propelled by a convergence of interests between four sectors: governments with an interest in tax revenue, local entrepreneurs with an interest in commercial growth, international gambling corporations

6 Peter J. Adams

with an interest in consolidated power and community organisations with an interest in knock-on funding opportunities. In the political determinants frame, these four parties are not viewed as simply peripheral beneficiaries of the central activity of consuming gambling products. On the contrary, the central activity associated with gambling is identified as the production of profits with the core form of consumption, the consumption of these profits (Adams, 2009). Furthermore, as consumption of these profits becomes established, the demand for these profits becomes embedded into social and financial structures, which in turn provide the impetus for further increased demand.

This chapter will summarise concerns regarding the capacity for commercial gambling to degrade key parts of democratic systems due to deepening reliance on the consumption of gambling profits.

Progressive degradation

The key issue with gambling and democracy has to do with money and power, in other words, how elites are able to deploy their financial resources to control or influence political actors. Francis Fukuyama in a series of books has highlighted how strong democracies are built on strong government institutions with clear and impartial accountability processes overseen by a commitment to the rule of law (Fukuyama, 2014, 2017). Other governance scholars have emphasised the role of certain key principles in protecting these institutions. For example, Alina Mungiu-Pippidi (2015) points to what she calls "ethical universalism in public life" as a fundamental principle in the battle to contain what she termed "particularism" where governance becomes locked into personal rather than public agendas. Michael Johnston (2014) describes how the processes of what he calls "deep democratization", such as increasing pluralism, reform activism and maintaining accountability, are crucial in state formation. Similarly, Acemoglu and Robinson (2012) argue that the quality of man-made political and economic institutions play a central role in the development of flourishing and adaptive nation states.

Gambling possesses several aspects capable of disrupting the integrity of these principles and processes. Gambling profits come disproportionally from those experiencing gambling-related harm and thereby exploit and contribute to rising inequalities (Rintoul, Livingstone, Mellor, & Jolley, 2013) see also Chapter 15. Gambling, as an extractive industry, generates large amounts of unattached and discretionary profits which governments and corporations can deploy to protect financial interests (Adams & Livingstone, 2015). Indeed, Mungiu-Pippidi (2015) draws attention to how governments with large amounts of concentrated discretionary money (such as the profits from oil or mining) are particularly vulnerable to corruption. Furthermore, gambling is often associated with various forms of corruption whether that be match-fixing in Indian cricket, its links to organised crime, money laundering and fraudulent practices in gambling retailing (Ferentzy & Turner, 2009; Goodman, 1995). For example, when the Canadian Ombudsman André Marin (2007) scratched the surface of Ontario Lotteries, he uncovered a range of ethically questionable practices. Finally, governments are often conflicted by their own vested interests in profits from gambling, with many relying on it for significant portions of their tax revenue (as in the Australian states of Victoria and New South Wales, ABS, 2002) and many others actually owning large parts of the industry (as happens in the provinces of Canada and Nordic countries, Korn, 2000). This immediately raises questions as to where, inside such governments, there might be sufficient independent accountability to guard against corrupt and particularistic practices (Smith & Rubenstein, 2011).

Vested interests in gambling, both inside and outside government, lead to the gradual erosion of accountability systems. Michael Johnston (2014) argues that corruption is a key threat to a nation achieving the levels of accountability required to form effective governance structures. He identifies corruption as "the abuse of public roles or resources for private benefit" (p. 8) and contends that no political structure is immune from its effects. He also makes the point that different systems of corruption require different remedies and in order to look at solutions we first need to recognise which type of corruption is taking place. He identifies four separate "syndromes of corruption": first, "Official Mogul" corruption (such as in China, Kenya and Egypt) has very weak democratic institutions, which enables a few powerful figures to dominate both the politics and resources of such countries. Second, "Oligarchs and Clans" corruption (such as in Russia, the Philippines and Mexico) involves overlapping networks of political leaders, business leaders and powerful families who together easily manipulate weak government institutions. Third, "Elite Cartel" corruption (such as Argentina, South Korea and Italy) have moderately strong state institutions but elite networks of business, military and political leaders collude to dominate government institutions. Fourth, and most interestingly, "Influence Market" corruption (such as in Australia, the United States and the Netherlands) occurs in countries with vibrant market economies and strongly established democratic institutions, but rather than corrupt practices occurring with specific individuals, corruption occurs within formal systems between political actors and coalitions of corporate entities such as banks and businesses.

> Influence Market corruption works through the system in many ways, rather than undermining it fundamentally: after all, those who trade in wealth or power are generally well served by existing arrangements.
>
> *(Johnston, 2014, p. 21)*

Johnston also argues that in terms of strengthening governance and weakening corruption, what might improve the situation for one syndrome is different from what is needed with another syndrome.

Gambling is most likely to flourish in Influence Market contexts because commercialised gambling rely strongly on stable and well-managed market economies. Other syndromes of corruption lead to governments that struggle to establish stable and predictable markets, the sort of instability and corruption in which complex operations such as casinos and electronic gaming machine (EGM) parlours

8 Peter J. Adams

are unlikely to flourish. High volume and commercialised forms of gambling rely heavily on systems that enable players to honour their deals.

Compromised public good

In the book *Moral Jeopardy: Risks of Accepting Money from The Alcohol, Tobacco and Gambling Industries* (Adams, 2016), I examine how addictive consumption industries exert influence over policymakers by enlisting the support of an interlinked series of paid intermediaries such as lobbyists, researchers, community groups and industry front groups. I organise these links into three chains of influence: the public good chain, the knowledge chain and the political chain. Each chain is made up of a series of interlinked individuals and groups that cooperate together in influencing those in the policy decision-making arena.

The public good chain is the most visible chain because it seeks to advance corporate interests by pushing key messages in the public mind and thereby influencing policymakers. The first key message is that gambling industries are contributing positively to public good by contributing visibly to economic development, employment and charitable causes. For example, corporate social responsibility programmes are a well-established way to advance a positive image of corporations (Tesler & Malone, 2008). They have been adopted widely by tobacco and alcohol companies in their contributions to causes of high public anxiety such as violence against women, HIV epidemics and environmental threats (Fooks & Gilmore, 2013; Yoon & Lam, 2013). Gambling organisations, such as casinos and online gambling providers, have followed suit in much-heralded contributions to charitable causes such as cancer and poverty (Cai, Jo, & Pan, 2012; Pratten & Walton, 2008). Such initiatives have been criticised as primarily aimed at reinforcing industry legitimacy and at diverting attention away from their ethically questionable relationship to gambling harm (Baumberg et al., 2014; Leung & Snell, 2017).

The second key message is that gambling providers are doing something about gambling-related harm including problem gambling. This provides a further boost to their corporate image but, more importantly, it reassures governments that, for those few people who are experiencing harms, responsible providers are doing all they can to ameliorate the damage. These measures include industry-funded gambling awareness campaigns and behavioural interventions, but perhaps most effort so far has focused on the types of host responsibility programmes first developed by the alcohol industry. These typically consist in a suite of measures that include training staff to recognise and intervene with people who gamble problematically, information on where to get help and self-exclusion initiatives (Hing, Russell, & Hronis, 2017). The main criticisms of these approaches are their poor evidence of effectiveness (Rintoul, Deblaquiere, & Thomas, 2017) and that they are intended more as window dressing rather than serious attempts to reduce play by people who gamble problematically (Adams & Rossen, 2012; Hancock, Schellinck, & Schrans, 2008).

The third and arguably most important message along the public good chain is that the downsides of gambling originate from individuals and not from the systems and environments in which gambling takes place. If only players could learn to play more responsibly then most harms from gambling could be avoided. This message is reinforced by industry and government initiatives targeting individual attitudes and behaviour such as host responsibility programmes. It is further advanced through industry communications such as government submissions, advertising and industry statements in the media. As with alcohol and tobacco, gambling industry influence is used to mobilise individualised perspectives and to distract, divert and obscure what is possible in terms of effective public health interventions (Borrell, 2008; Livingstone & Woolley, 2007).

Compromised knowledge

Along the knowledge chain, the processes by which research is conducted plays an important role in how a society responds to gambling-related harm. The knowledge acquired forms the basis of media reports and helps shape policy responses. This chain includes those who set research agendas, those who fund the research, those who judge the quality of the work and those who interpret and communicate this knowledge. At each point along this chain those associated with the gambling industry and governments with vested interests in profits have opportunities to influence and manipulate what goes on. Strategies include industry input into defining priorities, biased funding and review processes, selection of industry compliant panels and reviewers and the disguising of industry links by transferring funds via intermediaries (Adams, 2011). Rebecca Cassidy and colleagues (Cassidy, 2014; Cassidy, Loussouarn, & Pisac, 2013) interviewed a range of stakeholders in gambling research and found a broad range of concerns about the way gambling research is managed.

But behind these distorting processes, the primary reason for why our knowledge of gambling is severely compromised is because most researchers are willing to accept money either directly or indirectly from industry sources (Livingstone & Adams, 2016). What comes with accepting this money are distortions in research agendas in terms of the questions selected for investigation, the types of methods employed and the ways in which research is reported (Young, 2013). Whereas alcohol and tobacco have to a large extent shaken off direct influence from industry, industry influence with gambling still continues as normal and acceptable, with little sign of changing. The extent of this is revealed in the nature of gambling conferences where the majority, including the European Association for the Study of Gambling (EASG) in Europe, the National Association for Gambling Studies Australia (NAGS) and the International Conference on Gambling and Risk Taking (ICGRT) in the United States, are not only primarily funded from gambling industry sources but also tend to occur in gambling venues such as casino hotels (Adams, 2007; Livingstone, 2018; see also Chapter 9).

A concerned group of gambling researchers has been seeking ways of challenging the reliance of researchers on industry money (Livingstone et al., 2018). In one article we called on gambling researchers to support a set of ethical principles aimed at reducing industry influence (Livingstone & Adams, 2016). These

10 Peter J. Adams

principles included not accepting money from industry sources, research priorities being set independently of the beneficiaries of gambling, not attending conferences and other events influenced by industry and full disclosure of conflicts of interest.

The pressure on gambling researchers to accept industry funding is understandably stronger in environments where alternative sources of funding are scarce. A key way of reducing this pressure could involve creating other sources of funding that are not derived from the profits of gambling. These sources would, as long as independence is assured at every point along the funding process, provide sustained support for high quality research in this emerging field.

Compromised politics

Why, over the last 50 years, have successive governments in many Influence Market economies consistently favoured more individualised and less effective interventions for gambling over what public health research indicates are more effective interventions?

A key aspect to the commercialisation of the addictive consumptions like alcohol and gambling is their ability to generate profits over-and-above what occurs with ordinary nonaddictive consumptions such as buying petrol or televisions. For example, a pivotal feature of addictive gambling is consumption that goes well beyond what might be considered sensible. Addicted consumers, by the very nature of addictive behaviour, will consume to excess. They may be relatively small in number compared to non-addicted consumers, but they invest heavily and, accordingly, contribute far more to the profits. The resultant profit surplus underpins not only the motive force for seeking to increase consumption but also the resource base for a range of proconsumption initiatives that seek to guard against potential threats, particularly those associated with policy and regulation. Ways of gaining influence are not limited to exchanges of money such as those involved in advertising or paying political lobbyists (Bond, Daube, & Chikritzhs, 2009). Benefits can include appointments (e.g., of retired politicians to boards), cross-board memberships (e.g., company executives on government advisory committees), exchanges in kind (e.g., contributing to a hospital with an understanding of looser regulations) and currying public favour (e.g., funding local sporting or cultural events).

The political chain of influence is a low visibility chain built around industry actors forming relationships of mutual obligation with key government actors. Whilst it has proved difficult to research, recent studies in the UK have exposed some of the pathways by which alcohol industry corporations penetrate government contexts and have highlighted how building these relations typically involves long-term industry investment in relationship building, including the targeting of opposition politicians (Hawkins & Holden, 2013; McCambridge, Hawkins, & Holden, 2014). Our knowledge of the processes of influence along the political chain is meagre both because of the corruption of the knowledge chain described in the previous section and because of the politically sensitive nature of such inquiry (Young & Markham, 2015).

Conclusion

Yani-de-Soriano, Javed, and Yousafzai (2012) posed an interesting question: can the gambling industry be considered socially responsible if its products harm consumers? This stabs at the heart of why the industrialisation of gambling poses a threat to democracy. High intensity gambling has flourished in environments shaped by well-formed democratic institutions and strong market economies, and it is in these environments that Influence Market corruption flourishes. But, according to the prior analysis, the primary problem with gambling is not the person who gambles problematically, rather the escalating consumption of gambling profits. Whether the main consumer of gambling profits are private corporates or whether they are government or community agencies, as the scale of profit production increases so does entrenched forms of reliance on such consumption. Accordingly, the way forward in terms of delivering a public health approach to gambling harm will depend on the willingness of profit consumers to consider limiting their reliance on this form of addictive consumption. This leads to asking: in what circumstances might local entrepreneurs consider constraining their profits? What might lead international corporates to consider scaling down their promotion practices? What might lead community beneficiaries to consider reducing their reliance on such profits? And, what pressures might prompt governments to consider reductions in revenue from gambling? These are perplexing questions with no obvious or easy solutions. But they cut to the heart of the problem: reduction of harm from gambling is closely intertwined with reductions in the consumption of gambling profits.

References

ABS. (2002). Service industries special article: Gambling in Australia. In *Year Book Australia*. Canberra: Australian Bureau of Statistics.

Acemoglu, D., & Robinson, J. A. (2012). *Why Nations Fail: The Origins of Power, Prosperity and Poverty*. London: Profile.

Adams, P. J. (2007). Chapter 7: Researchers gambling, freedom and democracy. In *Routledge Studies in Social and Political Thought* (pp. 101–123). New York: Routledge.

Adams, P. J. (2009). Redefining the gambling problem: The production and consumption of gambling profits. *Gambling Research*, *21*(1), 51–54.

Adams, P. J. (2011). Ways in which gambling researchers receive funding from gambling industry sources. *International Gambling Studies*, *11*(2), 145–152.

Adams, P. J. (2016). *Moral Jeopardy: The Risks of Accepting Money from Tobacco, Alcohol and Gambling Industries*. Cambridge: Cambridge University Press.

Adams, P. J., & Livingstone, C. (2015). Addiction surplus: The add-on margin that makes addictive consumptions difficult to contain. *International Journal of Drug Policy*, *26*(1), 107–111.

Adams, P. J., & Rossen, F. (2012). A tale of missed opportunities: Pursuit of a public health approach to gambling in New Zealand. *Addiction*, *107*(6), 1051–1056.

Australian Productivity Commission. (2010). *Gambling: APC Report No. 50*. Canberra: Productivity Commission. Retrieved from www.pc.gov.au/projects/inquiry/gambling-2009/report

12 Peter J. Adams

Baumberg, B., Cuzzocrea, V., Morini, S., Ortoleva, P., Disley, E., Tzvetkova, M., . . . Beccaria, F. (2014). *Corporate Social Responsibility* (Deliverable 2, Work Package 11). Addiction and Lifestyles in Contemporary Europe: Reframing Addictions Project (ALICE RAP).

Bond, L., Daube, M., & Chikritzhs, T. (2009). Access to confidential alcohol industry documents: From "Big Tobacco" to "Big Booze". *Australian Medical Journal, 1*(3), 1–26.

Borrell, J. (2008, December). A thematic analysis identifying concepts of problem gambling agency: With preliminary exploration of discourses in selected industry and research documents. *Journal of Gambling Issues, 22*, 195–218.

Cai, Y., Jo, H., & Pan, C. (2012). Doing well while doing bad? CSR in controversial industry sectors. *Journal of Business Ethics, 108*(4), 467–480.

Cassidy, R. (2014). Fair game? Producing and publishing gambling research. *International Gambling Studies, 14*(3), 345–353.

Cassidy, R., Loussouarn, C., & Pisac, A. (2013). *Fair Game: Producing Gambling Research: The Goldsmiths Report.* London: Goldsmiths, University of London.

Ferentzy, P., & Turner, N. (2009, June). Gambling and organized crime: A review of the literature. *Journal of Gambling Issues, 23*, 111–148.

Fooks, G. J., & Gilmore, A. B. (2013). Corporate philanthropy, political influence, and health policy. *PLoS One, 8*(11), e80864.

Fukuyama, F. (2014). *Political Order and Political Decay.* London: Profile.

Fukuyama, F. (2017). *State Building: Governance and World Order in the 21st Century.* London: Profile.

Goodman, R. (1995). *The Luck Business: The Devastating Consequences and Broken Promises of America's Gambling Explosion.* New York: Free Press.

Hancock, L., Schellinck, T., & Schrans, T. (2008). Gambling and corporate social responsibility (CSR): Re-defining industry and state roles on duty of care, host responsibility and risk management. *Policy & Society, 27*(1), 55–68.

Hawkins, B., & Holden, C. (2013). Framing the alcohol policy debate: Industry actors and the regulation of the UK beverage alcohol market. *Critical Policy Studies, 7*(1), 53–71.

Hing, N., Russell, A. M., & Hronis, A. (2017). A definition and set of principles for responsible consumption of gambling. *International Gambling Studies*, 1–24. Retrieved from www.tandfonline.com/doi/pdf/10.1080/14459795.2017.1390591?needAccess=true

Johnston, M. (2014). *Corruption, Contention and Reform: The Power of Deep Democratization.* Cambridge: Cambridge University Press.

Korn, D. A. (2000). Expansion of gambling in Canada: Implications for health and social policy. *Canadian Medical Association Journal, 163*(1), 61–64.

Leung, T. C. H., & Snell, R. S. (2017). Attraction or distraction? Corporate social responsibility in Macao's gambling industry. *Journal of Business Ethics, 145*(3), 637–658.

Livingstone, C. (2018). A case for clean conferences in gambling research. *Drug & Alcohol Review, 37*(5), 683–686.

Livingstone, C., Adams, P., Cassidy, R., Markham, F., Reith, G., Rintoul, A., . . . Young, M. (2018). On gambling research, social science and the consequences of commercial gambling. *International Gambling Studies, 18*(1), 56–68.

Livingstone, C., & Adams, P. J. (2016). Clear principles are needed for integrity in gambling research. *Addiction, 111*(1), 5–10.

Livingstone, C., & Woolley, R. (2007). Risky business: A few provocations on the regulation of electronic gaming machines. *International Gambling Studies, 7*(3), 361–376.

Marin, A. (2007). *A Game of Trust: Ombudsman Report: Investigation into the Ontario Lottery and Gaming Corporation's Protection of the Public from Fraud and Theft.* Retrieved February 29, 2012, from www.webcitation.org/65ntUvKEi

McCambridge, J., Hawkins, B., & Holden, C. (2014). The challenge corporate lobbying poses to reducing society's alcohol problems: Insights from UK evidence on minimum unit pricing. *Addiction, 109*(2), 199–205.

Mungiu-Pippidi, A. (2015). *The Quest for Good Governance: How Societies Develop Control of Corruption.* Cambridge: Cambridge University Press.

Pratten, J. D., & Walton, S. (2008). *Policy and Reality: Corporate Social Responsibility in the UK Gambling Industry.* Manchester: Manchester Metropolitan University. Retrieved from www.crrconference.org/downloads/prattenwalton.pdf

Rintoul, A., Deblaquiere, J., & Thomas, A. (2017). Responsible gambling codes of conduct: Lack of harm minimisation intervention in the context of venue self-regulation. *Addiction Research & Theory, 25*(6), 451–461.

Rintoul, A. C., Livingstone, C., Mellor, A. P., & Jolley, D. (2013). Modelling vulnerability to gambling related harm: How disadvantage predicts gambling losses. *Addiction Research & Theory, 21*(4), 329–338.

Schull, N. D. (2012). *Addiction by Design: Machine Gambling in Las Vegas.* Princeton, NJ: Princeton University Press.

Smith, G., & Rubenstein, D. (2011, June). Socially responsible and accountable gambling in the public interest. *Journal of Gambling Issues, 25*, 54–67.

Tesler, L. E., & Malone, R. E. (2008). Corporate philanthropy, lobbying, and public health policy. *American Journal of Public Health, 98*(12), 2123–2133.

Williams, R. J., Volberg, R. A., & Stevens, R. M. G. (2012). *The Population Prevalence of Problem Gambling: Methodological Influences, Standardized Rates, Jurisdictional Differences, and Worldwide Trends . . . .* Toronto: Report Prepared for the Ontario Problem Gambling Research Centre and the Ontario Ministry of Health and Long Term Care. Retrieved from http://hdl.handle.net/10133/3068

Yani-de-Soriano, M., Javed, U., & Yousafzai, S. (2012). Can an industry be socially responsible if its products harm consumers? The case of online gambling. *Journal of Business Ethics, 10*(4), 481–497.

Yoon, S., & Lam, T. H. (2013). The illusion of righteousness: Corporate social responsibility practices of the alcohol industry. *BMC Public Health, 13*, 630.

Young, M. (2013). Statistics, scapegoats and social control: A critique of pathological gambling prevalence research. *Addiction Research & Theory, 21*(1), 1–11.

Young, M., & Markham, F. (2015). Beyond disclosure: Gambling research, political economy, and incremental reform. *International Gambling Studies, 15*(1), 6–9.

2

MEASURING HARM FROM GAMBLING AND ESTIMATING ITS DISTRIBUTION IN THE POPULATION

Matthew Browne

The gambling-industry represents itself as another segment of the wider entertainment industry, with the frequent use of the word "gaming" used as public reminder that gambling is simply another form of fun. In this conception, gambling is similar to going to the cinema, playing a computer game, or watching professional sporting events. It is fair to acknowledge that it provides similar benefits (i.e., consumer surplus) in providing opportunities for entertainment, social contact, and the alleviation of boredom (Shaffer & Kidman, 2004). Moreover, gambling has a cost, although the cost is perhaps less transparent than some other forms of entertainment. However, gambling differs from most entertainment alternatives, in the degree to which it fosters excessive consumption and behavioural addiction, which can lead to various harms (Griffiths, 2005). Nevertheless, nonproblematic gambling is generally socially acceptable, by degrees, and the rate of participation is high in jurisdictions in which it is legal. In these respects, gambling is quite similar to alcohol – another legal recreational product which is prone to overconsumption and dependence, leading to harms for some users. Another similarity is that; in addition to a small proportion of individuals being affected by severe dependence and harm; a much broader segment of the population experiences mild to moderate harm due to chronic or episodic overconsumption (Korn & Shaffer, 1999; Korn, Gibbins, & Azmier, 2003; Marshall, 2009). This has been termed the "prevention paradox" by some, since prevention of the most severe forms of overconsumption only reduces a fraction of the total harms in the community.

A theoretical model of gambling-related harm

The immediate consequences of excessive gambling can be described quite simply as the loss of money, loss of time, as well as the social and psychological impacts associated with preoccupation and dependence (Blaszczynski, Ladouceur, Goulet, &

Savard, 2006). Of these, the financial losses arguably present the greatest source of harm to the person who gambles and those connected to them. However, people who gamble usually have difficulty reliably reporting their investment of time and money (Rockloff, 2012). Further, the threshold that determines excessive expenditure varies greatly depending on the capacity of the person to support such costs. For example, a wealthy person with few commitments, social or work obligations would have more capacity to support a given level of gambling than a person with both a heavy workload and family obligations, and little discretionary income. Finally, these immediate losses of time and/or money are not themselves the instrumental drivers of harm, which can be understood instead as a detrimental effect on an individual's well-being or quality of life (Allister McGregor, Camfield, & Woodcock, 2009). Rather, it is the life events and situations that are a *consequence* of these losses that are instrumental. To illustrate, it is not loss of money *per se* that directly impacts well-being but rather the implications of an unaffordable financial loss, such as inability to pay rent and, for example, arguments over money. These in turn lead to other consequences, such as loss of autonomy, deterioration of relationships and distress over failing to adequately meet responsibilities. The ultimate result of these diverse events and life circumstances – and the outcome that is arguably of most relevance – is a decrease in subjective quality of life and well-being for the individuals involved. Accordingly, a public health approach treats gambling harm as morbidity and assesses the societal cost in terms of aggregate human suffering. Although costings of the economic burden of gambling are commonly undertaken; until recently, public health-oriented assessments of the "burden of harm" have been lacking.

Figure 2.1 illustrates the conceptual model outlined in the previous section. The established construct of "gambling problems", measured for instance using the Problem Gambling Severity Index (Wynne, 2003), encompasses symptoms of behavioural addiction, excessive consumption and negative consequences. However, gambling-related harm refers specifically to the negative *consequences* of maladaptive gambling-related behaviour and cognitions. Specific harms can be organised into domains, with examples provided in the dashed box in Figure 2.1. The probability of the occurrence of each specific symptom often depends not only on the degree of problematic/excessive gambling but tends to be highly dependent on an individual's particular life situation. The combined effect of these symptoms is understood to diminish quality of life, which in public health terms is a decrement to a person's potential to live in a state of ideal health and well-being. The distinction between gambling problems (which encompasses excessive gambling, behavioural addiction and negative consequences) versus harm becomes more important when considering the lower end of the continuum of excessive gambling, in which some degree of harm may be present, without the individual necessarily meeting clinical criteria to be categorised as a problem gambler. That is, it is possible to experience some minor harms without showing particularly excessive gambling behaviour, and without traits of behavioural addiction such as tolerance or preoccupation with gambling.

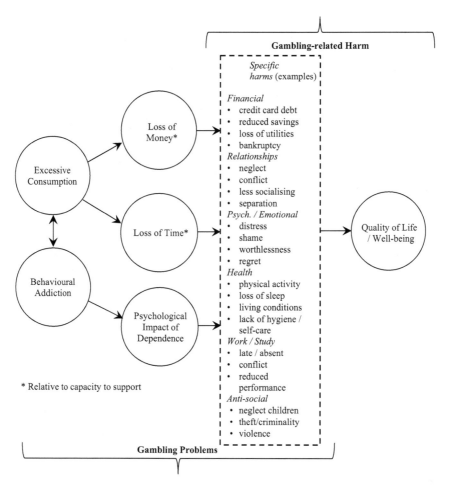

FIGURE 2.1 Conceptual model of the relationship between gambling problems and quality of life

Figure 2.2 illustrates the concept of harm occurring along a continuum (Canale, Vieno, & Griffiths, 2016), which can range from mild to very severe (Korn et al., 2003; Marshall, 2009). It shows the relative impact of harms and benefits, with respect to the gambling population ordered in relation to relative consumption. The idea that most harm in the population stems from subclinical gambling (Figure 2.2; B) rather than problem gambling (Figure 2.2; A) is an illustration of the previously mentioned "prevention paradox" (Abbott et al., 2015; Rose, 1981). This parallels alcohol related problems: although heavy drinkers have higher individual risk, low-risk drinkers contribute the greatest burden of disease because of the greater number of individuals in this group. The implication of this public health model is a shift in focus from measuring discrete cases of pathological gambling to evaluating harm at all levels of participation (Blaszczynski, 2009; Canale et al.,

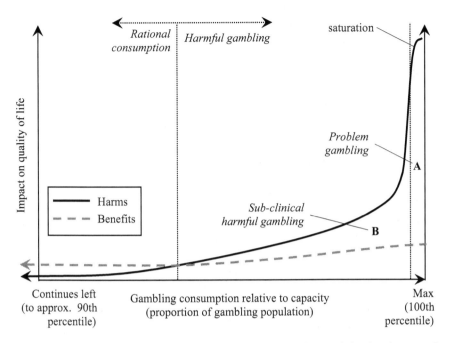

FIGURE 2.2 Conceptual illustration of the "prevention paradox" and the distribution of harms and benefits from gambling in the population

2016; Rodgers, Caldwell, & Butterworth, 2009). It is important to acknowledge that Figure 2.2 shows only the extreme upper range of gambling involvement: approximately 90% of people who gamble are likely to be "rational consumers", that is, experiencing more benefit than harm from their gambling involvement. Integrated over the entire population, gambling may yield a net social benefit, whilst also being mildly or severely harmful for some (Rockloff, Russell, Browne, & Hing, n.d.). An intriguing question raised by this observation is whether liberalised gambling policy represents a "tyranny of the majority" (Mill, 1869) in which the majority realises modest benefits at the expense of a minority who is relatively severely harmed.

Although the general model described in Figure 2.2 is generally well accepted, relatively little empirical research has focused on the distribution of gambling harms and benefits in the population (Currie, Miller, Hodgins, & Wang, 2009). Despite calls for a public health approach to gambling, only recently has research effort begun to shift from the exclusive focus on gambling problems and related problem-gambling screens. As a result, many key issues, such as the threshold at which harmful gambling occurs, i.e., when harms exceed benefits, are not well understood. This may be because a harm-centred methodological approach is intrinsically challenging. First, the set of specific harms that can potentially arise from gambling is large and diverse, with the particular pattern of "symptoms" varying greatly from person to person. As a consequence, it is difficult to define

18 Matthew Browne

a single "condition", or set of conditions, that adequately describe the impact of gambling at different points on the continuum in a population-representative manner. Few studies have attempted to apply public health protocols in order to elicit a consensus estimate of impact on quality of life. Furthermore, to the extent that gambling harm has a "long tail"; i.e., milder harms occurring to a larger proportion of people who gamble, it becomes increasingly important to also take into account the benefits of gambling (Figure 2.2, grey dashed line). It cannot be assumed, as it often is for the most severe gambling problems, that harms necessarily exceed benefits.

Empirical findings on the distribution of gambling-related harm

Currie et al. (2009) measured gambling harm using items combined from several problem gambling screens, rather than applying a dedicated measure of harm. Nevertheless, they found responses to be reliably related to indices of consumption, such as frequency of play, and percentage of gross income spent on gambling. For example, people who gamble and were free of harmful symptomatology typically spent an average of 0.86% of their income on gambling, whereas those with one or more symptoms spent 5.0%, and those with moderate-risk or problem gambling spent an average of 8.7% of their income on playing. As the authors note, those who met the most liberal definition of harm (at least one symptom – which in their conception may or may not have been an actual "harm") could be differentiated from people with no symptoms, on many indices of consumption.

In a population representative survey in Britain, Canale et al. (2016) found similar strong relationships between excessive consumption and harm but also observed that harms were distributed across low to moderate-risk gambling and not confined to problem gambling. Although per-person risk of harm was highest for high playing-time and large-spend gambling, most individuals experiencing at least one harm were drawn from lower time/spend groups. Canale et al. (2016) defined "social harms" using four items derived from the DSM-IV: illegal acts, problems with spouse and/or other people, work-related problems and financial problems. They acknowledge that this assessment was not completely satisfactory and may not fully capture all domains of harm. However, in our view, this limitation does not detract from the empirical support provided for the "prevention paradox" model illustrated in Figure 2.2. Despite a lack of sensitivity for low-range harms, Britain, according to Canale et al. (2016), still observed a widespread quantum of harm for low-risk gambling.

In a national Finnish telephone survey, Raisamo, Mäkelä, Salonen, and Lintonen (2015) also demonstrated a close coupling between excessive expenditure and harm, noting that harms were reported even at low gambling frequency and expenditure levels. They also concluded that the results supported a population approach, suggesting a shift in focus towards harm occurring at the lower end of the continuum.

Measuring harm from gambling   **19**

The authors acknowledged that the study was limited by the use of the Problem Gambling Severity Index as a proxy for gambling harm. This nine-item instrument contains five items that imply negative consequences: unaffordable losses, borrowing or selling items to fund gambling, health/stress/anxiety problems, financial problems and feelings of guilt. The remaining items relate to behavioural dependence or symptomatic "problems" in general.

From this brief review it can be seen that a recurring and acknowledged limitation has been the lack of a dedicated and comprehensive measure of gambling harm. Furthermore, until very recently, there has been no attempt to link the experience of harm to a metric that describes the total impact on a person's quality of life. Also, no work has taken into account the benefits that may accrue from gambling. A programme of research by our group conducted in Australia (Browne, Langham, et al., 2016) and New Zealand (Browne, Rawat, et al., 2017) has attempted to address these gaps. A comprehensive checklist of 72 specific harms, organised into six domains, were developed from a literature review and qualitative interviews (Langham, Thorne, et al., 2016), examples of which are given in Figure 2.1. From this, a profile of harm can be generated for an individual based on whether each harm has occurred to them or not in the nominated time frame. The harms are applicable both to people who gamble and "concerned significant others", e.g., a spouse or parent. Item-response theoretic analysis demonstrates that specific harms vary widely in their severity (Li, Browne, Rawat, Langham, & Rockloff, 2016): e.g., reduced available spending on entertainment is the least severe financial harm, whilst bankruptcy is the most severe financial harm. Like previous research, it was found that harm symptomatology was distributed across the continuum of problem severity. Harms also appear to be unidimensional. That is, an affected individual is likely to experience a range of harmful outcomes from across the six domains. This is true also for concerned significant others (those affected by someone's gambling), although the specific pattern of harms within each domain differs. For example, spouses are more likely to experience the emotional harms of vulnerability, hopelessness, and distress; whilst people who gamble are more likely to report feelings of worthlessness, shame, and failure (unpublished analysis). A ten-item short screen for gambling harm was also developed, with scores being strongly correlated with the full checklist ($r = 0.93$), and linearly related to decreases in self-reported quality of life (Browne, Goodwin, & Rockloff, 2017). Thus, our work creates a link between the experience of harm and its impact on well-being. This is an important link, since it allows a calculation of both individual impacts and the population-level impacts of gambling harm on the community.

The prior research has dealt with the objective of establishing a comprehensive index of gambling harm, as well as a dedicated measurement instrument. Related work has adapted public health methodologies (Arnold, Girling, Stevens, & Lilford, 2009; Krabbe, Essink-Bot, & Bonsel, 1997) for the purpose of translating these symptoms into total measure of impact on an individual's quality of life. Harm symptomatology profiles across the continuum were converted into a large set of

20 Matthew Browne

natural language vignettes in order to directly elicit state valuations from an Australian community sample (Browne, Rawat, et al., 2017). Given a health state scale from zero (a life not worth living) to one (perfect health and well-being), low-risk, moderate-risk and problem gambling were associated with an average decrement of 0.13, 0.29 and 0.44 respectively. These per-person decrements were then applied to the population prevalence of these categories of gambling (Browne, Greer, Rawat, & Rockloff, 2017). The majority of harm calculated from aggregation was found to accrue to low to moderate-risk gambling, due to the higher prevalence of individuals in these groups. Similar findings were also reported in New Zealand (Browne, Bellringer, et al., 2017).

Conclusion

Early research on gambling harm has conflated the gambling harms with related but distinct constructs of behavioural dependence and excessive consumption. More recent work, based on the theoretical model presented earlier, has focused specifically on harm as the negative consequence of excessive gambling. Using new tools, some borrowed from epidemiology and public health, our research has supported earlier findings; that harm from gambling is not restricted to the 1–2% of individuals categorised as problem gamblers but rather is distributed more widely across the continuum of gambling involvement. Given that our focus is consequently drawn to milder forms of gambling harm, the benefits of gambling for these individuals should also be taken into account. Translation of harm into a total quality of life decrement involves many methodological challenges. Accordingly, our preliminary results need to be confirmed using alternative elicitation protocols. Moreover, it is important to measure harm in a population-representative survey in the future, since our prior work has projected harm to the population based on the past estimates of the composition of low-risk, moderate-risk and problem-gambling, rather than direct measurement.

Research on gambling-harms using the new methods described here, that relate harm (negatively) to population well-being, have potentially profound implications for how we address gambling as a public good or evil. It appears that a majority of participants are experiencing more benefits than harm: a large minority are experiencing minor to moderate harms and a small minority are experiencing severe harm. When a full accounting of benefits is considered, it may be that gambling yields a net societal benefit, albeit potentially a minor one. Nevertheless, it must be acknowledged that the costs are unfairly distributed to a minority of participants, particularly poorer and more socially disadvantaged people. A challenge for the future is to improve the aggregate societal outcome of gambling involvement, as well as finding ways to distribute the benefits more fairly amongst everyone involved. In our estimation, we must move away from a prevention paradigm of limiting transitions to "problem gambling" and rather focus on maximising net outcomes and equity amongst participating individuals.

References

Abbott, M., Binde, P., Clark, L., Hodgins, D., Korn, D., Pereira, A., . . . Williams, R. (2015). Conceptual framework of harmful gambling: An international collaboration. *Gambling Research Exchange Ontario (GREO)*. Retrieved from http://dspace.ucalgary.ca/handle/1880/51023

Allister McGregor, J., Camfield, L., & Woodcock, A. (2009). Needs, wants and goals: Well-being, quality of life and public policy. *Applied Research in Quality of Life, 4*(2), 135–154.

Arnold, D., Girling, A., Stevens, A., & Lilford, R. (2009). Comparison of direct and indirect methods of estimating health state utilities for resource allocation: Review and empirical analysis. *BMJ, 339*, b2688.

Blaszczynski, A. (2009). Problem gambling: We should measure harm rather than "cases". *Addiction, 104*(7), 1072–1074.

Blaszczynski, A., Ladouceur, R., Goulet, A., & Savard, C. (2006). "How much do you spend gambling?": Ambiguities in questionnaire items assessing expenditure. *International Gambling Studies, 6*(2), 123–128.

Browne, M., Bellringer, M., Greer, N., Kolandai-Matchett, K., Rawat, V., Langham, E., . . . Abbott, M. (2017). *Measuring the Burden of Gambling Harm in New Zealand*. New Zealand Ministry of Health.

Browne, M., Goodwin, B. C., & Rockloff, M. J. (2017). Validation of the Short Gambling Harm Screen (SGHS): A tool for assessment of harms from gambling. *Journal of Gambling Studies, 32*(2), 499–512. https://doi.org/10.1007/s10899-017-9698-y

Browne, M., Greer, N., Rawat, V., & Rockloff, M. (2017). A population-level metric for gambling-related harm. *International Gambling Studies, 17*(2), 1–14.

Browne, M., Langham, E., Rawat, V., Greer, N., Li, E., Rose, J., . . . Best, T. (2016). Assessing gambling-related harm in Victoria: A public health perspective. *Victorian Responsible Gambling Foundation*.

Browne, M., Rawat, V., Greer, N., Langham, E., Rockloff, M., & Hanley, C. (2017). What is the harm? Applying a public health methodology to measure the impact of gambling problems and harm on quality of life. *Journal of Gambling Issues, 36*, 28–50.

Canale, N., Vieno, A., & Griffiths, M. D. (2016). The extent and distribution of gambling-related harms and the prevention paradox in a British population survey. *Journal of Behavioral Addictions, 5*(2), 204–212.

Currie, S. R., Miller, N., Hodgins, D. C., & Wang, J. (2009). Defining a threshold of harm from gambling for population health surveillance research. *International Gambling Studies, 9*(1), 19–38.

Griffiths, M. (2005). A "components" model of addiction within a biopsychosocial framework. *Journal of Substance Use, 10*(4), 191–197.

Korn, D. A., Gibbins, R., & Azmier, J. (2003). Framing public policy towards a public health paradigm for gambling. *Journal of Gambling Studies/Co-Sponsored by the National Council on Problem Gambling and Institute for the Study of Gambling and Commercial Gaming, 19*(2), 235–256.

Korn, D. A., & Shaffer, H. J. (1999). Gambling and the health of the public: Adopting a public health perspective. *Journal of Gambling Studies/Co-Sponsored by the National Council on Problem Gambling and Institute for the Study of Gambling and Commercial Gaming, 15*(4), 289–365.

Krabbe, P. F., Essink-Bot, M. L., & Bonsel, G. J. (1997). The comparability and reliability of five health-state valuation methods. *Social Science & Medicine, 45*(11), 1641–1652.

Langham, E., Thorne, H., Browne, M., Donaldson, P., Rose, J., & Rockloff, M. (2016). Understanding gambling related harm: A proposed definition, conceptual framework, and taxonomy of harms. *BMC Public Health, 16*(1), 80.

Li, E., Browne, M., Rawat, V., Langham, E., & Rockloff, M. (2016). Breaking bad: Comparing gambling harms among gamblers and affected others. *Journal of Gambling Studies, 33*(1), 223–248. https://doi.org/10.1007/s10899-016-9632-8

Marshall, D. (2009). Gambling as a public health issue: The critical role of the local environment. *Journal of Gambling Issues, 23*, 66–80.

Mill, J. S. (1869). On liberty. *Longmans, Green, Reader, and Dyer.* London, J.W. Parker and Son.

Raisamo, S. U., Mäkelä, P., Salonen, A. H., & Lintonen, T. P. (2015). The extent and distribution of gambling harm in Finland as assessed by the Problem Gambling Severity Index. *European Journal of Public Health, 25*(4), 716–722.

Rockloff, M. J. (2012). Validation of the Consumption Screen for Problem Gambling (CSPG). *Journal of Gambling Studies/Co-Sponsored by the National Council on Problem Gambling and Institute for the Study of Gambling and Commercial Gaming, 28*(2), 207–216.

Rockloff, M. J., Russell, A., Browne, M., & Hing, N. (n.d.). *The Utility of Gambling for Entertainment.* Presented at the AGRI Conference 2017, Central Queensland University, Banff, Canada.

Rodgers, B., Caldwell, T., & Butterworth, P. (2009). Measuring gambling participation. *Addiction, 104*(7), 1065–1069.

Rose, G. (1981). Strategy of prevention: Lessons from cardiovascular disease. *British Medical Journal, 282*(6279), 1847–1851.

Shaffer, H. J., & Kidman, R. (2004). *Gambling and the Public Health.* Washington DC: American Psychiatric Publishing, Inc.

Wynne, H. (2003). *Introducing the Canadian Problem Gambling Index.* Edmonton, AB: Wynne Resources. Retrieved from http://classes.uleth.ca/201201/hlsc3700a/The%20Canadian%20Problem%20Gambling%20Index.pdf

3

THE SOCIAL COST OF EXCESSIVE GAMBLING

Claude Jeanrenaud, Mélanie Gay, Dimitri Kohler, Jacques Besson and Olivier Simon

Introduction

Excessive gambling has a wide range of adverse impacts on people who gamble, their relatives, their social environments and the community. Individuals with a gambling disorder or gambling problem often experience various other issues: mental health disorders, nonmedical use of psychoactive substances (alcohol, tobacco, and controlled substances), criminal behaviour, domestic violence, verbal and physical abuse, problems at work, increased risk of unemployment, stress resulting from indebtedness and bankruptcy and higher suicide rates (Lorains, Cowlishaw, & Thomas, 2011; National Research Council (NRC), 1999; Productivity Commission, 1999). Spouses of individuals with a gambling disorder have reported often suffering from chronic or severe headache, stomach problems, dizziness and breathing difficulty, along with emotional issues of anger, depression and isolation (Lorenz & Yaffee, 1988, as cited in NRC, 1999). In Switzerland, there are on average 1.4 other family members in the household of each individual with a gambling disorder and 1.2 in the house of each person with problematic gambling. Friends, co-workers, and people involved in a financial relationship with individuals who have a gambling disorder are also affected by their addiction (Reith, 2006). The Australian Productivity Commission (1999) stated that five to ten people are affected by every individual with a gambling disorder. There are no indications that this number is lower in other countries.

Social cost is the sum of three components: direct cost (i.e., the resources devoted to medical treatments and police or judicial investigations); indirect cost, or productivity cost, includes reduced on-the-job productivity, short-term work incapacity, disability and long-term unemployment; and human cost (i.e., loss in the quality of life of people who gamble or their relatives because of their gambling behaviours).

In studies devoted to evaluating the cost of nonmedical substance use (tobacco, alcohol) or the cost of nonsubstance addiction, the term social cost

24 Claude Jeanrenaud et al.

has an unusual meaning. Social cost refers to part of the internal cost that is not "freely and knowingly borne by the consumer himself" plus the cost that falls on the rest of the community. In the usual economic terminology, these costs are called negative externalities. Following this definition, the total cost of excessive gambling to the community can be divided into two components – private cost and social cost (Collins & Lapsley, 2003; Markandya & Pearce, 1989). This practice is not straightforward because the burden that the consumer bears is usually considered private. However, the condition is that the consumers behave rationally and are aware of the cost they bear, including difficulties at work and the risks of losing their job, of receiving a lower salary and of a reduced health state. If consumers neither act rationally nor consider these impacts when they decide to undertake the activity, the adverse side-effects of gambling will be included in the social cost.

Three studies have attempted to estimate the social cost of gambling disorder in Switzerland. The first study concluded that the social cost of gambling in Switzerland in 2002 amounts to CHF100 million (Künzi, Fritschi, & Egger, 2004). The bulk of this amount – CHF70 million – is for loans that remain unpaid. These unpaid loans are transfers, not a real cost. They should be ignored when estimating the burden of gambling on a community. Therefore, the true cost of excessive gambling amounts to CHF30 million. The second study focused on the social cost of casino gambling. Direct and indirect costs altogether amount to CHF70 million (Künzi, Fritschi, Oesch, Gehrig, & Julien, 2009). Kohler (2014) used a generic instrument to measure changes in the quality of life of individuals with gambling disorder and observed that gambling disorder leads to a loss of 0.076 quality-adjusted life years (QALY).

The Australian Productivity Commission (1999) estimated that the cost of excessive gambling for the Australian population is about AUD1.8 billion to 5.6 billion, which amounts to AUD6,000–19,000 per individual with a gambling problem (between CHF4,500 and CHF14,200 at the current exchange rate). The relevance of this study lies in the fact that the loss in quality of life is part of the social cost estimate. Loss in quality of life represents the most significant share of the social cost (about three quarters). The Victorian Responsible Gambling Foundation recently conducted a study on the adverse effects of gambling in the state of Victoria, Australia (Browne et al., 2016). The authors estimated the annual years lost due to disability (YLD) for low-risk, moderate risk and problem gambling using direct methods (time trade-off and visual analogue scale). Financial harm is one of the dimensions considered, with the result that the utility loss estimate probably entails some non-health-related costs (reduced living standard, erosion of savings, and sale of personal items). The loss of utility due to gambling was measured at 0.13, 0.29 and 0.44 for low-risk, moderate risk, and problem gambling, respectively (with 1.0 signifying full health). The annual number of years lost due to disability (YLD) for people who gamble is 101,700 and for their relatives is 16,200. The adult population of the state of Victoria is 4.4 million, which corresponds to 62% of the Swiss population aged 18 and over. Using the value government agencies place on human life (value of a statistical life year VSL), AUD182,500 (Australian Government, 2014), the annual quality of life cost of an individual with gambling disorder (the most severe category in the study) is AUD80,100 (CHF59,800), which seems surprisingly high. The monetary equivalent of the quality of life loss for a person with gambling disorder in Switzerland estimated by Kohler (2014) is only a fraction of this amount (between CHF3,800 and CHF6,380).

The cost of excessive gambling in Switzerland

Context and results

Our study on the social cost of excessive gambling in Switzerland is the result of a collaboration between the Institute of Economic Research in Neuchâtel and the Centre for Excessive Gambling, Community Psychiatric Service, Lausanne University Hospital. The social cost estimate is based on data provided by the 2007 Swiss Health Survey. The Federal Gaming Board retained a three-item instrument to screen for gambling disorder, the extended Lie/Bet questionnaire[1] (Eidgenössische Spielbankenkommission ESBK, 2009; Tomei et al., 2009). Individuals with a gambling problem and those with gambling disorders make up 1.5% and 0.5% of the adult population, respectively. Therefore, people who gamble excessively account for 2.0% of the population over 18 years or 120,000 individuals. The small number of people who gamble excessively in the survey sample (219 individuals with a gambling problem and 69 with a gambling disorder out of a total of about 20,000 survey respondents) made it difficult to construct a statistical model. Furthermore, the Swiss Health Survey is a cross-sectional survey, not a panel, because it provides data from the Swiss population at a specific point in time. In the absence of longitudinal data, it is difficult to ascertain whether the onset of problem gambling precedes health impairment and thus to identify the causal factor. Numerous clinical studies have observed an association between depression and gambling disorder but are unsure about which of the two came first (NRC, 1999). There are similar problems regarding the relationship between gambling and work-related difficulties or long-term unemployment.

Social cost studies usually make a distinction between direct cost (medical and nonmedical), indirect cost (loss in production) and human cost (reduced quality of life). The adopted counterfactual scenario is an alternative state of affairs in which there is no excessive gambling.

Medical and gambling addiction treatment

The Swiss Health Survey shows that people who gamble excessively visit physicians more frequently than individuals without gambling problems. However, this result does not provide evidence that increased morbidity is the consequence of problem gambling, and it is not easy to find a proper instrument to control for

26 Claude Jeanrenaud et al.

reverse causality. We, therefore, considered the direct cost estimate from the Swiss Federal Gaming Board commissioned study (Künzi et al., 2009). The following cost categories are considered: medical and addiction treatment costs, judicial and police administrative costs and legal expenditures attributable to divorces. The yearly direct cost of excessive gambling amounts to CHF8.5 million.

Loss of resources and forgone production

The indirect cost includes reduced production because of frequent absence, lower productivity, and early retirement. We observed that individuals with gambling disorder or gambling-related problem have, on average, a lower labour force participation rate than the general population (42.1% and 41.3% for problem gambling and gambling disorder, respectively, against 50.4% for the general population). They also have a lower average income (CHF3,630 and CHF3,160 for problem gambling and gambling disorder, respectively, against CHF4,120 for the general population). However, the characteristics of the two communities – people who gamble excessively and the general population – differ, and these differences may explain the reduced participation rate and income of people who gamble excessively. Therefore, we used a statistical model to control for the set of individual characteristics that can influence productivity, work participation and compensation.

The first model has the following form:

$$employrate_i = \alpha + \beta_1 gambproblem_i + \beta_2 gambdisorder_i + \gamma socio_i + e_i$$

$Employrate_i$ (the dependent variable) is the economic activity rate (between 0 and 100), $gambproblem_i$ and $gambdisorder_i$ are the variables to identify people who gamble excessively, $socio_i$ is the vector of variables describing the individuals' socioeconomic characteristics (control variables) and e_i is the error term.

The income estimation model has an identical form, with the dependent variable being $income_i$, the monthly income in Swiss francs (CHF).

$$income_i = \alpha + \beta_1 probgambler_i + \beta_2 gambdisorder_i + \gamma socio_i + e_i$$

The two models contain the following control variables: age (and square of age), age groups (agegroup1: 15–24 years, agegroup2: 25–44 years, and agegroup3: 45–64 being the reference category), gender (male = 1), highest level of education (edu1: elementary school, edu2: high school, and tertiary education), Swiss citizenship, self-employment status and alcohol problems.

After controlling for these variables, we observed that the employment rate for individuals with a gambling disorder was 28% lower (or 14.1 points, see Table 3.1, model 5) than that of a match sample with no gambling disorder, the monthly income being 24% lower (or CHF1,020, Table 3.1, model 4). β is highly significant ($p<0.0001$). After controlling for socioeconomic characteristics, we observed no significant relationship between problem gambling and employment rate or monthly income.

TABLE 3.1 OLS regressions modelling the impact of gambling on employment rate and monthly income

	Dependent variable: employment rate					Dependent variable: monthly income				
	(1) employrate	(2) employrate	(3) employrate	(4) employrate	(5) employrate	(1) income	(2) income	(3) income	(4) income	(5) income
agegroup1	3.511*			2.044		-2687.7***	-2720.7***			
	-2.14			-1.01		(-26.60)	(-27.14)			
agegroup2	21.03***			22.05***		-181.7*	-198.9*			
	-23.07			-21.08		(-2.15)	(-2.35)			
man	29.11***	28.38***	30.45***	29.22***	29.46***	2574.2***	2587.3***	2564.3***	2563.4***	2595.5***
	-40.66	-38	-43.68	-34.5	-41.93	-37.99	-37.82	-38.46	-38.13	-32.92
edu1	-22.83***	-28.53***	-21.26***	-21.20***	-20.51***	-2990.6***	-3018.8***	-3013.6***	-3017.7***	-3150.1***
	(-14.84)	(-17.72)	(-14.03)	(-11.46)	(-13.64)	(-27.95)	(-28.84)	(-28.03)	(-29.07)	(-23.09)
edu2	-7.610***	-10.55***	-7.518***	-7.448***	-7.222***	-2067.5***	-2069.3***	-2110.8***	-2109.9***	-2245.9***
	(-10.35)	(-14.15)	(-10.27)	(-8.88)	(-9.92)	(-24.47)	(-24.25)	(-25.31)	(-25.18)	(-22.04)
gambdisorder	-14.67*	-17.95**	-15.03*	-14.64*	-14.09*	-1014.0***	-1028.9***	-1022.4***	-1021.7***	-1342.1***
	(-2.35)	(-2.76)	(-2.47)	(-2.12)	(-2.32)	(-3.71)	(-3.76)	(-3.67)	(-3.66)	(-4.48)
Gambproblem	-4.093	-6.398	-4.708	-4.247	-4.155	-599.6	-609.9	-635.3	-635.7	-1075.6***
	(-1.03)	(-1.58)	(-1.16)	(-1.00)	(-1.04)	(-1.64)	(-1.67)	(-1.75)	(-1.75)	(-4.74)
Swiss citizen	-3.561**	-6.059***	-2.232*	-2.257	2.726*	96.65		28.9		44.1
	(-3.18)	(-5.27)	(-2.01)	(-1.77)	(-2.46)	-0.8		-0.24		(-0.29)
self-employed	14.65***	16.24***		14.72***	14.40***	252.2		118.6	119.7	136.3
	-16.41	-18.11		-14.66	-15.93	-1.71		-0.81	-0.81	-0.78

(Continued)

TABLE 3.1 (Continued)

	Dependent variable: employment rate					Dependent variable: monthly income				
	(1) employrate	(2) employrate	(3) employrate	(4) employrate	(5) employrate	(1) income	(2) income	(3) income	(4) income	(5) income
age		−0.277*** (−8.42)	4.628*** −25.13		4.479*** −24.46			300.3*** −24.23	299 9*** −24.16	3331*** −21.37
agesquare			−0.0591*** (−27.26)		−0.0578*** (−26.93)			−2.975*** (−18.79)	−2.970*** (−18.80)	−3.304*** (−17.00)
prob alcohol				1.208 −0.87						231.8 −1.35
_cons	45.02*** −30.07	75.76*** −41.69	−20.78*** (−5.15)	43.10*** −25.21	−17.88*** (−4.44)	4891.4*** −32.63	5015.8*** −52.9	−2280.7*** (−8.61)	−2249.3*** (−9.39)	−2843.1*** (−8.46)
N	10601	10601	10602	7639	10601	10141	10142	10141	10141	7322
r2	0.242	0.2	0.25	0.256	0.2606	0.267	0.267	0.279	0.279	0.27
F	481.4	419	574.9	318.3	562.66	399.8	482.2	453	472.1	317.8

*P < 0.05

**P < 0.01

*** P < 0.001

The social cost of excessive gambling **29**

TABLE 3.2 Indirect cost of excessive gambling based on differences in participation rates

	Number	Participation rate	Hypothetical participation rate*	Monthly income (observed)	Loss of monthly income (CHF)**	Total annual loss of income, CHF million
Person with gambling disorder	34,900	41.3	55.4	3,160	1,078	451.6
Person with gambling problem	85,700	42.1	not significant	3,264		

*Participation rate of an individual from the general population with the same characteristics as the average person with a gambling disorder.

**Loss of monthly income due to reduced participation rate (34.1% of CHF 3,160).

TABLE 3.3 The indirect cost of excessive gambling based on differences in monthly income

	Number	Monthly income (CHF)	Hypothetical monthly income* (CHF)	Loss of monthly income (CHF)	Total annual loss of income, CHF million
Person with gambling disorder	34,900	3160	4181.7	1021.7	427.9
Person with gambling problem	85,700	3626	not significant		

*The income of an individual from the general population with the same characteristics as the average person with a gambling disorder.

The indirect cost of excessive gambling in the Swiss population amounts to CHF452 million per year (Table 3.2). We assumed that income varies proportionally to the employment rate. The loss of income attributable to gambling disorder corresponds to the difference between the income of individuals with a gambling disorder and their hypothetical income had they not developed a gambling disorder.

An alternative way to estimate the indirect cost of gambling disorder consists of measuring the differences between the actual monthly income of an individual with gambling disorder and the hypothetical income of an individual with the same characteristics from the general population (with the exception of gambling disorder). The indirect cost estimated this way amounts to CHF428 million (Table 3.3).

Reduced quality of life

In a seminal article, Kohler (2014) estimated the loss of health-related quality of life (HRQoL) due to gambling disorder in Switzerland. The group with gambling disorder (N = 52) consisted of people in treatment from centres in Western Switzerland,

30 Claude Jeanrenaud et al.

TABLE 3.4 Reduced quality of life for people who gamble excessively and their relatives

Excessive gambling	Person who gambles	Relatives*	QALY lost	Social cost in CHF million	
				Low estimate	High estimate
Person with gambling disorder	34,900	48,860	1,926	96.3	161.8
Person with gambling problem	85,700	102,840	377	18.9	31.7
Total	120,600	151,700	2,303	115.2	193.5

*According to the Swiss Health Survey in 2007, there are, on average, 1.4 relatives in the household of an individual with a gambling disorder and 1.2 relatives in the family of a person with problem gambling.

and the control group (N = 93) consisted of individuals from the general population. The two item Lie/Bet screening test was used to identify individuals with gambling disorders, and a generic preference-based method (SF-6D) was applied to measure the loss in the HRQoL for individuals with a gambling disorder. Kohler conducted a Tobit regression to control for the effect of confounding variables on HRQoL, comorbidities (depression, chronic diseases, or disabilities), individual characteristics (age), behaviour (smoking) and problematic use of alcohol screened with CAGE. Thus, we can observe the effect of gambling disorder on the quality of life, with all other variables being held constant. A fundamental assumption is that the comorbidities are not caused by gambling addiction. The regression model shows that gambling disorder is associated with loss in the quality of life by 0.076 QALY. Disease severity in people at the treatment centres was however significantly higher than that in an average person with gambling disorder in the Swiss Health Survey. A disease severity index based on responses to the Lie/Bet questionnaire confirms this hypothesis: The disease severity index amongst people at treatment centres is approximately three times the average value for people with gambling disorder (Jeanrenaud, Gay, Kohler, Besson, & Simon, 2012). The HRQoL loss amounts to 0.023 QALY for an average person with gambling disorder and 0.002 QALY for problem gambling. We assume that the loss of quality of life is the same for people who gamble excessively and their relatives. To express the QALY loss in monetary terms, we need to know the value of a life year (VOLY). According to a study by Jeanrenaud, Marti, and Pellegrini (2008), the VOLY is between CHF50,000 and CHF84,000 (see also Desaigues et al., 2011). The quality of life cost of excessive gambling lies in the range of CHF115.2 to 193.5 million (Table 3.4).

Social cost

The social cost of excessive gambling is the sum of direct cost (treatments of problem gambling and gambling addiction, judicial and legal expenses), indirect cost (reduced employment and productivity) and quality of life cost (personal and

The social cost of excessive gambling **31**

TABLE 3.5 The annual social cost of excessive gambling

Cost categories	Low	High
	CHF million	
Medical expenses and treatment of addictive behaviour (direct cost)	8.5	8.5
Productivity and employment costs (indirect cost)	427.9	451.6
Personal and family impact (quality of life cost)	115.2	193.5
Social cost	551.6	653.6

familial impact). The annual social cost of excessive gambling is in the range of CHF552 to 654 million (Table 3.5).

Discussion

Studies regarding the adverse economic impact of excessive gambling pose plenty of challenges. Gambling problems often coexist with substance disorders, mental health disorders and other comorbidities, and it is, therefore, difficult to separate the impact of one condition or behaviour from the others (Reith, 2006). The primary challenge in estimating the effect of excessive gambling on productivity and employment is simultaneous causality. Are long-term unemployed people more prone than the general population to developing a gambling disorder, or are people with gambling disorder at higher risk of losing their jobs? In other words, is unemployment a risk factor for excessive gambling or is excessive gambling a risk factor for unemployment? It is also possible that employment difficulties and problem gambling have a common causal factor: the literature indicates that mental health disorders make people more susceptible to gambling regularly and, in some instances, developing gambling problems (Abbott, Williams, & Volberg, 2004). They also make people more susceptible to encountering difficulties in relation to their employment. Unless we have longitudinal data and information about the chronology of events, we cannot establish whether problem gambling predates employment difficulties. The Swiss Health Survey is performed every five years with a new sample and does not provide information about the chronology of events.

There is evidence to suggest that, in most cases, the onset of problem gambling precedes employment-related problems. We suggest that the reduced productivity and employment rate of people with gambling disorders is attributable to problem gambling and not the other way around. The work behaviour of those with gambling disorders exposes them to a higher risk of losing their job or being less productive at work. They are often late to work, leave work early to gamble, take extended breaks, steal from other employees, are frequently absent, use work hours for personal purposes and have poor job performance (Nower, 2003). Evidence shows that a significant proportion (25%–30%) of people with a gambling disorder

32 Claude Jeanrenaud et al.

have reported losing their job as a consequence of their disorder (Lesieur, 1998, cited in Nower, 2003). The prevalence of depression and problematic alcohol use or dependence is high in this population. Therefore, we have to examine whether depression could be a common risk factor for gambling disorder and work-related difficulties. In an early study devoted to solving this question, McCormick, Russo, Ramirez, and Taber (1984) observed that gambling preceded depression in 86% cases (NRC, 1999). However, there are also studies that reached the opposite conclusion (Cunningham-Williams, Cottler, Compton, & Spitznagel, 1998; Martin, 2004). Martin (2004) observed that for many people who gamble problematically, mood disorders seem to predate the onset of gambling disorder. This observation does not question the method used to estimate production losses. We should be aware that when the economic cost of both depression and gambling disorder are measured, there is a risk of double counting.

The indirect cost estimate is based on the human capital method, which equates the economic cost to the value of the forgone production. Every hour not worked represents a productivity cost. The alternative approach, the friction cost method, only counts lost hours until another employee replaces the absent employee. The value of lost production is significantly lower when the friction cost approach is applied. The reasons for not choosing the friction cost method is that the underlying assumptions are not realistic (indirect costs only occur during the short period it takes to find and train a new employee). Johannesson and Karlsson (1997) consider the friction cost method as an inappropriate substitute method to human capital in the estimation of indirect costs.

The quality of life losses due to gambling disorder for Switzerland are surprisingly low. The HRQoL weight is 97.3, pretty close to full heath, for an average disorder and 92.4 for the most severe cases recruited from treatment centres in Western Switzerland. By comparison, the HRQoL weights found in the literature for alcohol dependency are substantially lower: 67 for alcohol dependence by Kraemer et al. (2005); 89 for problem drinking and 45 for alcohol dependency by Stouthard et al. (1997); 92, 83 and 66 for three levels of alcohol dependency by Sanderson, Andrews, Corry, and Lapsley (2004); and between 56 (problem gambling) and 87 (low risk gambling) in a recent study measuring gambling-related harm (Browne et al., 2016). These studies have adopted a direct approach (standard gamble, time trade-off and visual analogue rating scale) based on the preferences of the general population or physicians. These differences – a person with gambling disorder having a quality of life that is close to that of a person with perfect health but an alcohol-dependent person having a severely reduced quality of life – seems implausible. This view is confirmed by a comparison of the estimated direct cost of gambling and alcohol dependence. The monetary equivalent of the loss of quality of life for a person with gambling disorder in Switzerland lies in the range of CHF1,150 and CHF1,930 per year, whereas the same indicator for an alcohol-dependent person in treatment is close to CHF14,000 (Jeanrenaud, Priez, Pellegrini, Chevrou-Severac, & Vitale, 2003; see also Abbott, 2017). The substantial difference may be the consequence of applying two different instruments – a generic tool and a direct approach – to measure changes in the quality of life caused by problematic alcohol use and gambling disorder, respectively. In Browne et al.'s study on the population of Victoria (2016), the yearly quality-of-life cost for a person who gambles problematically was close to CHF60,000.

Generic instruments focus on physical incapacity and probably underestimate the loss of quality of life caused by alcohol dependency or gambling disorder. As Luquiens, Reynaud, Falissard, and Aubin (2012) note, the non-disease specific instruments currently used to assess HRQoL, such as SF-36/12 or EQ-5D, do not collect information that is both relevant and accurate to the lives of these individuals. Rodriguez-Miguez and Mosquera Nogueira (2017) expressed a similar point of view when they concluded that a narrow focus can lead to a substantial underestimation of the impact of substance use disorder or nonsubstance addictive behaviour on quality of life. To adequately measure the HRQoL loss associated with gambling disorder, an instrument with the capability to account not only for physical incapacity but also psychosocial incapacity and capture the person's overall state of well-being must be developed. Another solution would be to assess HRQoL losses using a direct approach, such as time trade-off (respondent trade health state for different risks of death) or standard gamble (respondent trade health state for months/years of remaining life).

The last question of interest remains whether people with gambling disorder pay their way? A small share of medical costs is borne by people who gamble excessively, such as copayments and deductibles, whereas the most substantial part is borne by the general population through the health insurance system and taxation because public funds cover half of the hospital expenditure, and subsidies to reduce health insurance premiums are funded through taxes. Productivity costs are also shared because a significant part is borne by people who gamble excessively (lower income, extended periods of unemployment and premature retirement), the general population provides the remainder through compulsory unemployment insurance contributions, social insurance contributions and taxation. People who gamble excessively and their relatives only bear the entirety of the quality-of-life costs.

Note

1 In this chapter, "gambling disorder" (terminology from DSM-5, 2013) corresponds to the definition of pathological gambling according to DSM IV (2004), and "problem gambling" refers to the subclinical categories of DSM-IV (3–4 criteria). The adapted Lie-Bet (2007) includes three questions; a score of more than 2 indicates "gambling disorder" and 1 indicates "problem gambling".

References

Abbott, M. W. (2017). The epidemiology and impact of gambling disorder and other gambling-related harm. In *Who Forum on Alcohol, Drugs and Addictive Behaviours* (pp. 1–9). Geneva: World Health Organization.

Abbott, M. W., Williams, M. M., & Volberg, R. A. (2004). A prospective study of problem and regular nonproblem gamblers living in the community. *Substance Use & Misuse, 39*(6), 855–884. doi:10.1081/ja-120030891

34 Claude Jeanrenaud et al.

Australian Government, Department of the Prime Minister and Cabinet, Office of Best Practice Regulation. (2014). *Best Practice Regulation Guidance Note: Value of Statistical Life.* Retrieved from www.pmc.gov.au/sites/default/files/publications/Value_of_Statistical_Life_guidance_note.pdf

Browne, M., Langham, E., Rawat, V., Greer, N., Li, E., Rose, J., . . . Best, T. (2016). *Assessing Gambling-Related Harm in Victoria: A Public Health Perspective.* Melbourne: Victorian Responsible Gambling Foundation.

Collins, D., & Lapsley, H. (2003). The social costs and benefits of gambling: An introduction to the economic issues. *Journal of Gambling Studies, 19*(2), 123–148.

Cunningham-Williams, R. M., Cottler, L. B., Compton, W. M., & Spitznagel, E. L. (1998). Taking chances: Problem gamblers and mental health disorders-results from the St. Louis Epidemiologic Catchment Area Study. *American Journal of Public Health, 88*(7), 1093–1096. doi:10.2105/ajph.88.7.1093

Desaigues, B., Ami, D., Bartczak, A., Braun-Kohlová, M., Chilton, S., Czajkowski, M., . . . Urban, J. (2011). Economic valuation of air pollution mortality: A 9-country contingent valuation survey of value of a life year (VOLY). *Ecological Indicators, 11*(3), 902–910. doi:10.1016/j.ecolind.2010.12.006

Eidgenössische Spielbankenkommission ESBK. (2009). *Glücksspiel: Verhalten und Problematik in der Schweiz: Schlussbericht.* Bern.

Jeanrenaud, C., Gay, M., Kohler, D., Besson, J., & Simon, O. (2012). *Le coût social du jeu excessif en Suisse.* Lausanne: IRENE, Université de Neuchâtel et CJE, Service de psychiatrie communautaire.

Jeanrenaud, C., Marti, J., & Pellegrini, S. (2008). *The Cost of Reduced Life Expectancy Due to Air Pollution: Assessing the Value of a Life Year (VOLY) Using Contingent Valuation.* Poster at the 2nd Biennial Conference of the American Society of Health Economists. Durham, NC: Duke University.

Jeanrenaud, C., Priez, F., Pellegrini, S., Chevrou-Severac, H., & Vitale, S. (2003). *Le coût social de l'abus d'alcool en Suisse.* Neuchâtel: IRENE, University of Neuchâtel.

Johannesson, M., & Karlsson, G. (1997). The friction cost method: A comment. *Journal of Health Economics, 16*, 249–255.

Kohler, D. (2014). A monetary valuation of the quality of life loss associated with pathological gambling: An application using a health utility index. *Journal of Gambling Issues, 29*, 1–23.

Kraemer, K. L., Roberts, M. S., Horton, N. J., Palfai, T., Samet, J. H., Freedner, N., . . . Saitz, R. (2005). Health utility ratings for a spectrum of alcohol-related health states. *Medical Care, 43*(6), 541–550. doi:10.1097/01.mlr.0000163644.97251.14

Künzi, K., Fritschi, T., & Egger, T. (2004). *Glücksspiel und Spielsucht in der Schweiz: Empirische Untersuchung von Spielpraxis, Entwicklung, Sucht und Konsequenzen* (pp. 1–213, Tech.). Bern: BASS. Im Auftrag der Eidgenössischen Spielbankenkommission und des Bundesamtes für Justiz.

Künzi, K., Fritschi, T., Oesch, T., Gehrig, M., & Julien, N. (2009). *Sozialen Kosten des Glücksspiels in Casinos: Studie zur Erfassung der durch die Schweizer Casinos verursachten sozialen Kosten* (Rep.). Bern: Bass. Im Auftrag der Eidgenössischen Spielbankkommission ESKB.

Lesieur, H. (1998). Cost and treatment of pathological gambling. *Annals AAPSS, 556*, 153–171.

Lorains, F. K., Cowlishaw, S., & Thomas, S. A. (2011). Prevalence of comorbid disorders in problem and pathological gambling: Systematic review and meta-analysis of population surveys. *Addiction, 106*(3), 490–498. doi:10.1111/j.1360-0443.2010.03300.x

Lorenz, V. C., & Yaffee, R. A. (1988). Pathological gambling: Psychosomatic, emotional and marital difficulties as reported by the spouse. *Journal of Gambling Behavior, 4*(1), 13–26. doi:10.1007/bf01043525

Luquiens, A., Reynaud, M., Falissard, B., & Aubin, H. (2012). Quality of life among alcohol-dependent patients: How satisfactory are the available instruments? A systematic review. *Drug and Alcohol Dependence, 125*(3), 192–202. doi:10.1016/j.drugalcdep.2012.08.012

Markandya, A., & Pearce, D. W. (1989). The social costs of tobacco smoking. *British Journal of Addiction, 84*(10), 1138–1150.

Martin, N. (2004). *Mood Disorders and Problem Gambling: Cause, Effect or Cause for Concern*. Typescript, Mood Disorders Society of Canada. Retrieved from https://mdsc.ca/documents/Publications/MoodDisordersandProblemGamblingAReviewofLiterature.pdf

McCormick, R. A., Russo, A. M., Ramirez, L. F., & Taber, J. I. (1984). Affective disorders among pathological gamblers seeking treatment. *American Journal of Psychiatry, 141*, 215–218.

National Research Council. (1999). *Pathological Gambling: A Critical Review*. Washington, DC: The National Academies Press. https://doi.org/10.17226/6329

Nower, L. (2003). Pathological gamblers in the workplace. *Employee Assistance Quarterly, 18*(4), 55–72. doi:10.1300/j022v18n04_03

Productivity Commission. (1999). *Australia's Gambling Industries*. Report No. 10. Canberra: AusInfo.

Reith, G. (2006). *Research on the Social Impacts of Gambling: Final Report*. Edinburgh: The Scottish Executive Social Research.

Rodriguez-Miguez, E., & Mosquera Nogueira, J. (2017). Measuring the impact of alcohol-related disorders on quality of life through general population preferences. *Gaceta Sanitaria, 31*(2), 98–94.

Sanderson, K., Andrews, G., Corry, J., & Lapsley, H. (2004). Using the effect size to model change in preference values from descriptive health status. *Quality of Life Research, 13*(7), 1255–1264. doi:10.1023/b:qure.0000037482.92757.82

Stouthard, M., Essink-Bot, M., Bonsel, G., Barendregt, J., Kramers, P., Van de Water, H., . . . Van der Maas, P. (1997). *Disability Weights for Diseases in the Netherlands*. Rotterdam: Typescript, Erasmus University, Department of Public Health.

Tomei, A., Hardegger, S., Tichelli, E., & Rihs-Middel, M. (2009). *Validation du test LBE en langue française pour le dépistage du jeu pathologique dans la population adulte. Rapport final*. Villars-sur-Glâne: FERARIHS.

4

THE NORMALISATION OF DANGEROUS GAMBLING

An ethical issue

Jim Orford

Introduction

Commercial gambling is now on a colossal scale, with gross annual global revenue in the region of half a trillion US dollars (Sulkunen et al., 2019; see also Chapter 1). Pronouncements by gambling providers and supportive governments have increasingly portrayed gambling as harmless amusement, a leisure activity like any other such commodity, to which the public has a right, hindered by as few restrictions as possible. Gambling is to be seen as a source of cultural and economic enhancement and, above all else, as a good example of ordinary business which ought to be allowed to innovate and flourish. An important element of that now-dominant discourse about the proper place of gambling in modern life (Orford, 2011, 2020) is the idea that gambling is normal, and unproblematic for most people, who engage in it because they find it entertaining. That is convenient to those who profit from the provision of gambling and is contrary to the view that the central motive for all gambling is the chance of winning money besides which other motives are peripheral (Binde, 2013) and contrary to evidence that whenever people who gamble are asked why they do so, topping the list is the prospect of winning money (e.g., Clarke et al., 2006; Wardle et al., 2011). This is reflected in the way gambling is advertised. Studies from Sweden (Binde, 2009) and Britain (Banks, 2014), involving, respectively, analysis of newspaper, magazine, poster, direct mail, television and film advertisements for gambling and study of e-mail online gambling promotions, are amongst those that have reported an advertising emphasis on the possibility of winning, although the actual probability of winning is rarely alluded to. Both also found an overemphasis on the skill element in gambling and an underemphasis on chance or luck.

The argument of this chapter is that whilst commercialised gambling is becoming increasingly normalised, that normalisation is based on a deception. Gambling is promoted, particularly towards young people, with an offer of the prospect of winning money, masked as entertainment or sport, when in reality commercial gambling is designed to help people lose money. We will begin by considering modern Electronic Gambling Machine (EGM) gambling.

Is modern EGM gambling inherently deceptive?

A crucial question, mostly avoided by governments and regulators, is whether some forms of gambling are more dangerous than others. In Britain, for example, we have nothing for gambling similar to the Class A, B, C system, which is central to regulation of drug supply and consumption. In fact, such systems do exist for suggesting how dangerous a form of gambling might be – the Veikkaus Ray model from Finland being one. Survey results from around the world have consistently found that it is EGM gambling which is the form most often associated with higher problem gambling prevalence – in no less than 75 studies in one review (Williams, Volberg, & Stevens, 2012). One indication of dangerousness is the degree to which a form of gambling draws for its profits on those with problems. Analysis of data from the 2010 British Gambling Prevalence Survey found that the fixed odds betting terminals (FOBTs, the British example of modern high-intensity EGMs) topped the list in that respect with an estimated 23% of gross gambling yield being contributed by people with problems, rising to around 40% if those at moderate risk were included (Orford, Wardle, & Griffiths, 2013).

Because of the multi-level prize structure of EGMs there is a high degree of "volatility" in the potential outcome from bet to bet. Turner (2011), working in Canada, where some of the best work on the intricacies of modern machine gambling has come from, ran multiple simulations of playing EGMs. He was able to show why, during a relatively short period of play, it is so difficult to appreciate how it is that the chances of ending up a winner are decreasing all the time, sooner or later decreasing to virtually nothing. This inexorable downward trend is, as Turner put it, "masked by the number of wins". All the simulated "players" who persisted continued to win small amounts from time to time and there were some who won a comparatively large amount, although even they would give it back to the machine if they persisted in playing. For any short length of play, less than a few thousand spins, it is difficult for a player to appreciate the house advantage.

Why information about payback percentage is mostly misleading and irrelevant: The importance of skewed distributions of wins

Harrigan and Dixon (2009, 2010) went further, making the crucial point that averages, such as payback percentage figures, otherwise known as return-to-player (RTP) percentages, give a very distorted impression of the experience of the average person playing such machines because of the very skewed distributions of wins. The larger number of players, if they win at all, win relatively small amounts whilst smaller and

38 Jim Orford

yet smaller proportions of players win larger and yet larger amounts. Only a small minority of players win a lot, and their winnings contribute disproportionately to the average payback. This is why, even in jurisdictions such as Britain where it is a requirement to provide RTP information, this is misleading. An RTP of say 90% masks the fact that the majority of players will lose. Arguing that the medians were a better indication of the experience of the "average" player, they were able to show that the payback percentages that the median players could expect, instead of the advertised averages of 85% and 98% (from the low and high payback machines they studied, respectively) were 67% and 73%.

The same dishonest claim, that customers are being given the opportunity to win money when in fact nearly all are losing nearly all the time, applies to online gambling, as was shown by LaBrie, LaPlante, Nelson, Schumann, and Shaffer's (2007) study of eight months' records of over 40,000 people betting with a single sports gambling company. The mathematical average of total amount wagered was in the region of €700–€1400 and average net losses €85–€97 (figures differed for bets on outcomes and live-action bets). However, as already noted, averages are misleading because most of their measures were heavily skewed; the 1% who wagered the most wagered an average of nearly €23,000, and the 1% who ran up the heaviest net losses lost an average of nearly €3,500. The operator's own figures for RTP were 87% for outcome and 94% for live-action betting. However, if percent losses were calculated separately for each individual player and then averaged, the average RTPs appeared much less generous, at 68% and 77%. Small bettors, who bet less and therefore contributed less to the calculation of overall loss percentage, actually lost a higher percentage of everything they bet. RTP is a highly misleading index and is widely misunderstood. It gives the false impression that gambling can be priced like any other entertainment product, although if gambling is to be thought of as a "product", then it is a very unusual one because the price for it is only paid by those who lose.

Losses disguised as wins

One of the important features of many modern machines which the simulations described earlier were not able to examine is the option available on machines in many countries to play on more than one line at a time. The same group of Canadian researchers (Templeton, Dixon, Harrigan, & Fugelsang, 2014) exposed an important effect of this popular option. When players experience a "win" on one line they may have the impression that they have won on that spin even though the other lines bet on are losses on that spin. This impression is encouraged by the celebration of every win on a single line, for example with the playing of a celebratory song and the lighting up of winning symbols. These researchers referred to such outcomes as "losses disguised as wins" or LDWs. They confirmed that players tend to overestimate the amount they are winning because they misinterpret LDWs as wins. Combined with the confusing effects of volatility, plus a high frequency of *near misses* – that other, long-recognised way of encouraging an overinflated perception of the likelihood of winning – this idea of LDWs is highly significant. It gives us an important insight into how all commercial gambling works: promoter profit is assured by deceiving people who gamble into thinking they are winning, or are about to, when in fact they will lose or are already doing so. Modern EGMs in particular are designed to take advantage of these motivating and habit-forming processes (Schüll, 2012). What has changed is not the basic dynamics of the processes but rather the speed and intensity involved and the use made of advanced, 'sophisticated' technology.

The normalisation of online gambling and its dangers

The "aggressive" promotion of online gambling

Engagement in online gambling is increasing internationally and is more strongly associated with problem gambling and more heavily concentrated amongst younger adults than is the case for other forms of gambling (Gainsbury, 2012). There have been a number of studies that have exposed the "aggressive" promotion of online gambling. They include a British study in which people gambling online were interviewed about the attractions of that way of gambling (McCormack & Griffiths, 2012) and a study from Nova Scotia which studied online poker sites from a variety of jurisdictions (McMullan & Kervin, 2012). People who gambled liked the convenience of online games which made available "24-hour gambling". Sites were found to be highly sophisticated, fast and easy to navigate. Most went out of their way to encourage feelings that players were gambling globally, that poker was a legitimate consumption practice that is taking place constantly, somewhere in the world. Dominant on the sites was a continual emphasis on wins, winning and winners. Most sites used message boards and screen displays to report significant winnings to other players, giving the impression that consumers were constantly winning and that another big win was coming up. Three-quarters of the sites appeared to promote the belief that poker afforded an alternative means to financial and social success.

Almost all sites offered incentives, attractive to many online players, including deposit, sign-up, welcome and other bonuses, including "reward programmes" for playing longer and bonuses for recruiting new players, travel and holiday packages and opportunities to play in poker tournaments. The age, clothing and behaviour of the human images portrayed on the websites gave the unmistakable impression that poker was a glamourous activity for young people to engage in. The opportunity for inexperienced players, at poker for example, to practice for free or with very small stakes in order to gain experience, offered by almost all sites, not possible at a casino, was also an attraction for some. Three-quarters of sites published responsibility statements. But most of these were found to be "parsimonious in style when compared to the fanfare surrounding promotional incentives, sponsorships and endorsements" (McMullan & Kervin, 2012, p. 637).

40 Jim Orford

Gambling aligned with sport

In one Australian study (Thomas, Lewis, McLeod, & Haycock, 2012) participants described what they saw as the role of marketing in normalising gambling, with advertising often containing implicit messages about masculinity, team loyalty and being able to prove sporting knowledge. The alignment with sport may be particularly harmful, especially for young males, the group known to be most at risk from gambling problems. The growth of live-action or "in-play" sports betting, which provides many betting opportunities which come quick and fast in real-time during a sporting event, has increased the intensity of sports betting. Researchers, particularly in Australia, have explored the ways in which sports betting marketing has become embedded within sport and how it appeals to fan loyalty, with celebrities used to help promote gambling products and professional sporting teams linked to gambling products, with the effect, it has been argued, of reinforcing the idea that gambling is fun – a harmless leisure activity, an easy way to win money (Gainsbury, Delfabbro, King, & Hing, 2015; Hing, Lamont, Vitartas, & Fink, 2015). Others have shown how sports betting is becoming a normal and socially accepted activity amongst young male peer groups, a natural "add on" to sport, with clear indicators that sports wagering is becoming embedded within existing peer-based sporting rituals (Deans, Thomas, Derevensky, & Daube, 2017). There are clear lessons from the Australian experience for other countries, relating to the ways in which industry marketing tactics may combine with culturally valued activities such as sport to influence risky gambling behaviours.

The new grey area of online gambling and gaming

A further indication of the normalisation of gambling, and particularly the dangers for young people, is the convergence of gambling with digital media technologies, and the rapid pace of development of new technologies, which has led to confusion about what is gambling and what is not. That has made it difficult to identify all those who are in effect providing gambling of the kind that may be consumed by adolescents and children. Several forms of Internet activity fall into this grey area (King, Delfabbro, & Griffiths, 2009). One is online games, often mixing skill and chance, in which a player can win points that can be transferred into real money. Furthermore, some online games feature advertisements and direct links to online gambling sites. Another grey area is "non-monetary forms of gambling" such as video games which include gambling situations and games of chance: for example, offering the possibility to enter a "casino" and play to win in-game money. An even more starkly obvious variety of nonmonetary gambling is when traditional casino games like poker, blackjack and roulette are made available as stand-alone video games which can be downloaded and played on a personal computer, mobile phone or dedicated game console using online services or by playing gambling apps on social networking sites. King et al. (2009) suggest that these grey area forms of gambling "may be problematic for adolescents because they promote positive

The normalisation of dangerous gambling **41**

attitudes towards gambling, portray gambling in glamorised and/or misrepresenta-
tive ways, and that these activities are freely available and playable by adolescents and
children" (p. 177). Playing money-free games may act as an important pathway into
"real" gambling for young people. In a national British survey 12 to 15 year olds,
8% admitted to gambling online and nearly three in ten of those who had gambled
online reported playing free "demo" games (National Lottery Commission, 2013).

Wider harms to communities and society

Attention has been drawn to various harms from gambling to communities, including changes to the nature of an area and unintended local labour market changes
(Goodman, 1995; Grinols, 2003; Langham et al., 2016; see also Chapters 2 and 3).
There are also wider issues to be faced such as the contribution that commercialised
gambling may be making to economic and health inequalities. Research from many
countries shows there to be a tendency for gambling problems to be concentrated
amongst relatively disadvantaged groups such as those with lower incomes and of
lower socioeconomic status, including the unemployed, ethnic minorities and home-
less people (Williams et al., 2012). Research in several countries, including Australia
and Britain (Marshall, 2005; Wardle, Kiely, Astbury, & Reith, 2014), has also found
area EGM density to be correlated with area disadvantage. In both those countries
it is the relatively poor who have a higher concentration of gambling opportunities in their areas, who lose a much higher proportion of their incomes gambling
and from whose communities a greater proportion of their collective wealth drains
away. If gambling is seen as a form of wealth transfer, from most people who gamble
to operating companies, and other beneficiaries such as governments, then it is
predominantly a transfer from the relatively less well off to the better off, from the
relatively powerless to the relatively powerful (Sulkunen et al., 2019).

Public attitudes

Whilst the gambling industry may, understandably, be reluctant to acknowledge
the harm that the normalisation of gambling is doing to societies, and governments dependent on gambling revenue may be complacent about the costs being
incurred, there is evidence that citizens themselves are much more conscious of cultural and societal harms. The 2007 and 2010 British Gambling Prevalence Surveys
included questions about attitudes towards gambling (Wardle et al., 2007, 2011).
The results were clear-cut. Although most people were not in favour of prohibition of gambling, the weight of public opinion was on the side of believing that
gambling is foolish and dangerous, that on balance it is bad rather than good for
families, communities and society as a whole and that it should not be encouraged
(Orford, Griffiths, Wardle, Sproston, & Erens, 2009). Although men were more positive towards gambling than women, younger people were more positive than older,
and people who gambled frequently more positive than others, all groups, including
the majority of those who gambled, were on balance negative in their attitudes.

Australia, Canada, Israel and Finland are other countries where public attitudes towards gambling have been assessed with similar results (Australian Productivity Commission, 1999; Azmier, 2000; Gavriel-Fried, 2015; Salonen et al., 2014). However, when it comes to the cultural acceptance of gambling there is further evidence of restraint erosion. In the three years between the 2007 and 2010 British prevalence surveys attitudes had moved slightly but significantly in a positive direction (Wardle et al., 2011).

An issue of values and ethics

Policymakers also need to be asking, not just whether gambling is harmful or harmless in rather narrow utilitarian terms, but whether more gambling increases the quality of life for us all (see also Chapter 1). There is an apparent official reluctance to address wider questions of values and ethics with policymakers adopting a stance of apparent ethical neutrality (Skidelsky & Skidelsky, 2013). However, it has been pointed out that this apparently neutral position can mask a far from neutral unquestioning support for an industry that provides health-damaging products (Hancock & Smith, 2017). Meanwhile legal and regulatory changes have reduced many former restraints on gambling (Orford, 2012, 2020): new forms and modes of gambling have been added whilst more familiar forms of gambling remain, constraints on access to gambling and its promotion have steadily been dismantled and some particularly dangerous forms of gambling have become much more accessible.

References

Australian Productivity Commission (APC). (1999). *Australia's Gambling Industries.* Report No. 10. Canberra: Ausinfo.

Azmier, J. J. (2000). *Canadian Gambling Behaviour and Attitudes: Summary Report.* Calgary: Canada West Foundation.

Banks, J. (2014). *Online Gambling and Crime: Causes, Controls and Controversies.* Farnham, Surrey: Ashgate Publishing, Ltd.

Binde, P. (2009). Exploring the impact of gambling advertising: An interview study of problem gamblers. *International Journal of Mental Health and Addiction, 7*(4), 541–554.

Binde, P. (2013). Why people gamble: A model with five motivational dimensions. *International Gambling Studies, 13*, 81–97.

Clarke, D., Tse, S., Abbott, M., Townsend, S., Kingi, P., & Manaia, W. (2006). Key indicators of the transition from social to problem gambling. *International Journal of Mental Health and Addiction, 4*(3), 247–264.

Deans, E. G., Thomas, S. L., Derevensky, J., & Daube, M. (2017). The influence of marketing on the sports betting attitudes and consumption behaviours of young men: Implications for harm reduction and prevention strategies. *Harm Reduction Journal, 14*(1), 5.

Gainsbury, S. (2012). *Internet Gambling: Current Research Findings and Implications.* New York: Springer.

Gainsbury, S., Delfabbro, P., King, D., & Hing, N. (2015). An exploratory study of gambling operators' use of social media and the latent messages conveyed. *Journal of Gambling Studies, 32*(1), 125–141. doi 10. 1007/S10899-015-9525-2

The normalisation of dangerous gambling **43**

Gavriel-Fried, B. (2015). Attitudes of Jewish Israeli adults towards gambling. *International Gambling Studies*, *15*(2), 196–211.

Goodman, R. (1995). *The Luck Business: The Devastating Consequences and Broken Promises of America's Gambling Explosion.* New York: The Free Press.

Grinols, E. L. (2003). Cutting the cards and craps: Right thinking about gambling economics. In G. Reith (Ed.), *Gambling: Who Wins? Who Loses?* (pp. 67–87). New York: Prometheus.

Hancock, L., & Smith, G. (2017). Critiquing the Reno model I-IV international influence on regulators and governments (2004–2015): The distorted reality of "responsible gambling". *International Journal of Mental Health and Addiction*, *15*(6), 1151–1176.

Harrigan, K., & Dixon, M. (2009). PAR Sheets, probabilities, and slot machine play: Implications for problem and non-problem gambling. *Journal of Gambling Issues*, *23*, 81–110.

Harrigan, K., & Dixon, M. (2010). Government sanctioned "tight" and "loose" slot machines: How having multiple versions of the same slot machine game may impact problem gambling. *Journal of Gambling Studies*, *26*(1), 159–174.

Hing, N., Lamont, M., Vitartas, P., & Fink, E. (2015). Sports-embedded gambling promotions: A study of exposure, sports betting intention and problem gambling among adults. *International Journal of Mental Health and Addiction*, *13*(1), 115–135.

King, D., Delfabbro, P., & Griffiths, M. (2009). The convergence of gambling and digital media: Implications for gambling in young people. *Journal of Gambling Studies*, *26*(2), 175–187. doi:10.1007/s 10899-009-9153-9.

LaBrie, R., LaPlante, D., Nelson, S., Schumann, A., & Shaffer, H. (2007). Assessing the playing field: A prospective longitudinal study of internet sports gambling behavior. *Journal of Gambling Studies*, *23*(3), 347–362.

Langham, E., Thorne, H., Browne, M., Donaldson, P., Rose, J., & Rockloff, M. (2016). Understanding gambling related harm: A proposed definition, conceptual framework, and taxonomy of harms. *BMC Public Health*, *16*(1), 80. doi:10.1186/s 12889-016-2747-0

Marshall, D. (2005). The gambling environment and gambler behaviour: Evidence from Richmond-Tweed, Australia. *International Gambling Studies*, *5*(1), 63–83.

McCormack, A., & Griffiths, M. (2012). Motivating and inhibiting factors in online gambling behaviour: A grounded theory study. *International Journal of Mental Health and Addiction*, *10*(1), 39–53.

McMullan, J. L., & Kervin, M. (2012). Selling internet gambling: Advertising, new media and the content of poker promotion. *International Journal of Mental Health and Addiction*, *10*(5), 622–645.

National Lottery Commission. (2013). *The Young People Omnibus Survey 2013.* Conducted by Ipsos MORI for the Lottery Commission, UK.

Orford, J. (2011). *An Unsafe Bet? The Dangerous Rise of Gambling and the Debate We Should Be Having.* Chichester: Wiley-Blackwell.

Orford, J. (2012). Gambling in Britain: The application of restraint erosion theory. *Addiction*, *107*(12), 2082–2086.

Orford, J. (2020). *The Gambling Establishment: Challenging the Power of the Modern Gambling Industry and Its Allies.* Abingdon, Oxon: Routledge.

Orford, J., Griffiths, M., Wardle, H., Sproston, K., & Erens, B. (2009). Negative public attitudes towards gambling: Findings from the 2007 British Gambling Prevalence Survey using a new attitude scale. *International Gambling Studies*, *9*(1), 39–54.

Orford, J., Wardle, H., & Griffiths, M. (2013). What proportion of gambling is problem gambling? Estimates from the 2010 British Gambling Prevalence Survey. *International Gambling Studies*, *13*(1), 4–18.

Salonen, A., Castrén, S., Raisamo, S., Orford, J., Alho, H., & Lahti, T. (2014). Attitudes towards gambling in Finland: A cross-sectional population study. *BMC Public Health*, *14*(1), 982.

Schüll, N. D. (2012). *Addiction by Design: Machine Gambling in Las Vegas*. Princeton: Princeton University Press.

Skidelsky, R., & Skidelsky, E. (2013). *How Much Is Enough? Money and the Good Life*. London: Penguin Books.

Sulkunen, P., Babor, T., Cisneros Örnberg, J., Egerer, M., Hellman, M., Livingstone, C., . . . Rossow, I. (2019). *Setting Limits: Gambling, Science, and Public Policy*. Oxford: Oxford University Press.

Templeton, J., Dixon, M., Harrigan, K., & Fugelsang, J. (2014). Upping the reinforcement rate by playing the maximum lines in multi-line slot machine play. *Journal of Gambling Studies, 31*(3), 949–964. doi 10.1007/s10899-014-9446-5

Thomas, S., Lewis, S., McLeod, C., & Haycock, J. (2012). "They are working every angle": A qualitative study of Australian adults' attitudes towards, and interactions with, gambling industry marketing strategies. *International Gambling Studies, 12*(1), 111–127.

Turner, N. E. (2011). Volatility, house edge and prize structure of gambling games. *Journal of Gambling Studies, 27*(4), 607–623.

Wardle, H., Kiely, R., Astbury, G., & Reith, G. (2014). "Risky Places?": Mapping gambling machine density and socio-economic deprivation. *Journal of Gambling Studies, 30*(1), 201–212.

Wardle, H., Moody, A., Spence, S., Orford, J., Volberg, R., Jotangia, D., . . . Dobbie, F. (2011). *British Gambling Prevalence Survey 2010*. National Centre for Social Research/Gambling Commission. London: The Stationery Office.

Wardle, H., Sproston, K., Orford, J., Erens, B., Griffiths, M., Constantine, R., & Pigott, S. (2007). *British Gambling Prevalence Survey 2007*. National Centre for Social Research/Gambling Commission. London: The Stationery Office.

Williams, R., Volberg, R., & Stevens, R. (2012). *The Population Prevalence of Problem Gambling: Methodological Influences, Standardized Rates, Jurisdictional Differences, and Worldwide Trends*. Report Prepared for the Ontario Problem Gambling Research Centre and the Ontario Ministry of Health and Long-Term Care. Retrieved from www.uleth.ca/dspace/handle/10133/3068

5

FAMILY MEMBERS AFFECTED BY EXCESSIVE GAMBLING

Jim Orford

Introduction

From at least the 1980s onwards, the experiences of family members affected by their relatives' excessive gambling (Gambling-Affected Family Members or AFMs) have been detailed by a number of authors (Black, Moyer, & Schlosser, 2003; Custer & Milt, 1985; Dickson-Swift, James, & Kippen, 2005; Kalischuk, Nowatzki, Cardwell, Klien, & Solowoniuk, 2006; Krishnan & Orford, 2002; Lorenz & Yaffe, 1988; McComb, Lee, & Sprenkle, 2009; Tepperman, 2009; Valentine & Hughes, 2010). Velleman, Cousins, and Orford (2015) have previously summarised the main themes contained in that literature. This chapter updates that summary, drawing particularly on a number of relatively recent reports including the following: a study of a sample of Singapore residents who were either seeking help for a relative with a gambling problem (mostly their husbands, but in other cases parents, siblings, adult children or in-laws; Mathews & Volberg, 2013); the conceptual framework and taxonomy of harms developed in Australia by Langham et al. (2016) on the basis of a literature review and focus groups and interviews with professionals and individuals harmed by their own or another's gambling (see also Chapter 2); an insightful Australian interview study of partners of people who gamble (Holdsworth, Nuske, Tiyce, & Hing, 2013); a rare population-based study, carried out in Finland, which reported a lifetime prevalence of 9.3% for having a close family member with a gambling problem (Salonen, Alho, & Castrén, 2016); and our group's report of family members attending the National Problem Gambling Clinic in London (Orford, Cousins, Smith, & Bowden-Jones, 2017). The present chapter continues by suggesting that gambling-AFMs are often multiply stressed, abused and disempowered, and that this constitutes a human rights issue, concluding by asking what AFMs might reasonably expect from policy and from service providers.

46 Jim Orford

Impact on family finances

The prominence of financial harm distinguishes the experience of gambling-AFMs from that of AFMs facing other kinds of addictive behaviour problems. Holdsworth et al. (2013, pp. 5–6) described family financial impacts as, "substantial, detrimental and far-reaching, affecting their financial security and their relationships. . . . All suffered disruption and deterioration of their established ways of life and their sense of stability and security". Many of their participants spoke of not being aware of the financial consequences of the gambling until a financial or legal crisis occurred. Others have also documented how commonly excessive gambling remains completely hidden from family members for months or years. The discovery or disclosure of the problem then comes as a traumatic and devastating event for a family member (McComb et al., 2009).

More than half of the Singaporean families (Mathews & Volberg, 2013) had substantial family debts, ranging from tens to hundreds of thousands of dollars. Family members often had to make lifestyle adjustments, for example spouses with childcare responsibilities being forced into employment or family members having to work night shifts or take extra jobs. A quarter reported having had to sell their housing. Mathews and Volberg (2013), and Holdsworth et al. (2013) both refer to harassment from creditors.

As Langham et al. (2016) point out financial consequences for the family frequently include not only reduced spending on necessities such as clothing, transport, accommodation or food which has immediate consequences but also reduced capacity for discretionary spending on things like children's sports, erosion of savings, the need to manage cash flow problems by taking on additional employment, use of pawn and payday loan services and inability to spend on such things as insurance, repairs or maintenance which may result in chronic or delayed harms. What Langham et al. (2016) refer to as the "legacy consequences" of financial harms includes continued financial hardship, reliance on welfare, restricted credit and "'forced' cohabitation or involvement in unhealthy relationships due to financial constraint" (p. 14).

The "coping dilemmas" which partners, parents and others face when having a close relative with a gambling problem are actually very similar to those described by family members whose relatives have other types of addictive behaviours (Orford, Natera, Velleman, Templeton, & Copello, 2015), but those revolving around money are prominent, for example the difficult dilemma of whether to "loan" money to a relative who is in serious trouble, whilst suspecting that money will be misused for gambling (Krishnan & Orford, 2002). Family members frequently have to take up the role of managing family finances and controlling their relative's access to money (Suomi et al., 2013; Valentine & Hughes, 2010).

Impact on relationships

In common with substance-AFMs, for many gambling-AFMs it is the impact on relationships that is most deeply felt. Langham et al. (2016) found evidence for relationship harms which included: reduced amount and quality of time spent with the person who gambles, dishonest communication, feelings of unequal contribution to the relationship and reduced engagement in family or social events with the person who gambles. Holdsworth et al. (2013, p. 10) reported that the gambling eroded the partners' relationships because of the time and resources spent on gambling but also because of dishonesty and lies, "loss of shared goals" and "disruption of shared understandings". As these authors put it, "The notion of shared dreams, 'promises' and mutual respect that accompany commitments to intimate partner relationships were perceived to be disrespected and undermined by the gambling behaviour of partners" (Holdsworth et al., 2013, p. 9). One woman summed it up by saying:

> Gambling drives a wedge in your relationship and pulls it apart, and it becomes destructive. You feel like they are being unfaithful to you, because it takes up such a huge part of the relationship.
>
> *(Holdsworth et al., 2013, p. 8)*

High rates of domestic abuse

Of particular importance are the high rates of domestic abuse, both verbal and physical, which have been reported in families where one member gambles excessively (Afifi, Bownridge, MacMillan, & Sareen, 2010; Lesieur, 1989; Muelleman, DenOtter, Wadman, Tran, & Anderson, 2002). Salonen et al. (2016) found the same in their Finnish population study but found an even higher rate of emotional violence, such as blackmailing, pressurising or intimidation, reported by partners. It is interesting to note that in a mixed sample of both substance and gambling-affected partners, Petra (2014) found that, whilst reports of physical violence from their partners were common, experiences of emotional abuse and "coercive control" from their partners were even more the norm. An Australian study of family members with problem gambling relatives asked more closely about the link between gambling and abuse (Suomi et al., 2013). Using a relatively broad definition of domestic violence ("In the past 12 months, has a family member physically hurt you, insulted or talked down to you, threatened you with harm, or screamed or cursed at you?" – Suomi et al., 2013, p. 6.), violence victimisation from the problem gambling relative was reported by 56%, of whom over 70% thought the violence was related to the gambling. All of the latter believed that the problem gambling had preceded the violence, most often attributing the violence to financial losses and fights ensuing over money.

Relationship harm often extends beyond the person-who-gambles-AFM dyad to include strained relationships within the family unit, with the extended family, with neighbours and amongst friends, due to tensions and disagreements about the management of the problem (Langham et al., 2016; Mathews & Volberg, 2013; Suomi et al., 2013). There are also likely to be legacy consequences of relationship harms, amongst which Langham et al. (2016) list social isolation, ongoing resentment and feelings of guilt and shame, long-term damage or estrangement or distortion of relationship roles, effects on future relationships (difficulty in trusting others, hypervigilance, vulnerability to unhealthy relationships), as well as ongoing engagement with the legal system.

Impact on family members' health

The emotional and physical health impacts for AFMs have long been reported (Velleman et al., 2015). Amongst them, Langham et al. (2016) include family members' feelings of distress, insecurity, shame, guilt, low self-worth and the consequent increased risk of depression, anxiety and self-harm. They also include physical impacts such as tiredness, increased blood pressure, loss of sleep, migraine, nausea, diarrhoea, reduced levels of self-care and consequent increased risk to physical well-being, higher incidence of disease or injury and exacerbation of other disorders. They also list harms under the headings of reduced performance at work or study, due to tiredness or distraction, and absenteeism due to time spent managing problems. Under health impact, Holdsworth et al. (2013) report disturbances of sleeping and eating, and anxiety and depression, as the things most mentioned by partners. Mathews and Volberg (2013) estimated that over half the Singaporean families who took part in their study were experiencing high levels of emotional distress. Some reported feeling they were losing their sanity, having difficulties concentrating at work or school and spending a lot of time ruminating about their fears and feeling depressed. A number felt suicidal. In Salonen et al.'s (2016) Finnish population study, 61% of partners and 56% of parents of relatives with gambling problems reported experiencing emotional distress, such as restlessness, anxiety, depression, hopelessness or guilt. The average level of common psychological and physical symptoms reported by members of Orford et al.'s (2017) clinic-based sample was almost identical to that reported by family members recruited in services that treat substance misuse, a level of symptoms far in excess of levels found in the general population.

Particularly poignant is the guilt that many AFMs describe because they think they might have encouraged the gambling in its early stages or might otherwise have been responsible for their relatives' problems, or because, despite their efforts, they have been unable to do anything to stop the behaviour (Langham et al., 2016; Mathews & Volberg, 2013). Several of Holdsworth et al.'s (2013) partners had felt embarrassment and shame because of the social stigma attached to problem gambling and what it did to their feelings about themselves. As one said:

> Your self-confidence, I think, just gets destroyed. . . . I would go through his stuff to see if he was still gambling. I became the worst version of myself. I became someone who I hated.
>
> *(Holdsworth et al., 2013, p. 7)*

Consequences for children

The impact on children has also long been recognised. Lorenz (1987, p. 83) observed:

> Children of the pathological gambler are probably the most victimized by the illness. Usually underage, emotionally and financially dependent upon the gambler during the worst of the illness, it is the children who are the most

helpless. They hear the arguments, recriminations, apologies, broken promises, insults, lies, and fights. They hear their mother arguing with their father about not having money for food, clothes, or school items for the children.

Lesieur and Rothschild (1989) found that children of Gamblers Anonymous (GA) members in the United States and Canada, compared with nationally normed samples, were more likely to have been subjected to parental physical violence and abuse. Two-thirds reported feeling sad, over half emotionally hurt, depressed and confused, with between one-quarter and one-half feeling angry most or all of the time, pity for their parents' gambling, hateful, shameful, helpless, isolated, abandoned and guilty. Two other US studies compared children with problem gambling parents with control groups of children, finding the former to be at much greater risk for health-threatening behaviours such as smoking and alcohol or drug use, and for experiencing educational difficulties, conduct problems and emotional disorders, including depression and suicidal thoughts (Jacobs et al., 1989; Vitaro, Wanner, Brendgen, & Tremblay, 2008).

For AFMs who are exposed as children there are also what Langham et al. (2016) call "life course" consequences including having to take on parent-like responsibilities, delay in the occurrence of normal life course events, continuing financial insecurity, forced moves and loss of relationships and social connections. The Singapore family study also gave details of the heavy toll on children. Some had had to start work early in life, having to work alongside their schooling and having to support themselves during post-secondary education. Sometimes they had to make career decisions that they might not otherwise have taken. Children experienced substantial distress through constantly comparing themselves with others who had come from good financial backgrounds. Saving was impossible for many of the families for whom existing savings had been wiped out, including children's piggy bank savings. Inheritances and proceeds from property sales had often been used to pay off the debts, meaning the children had few resources and often had to postpone important life goals such as marriage and starting their own families. Grown-up children experienced guilt when having to distance themselves from their parents or having to deny their parents' money to pay the latter's gambling debts (Mathews & Volberg, 2013).

Understanding the experience of being a gambling-AFM: Multiply-stressed, abused and disempowered

How should we understand the experience of being a gambling-AFM? One way would be to borrow the concept of "harm to others" (HtO) which has been gaining momentum in the case of harm caused by alcohol (Casswell, Quan You, & Huckle, 2011). In gambling policy, too, there are signs of a movement away from a strict focus on individual gambling disorder towards a broader appreciation of gambling's harms (see Chapters 2 and 3). The harm that gambling-AFMs experience is damage to the institution – the family – which is universally acknowledged as being

50 Jim Orford

at the heart of any society. One of the main groups of victims is the very group – children – whom we are all most committed to protecting from harm. Gambling harm reduction must therefore embrace reducing family harm to a much greater degree than is presently the case.

But that may be insufficient as a way of conceptualising the experience of AFMs that does justice to that experience, is respectful of the stories that they have to tell, and which can form a basis for professional understanding, training and research. To that end, our group has developed the stress-strain-coping-support (SSCS) model, first developed in the context of substance addictive behaviours but always considered relevant in the case of gambling (Orford, Copello, Velleman, & Templeton, 2010; Orford et al., 2015). The focus of the model is deliberately on the experiences of, and outcomes for, AFMs. It is in the tradition of stress-coping models, popular in health psychology and related disciplines (Zeidner & Endler, 1996). It treats the affected family member as an ordinary person exposed to a set of seriously stressful circumstances or conditions of adversity. In contrast to a number of earlier models of addictive behaviours and the family, the SSCS model is designed to be non-pathological in its assumptions about AFMs and their thoughts, emotions and actions in relation to their relatives with addictive behaviour. In particular the model avoids any suggestion that blame for the development or maintenance of the relative's addictive behaviour problem can be attributed to family members' actions. In general, we think of AFMs as disempowered through close contact with their relatives, who are themselves disempowered through their addictive behaviour (Levy, 2006).

But that may not go far enough. In view of the mounting evidence that family members are very likely to be financially "exploited" (the word used by Lesieur, 1984, in his seminal book *The Chase*) and to be on the receiving end of coercion and abuse, this should also be seen as a human rights issue. There are at least two general social and community models which help place the literature on gambling-AFMs in such a broader perspective. One is Hobfoll's (1998) *conservation of resources* theory, which supposes that stress occurs when people's resources, necessary for survival and achievement of goals, are lost or threatened. By resources he had in mind a wide range of things, including *personal resources* such as occupational skills and self-esteem, *object resources* such as home and household possessions, *condition resources* such as health, employment and marriage and *energy resources* such as money, credit and knowledge. Many of those resources can be seen to be threatened when a close family relative has a gambling problem. The other is Nussbaum's (2000) *capabilities* approach based on the idea that each individual should be respected in her or his own right and should not be so constrained by other powerful people or by circumstances in such a way that basic human capabilities, such as bodily health, bodily integrity (including being secure against assault), emotions (including not being overwhelmed by fear and anxiety or suffering traumatic events of abuse or neglect), affiliation and play, are threatened. AFMs can be seen as people struggling to preserve their personal and family resources in the face of a relative's harmful gambling, and whose capabilities are diminished as a consequence, and who are subject to many of the same pressures as others in powerless and subordinate positions. Like the less powerful everywhere, they are ground down by their daily difficulties, they have little or no collective voice and they are ever ready to attribute to their own actions responsibility and blame for their circumstances (Orford, 2013).

What family members should expect from services and policy

Problem gambling treatment services should be much better at engaging AFMs in treatment provision. There are four ways in which they can do that.

- Include AFMs in their relatives' treatment, which evidence suggests confers benefits in the form of greater engagement in, reduced dropout from and greater likelihood of a successful conclusion to treatment (Ingle, Marotta, McMillan, & Wisdom, 2008; Jiménez-Murcia, Tremblay, Stinchfield, et al., 2017).
- Provide joint treatments such as community reinforcement and family therapy (Hodgins, Toneatto, Makarchuk, Skinner, & Vincent, 2007) or couple therapy (Lee, Rovers, & MacLean, 2008).
- Provide interventions that help family members to encourage their problem gambling relatives to enter treatment or to continue to engage in treatment such as a coping skills training programme (Rychtarik & McGillicuddy, 2006).
- Help family members in their own right, for example using methods such as the 5-Step Method which aims to allow AFMs to describe their experiences of living with a relative with a gambling problem, provide useful information and explore options for coping and social support (George & Bowden-Jones, 2015; Orford et al., 2015, 2017).

Service provision needs to be much more family-friendly. That will require improved professional training about gambling disorder and its effects on families. But that is not enough and anyway is unlikely to happen without changes in policy. Affected family members, both children and adults, are at the sharp end of the harm associated with gambling. They are one of the principal groups of "stakeholders" when it comes to thinking about gambling legislation and regulation. Or at least they should be. Sadly, however, theirs is a voice that has been little heard in the forums where gambling policy is discussed. This needs to change. The views of affected family members should be sought when it comes to gambling policy issues such as gambling advertising and the concentration of outlets for the sale of gambling products or the sale or promotion of such products to children or young people. Influential policy documents, such as national and local government plans and medical and other statements by professional bodies, should show greater awareness of how family members and family life is being harmed by gambling and how national policy may be putting people at risk. Relevant legislation should recognise the contribution and rights of AFMs.

References

Afifi, T., Bownridge, D., MacMillan, H., & Sareen, J. (2010). The relationship of gambling to intimate partner violence and child maltreatment in a nationally representative sample. *Journal of Psychiatric Research, 44*(5), 331–337.

Black, D., Moyer, T., & Schlosser, S. (2003). Quality of life and family history in pathological gambling. *Journal of Nervous and Mental Disorders, 191*(2), 124–126.

Casswell, S., Quan You, R., & Huckle, T. (2011). Alcohol's harm to others: Reduced wellbeing and health status for those with heavy drinkers in their lives. *Addiction, 106*(6), 1087–1094.

Custer, R., & Milt, H. (1985). *When Luck Runs Out: Help for Compulsive Gamblers and Their Families.* New York: Facts on File Publications.

Dickson-Swift, V. A., James, E. L., & Kippen, S. (2005). The experience of living with a problem gambler: Spouses and partners speak out. *Journal of Gambling Issues, 13*, 1–22.

George, S., & Bowden-Jones, H. (2015). Family interventions in gambling. In H. Bowden-Jones & S. George (Eds.), *A Clinician's Guide to Working with Problem Gamblers* (pp. 163–171). London: Royal College of Psychiatrists.

Hobfoll, S. (1998). *Stress, Culture and Community: The Psychology and Philosophy of Stress.* New York: Plenum.

Hodgins, D. C., Toneatto, T., Makarchuk, K., Skinner, W., & Vincent, S. (2007). Minimal treatment approaches for concerned significant others of problem gamblers: A randomized controlled trial. *Journal of Gambling Studies, 23*(2), 215–230.

Holdsworth, L., Nuske, E., Tiyce, M., & Hing, N. (2013). Impacts of gambling problems on partners: Partners' interpretations. *Asian Journal of Gambling Issues and Public Health, 3*(1), 1–14.

Ingle, P. J., Marotta, J., McMillan, G., & Wisdom, J. P. (2008). Significant others and gambling treatment outcome. *Journal of Gambling Studies, 24*(3), 381–392.

Jacobs, D., Marston, A., Singer, R., Widsman, K., Little, T., & Veizades. J. (1989). Children of problem gamblers. *Journal of Gambling Behavious, 5*(4), 261–268.

Jiménez-Murcia, S., Tremblay, J., Stinchfield, R., Granero, R., Fernández-Aranda, F., Mestre-Bach, G., . . . Aymamí, N. (2017). The involvement of a concerned significant other in gambling disorder treatment outcome. *Journal of gambling studies, 33*(3), 937–953.

Kalischuk, R. G., Nowatzki, N., Cardwell, K., Klien, K., & Solowoniuk, J. (2006). Problem gambling and its impact on families: A literature review. *International Gambling Studies, 6*(1), 31–60.

Krishnan, M., & Orford, J. (2002). Gambling and the family from the stress-coping-support perspective. *International Gambling Studies, 2*(1), 61–83.

Langham, E., Thorne, H., Browne, M., Donaldson, P., Rose, J., & Rockloff, M. (2016). Understanding gambling related harm: A proposed definition, conceptual framework, and taxonomy of harms. *BMC Public Health, 16*(1), 80. doi:10.1186/s 12889-016-2747-0

Lee, B. K., Rovers, M., & MacLean, L. (2008). Training problem gambling counsellors in Congruence Couple Therapy: Evaluation of training outcomes. *International Gambling Studies, 8*(1), 95–111.

Lesieur, H. (1984). *The Chase: The Career of the Compulsive Gambler.* Rochester, VT: Schenkman.

Lesieur, H. (1989). Current research into pathological gambling and gaps in the literature. In H. J. Shaffer, S. A. Gambino, & T. N. Cummings (Eds.), *Compulsive Gambling: Theory, Research, and Practice* (pp. 225–248). Toronto: Lexington Books.

Lesieur, H., & Rothschild, J. (1989). Children of gamblers anonymous members. *Journal of Gambling Behaviour, 5*(4), 269–281.

Levy, N. (2006). Autonomy and addiction. *Canadian Journal of Philosophy, 36*(3), 427–447.

Family members affected by excessive gambling   **53**

Lorenz, V. C. (1987). Family dynamics of pathological gamblers. In T. Galski (Ed.), *The Handbook of Pathological Gambling* (pp. 83–84). Springfield, IL: Charles C. Thomas.

Lorenz, V. C., & Yaffe, R. A. (1988). Pathological gambling: Psychosomatic, emotional and marital difficulties as reported by the spouse. *Journal of Gambling Behavior, 4*(1), 13–26.

Mathews, M., & Volberg, R. (2013). Impact of problem gambling on financial, emotional and social well-being of Singaporean families. *International Gambling Studies, 13*(1), 127–140. doi:10. 1080/14459795.2012.731422

McComb, J. L., Lee, B. K., & Sprenkle, D. H. (2009). Conceptualizing and treating problem gambling as a family issue. *Journal of Marital and Family Therapy, 35*(4), 415–431.

Muelleman, R. L., DenOtter, T., Wadman, M. C., Tran, T. P., & Anderson, J. (2002). Problem gambling in the partner of the emergency department patient as a risk factor for intimate partner violence. *Journal of Emergency Medicine, 23*(3), 307–312.

Nussbaum, M. C. (2000). *Woman and Human Development: The Capabilities Approach*. Cambridge: Cambridge University Press.

Orford, J. (2013). *Power, Powerlessness and Addiction*. Cambridge: Cambridge University Press.

Orford, J., Natera, G., Velleman, R., Templeton, L., & Copello, A. (2015). Addiction in the family is a major but neglected contributor to the global burden of adult ill-health. *Social Science & Medicine, 78*, 70–77.

Orford, J., Copello, A., Velleman, R., & Templeton, L. (2010). Family members affected by a close relative's addiction: The stress-strain-coping-support-model. *Drugs: Education, Prevention and Policy, 21*(Supplement 1), 36–43.

Orford, J., Cousins, J., Smith, N., & Bowden-Jones, H. (2017). Stress, strain, coping and social support for affected family members attending the National Problem Gambling Clinic, London. *International Gambling Studies, 17*(2), 259–275.

Petra, M. (2014). *Coping with Intimate Partners' Substance Abuse and Gambling Problems: The Role of Intimate Partner Violence* (Unpublished PhD thesis), George Warren Brown School of Social Work, Washington University in St Louis.

Rychtarik, R. G., & McGillicuddy, N. B. (2006). Preliminary evaluation of a coping skills training program for those with a pathological-gambling partner. *Journal of Gambling Studies, 22*(2), 165–178.

Salonen, A. H., Alho, H., & Castrén, S. (2016). The extent and type of gambling harms for concerned significant others: A cross-sectional population study in Finland. *Scandinavian Journal of Public Health, 44*(8), 799–804.

Suomi, A., Jackson, A. C., Dowling, N. A., Lavis, T., Patford, J., Thomas, S. A., . . . Cockman, S. (2013). Problem gambling and family violence: Family member reports of prevalence, family impacts and family coping. *Asian Journal of Gambling Issues and Public Health, 3*(1), 13.

Tepperman, L. (2009). *Betting Their Lives: The Close Relations of Problem Gamblers*. Don Mills, Ontario: Oxford University Press.

Valentine, G., & Hughes, K. (2010). Ripples in the pond: The disclosure to, and management of Internet problem gambling with/in the family. *Community, Work and Family, 13*(3), 273–290.

Velleman, R., Cousins, J., & Orford, J. (2015). Effects of gambling on the family. In H. Bowden-Jones & S. George (Eds.), *A Clinician's Guide to Working with Problem Gamblers* (pp. 90–103). London: Royal College of Psychiatrists.

Vitaro, F., Wanner, B., Brendgen, M., & Tremblay, R. (2008). Offspring of parents with gambling problems: Adjustment problems and explanatory mechanisms. *Journal of Gambling Studies, 24*(4), 535.

Zeidner, M., & Endler, N. (Eds.). (1996). *Handbook of Coping: Theory, Research, Applications*. London: Wiley.

6

NEUROCOGNITIVE COMPONENTS OF GAMBLING DISORDER

Implications for assessment, treatment and policy

Juan F. Navas, Joël Billieux, Antonio Verdejo-García and José C. Perales

Aims and scope

The present chapter aims to describe the psychobiological bases of gambling disorder (GD), and to identify how neuroscience research could inform better prevention and treatment strategies. In the first section, we describe the characteristics shared by people with gambling disorder (PGD) who are receiving treatment, and revisit the literature showing that GD is in essence a disorder of learning. Amongst vulnerabilities, we highlight factors incrementing the allure of gambling, making it more rewarding or strengthening its negatively reinforcing properties. Second, we pinpoint the variables contributing to individual differences within the PGD population, with a particular focus on emotion regulation. Dysfunction of automatic (model-free) emotion regulation is suggested to be a complicating factor of GD, and a transdiagnostic vulnerability factor for psychopathology beyond GD. Dysfunction of controlled (model-based) emotion regulation strategies, along with gambling-related cognitive distortions, are hypothesised to contribute to self-deceptive thinking in some people who gamble. Last, all these variables are integrated into a dimensional model (the *Gambling Space Model*), aimed at updating previous cluster-based proposals to subtype PGD, by incorporating recent neurocognitive evidence. The implications of the model are discussed, and we address its implications on policy and regulation. Additionally, we discuss whether or not other putative behavioural addictions should be ascribed the same consideration. Eventually, we analyse how better understanding individual differences could contribute to better treatment and prevention designs.

Homogeneity in gambling disorder: Incentive sensitisation as the mechanism of gambling conditioning

Gambling research has flourished in recent years and can be considered an example of integration of knowledge from different disciplines. The recent reconceptualisation of GD as an addictive disorder (American Psychiatric Association, 2013) and the ensuing translational advances would have not occurred without such cross-talk. In a joint attempt to define addictive disorders, animal and human research, behavioural neuroscience and cognitive neuroscience have converged in stressing the importance of progressive detachment of addictive behaviour from instrumental goals. According to some etiological models, addictive behaviours are problematic because they become *habit-driven* or *compulsive* (Everitt & Robbins, 2016). Other models stress that individuals with addictive disorder cannot help *craving* their addictive substance or activity (Skinner & Aubin, 2010). Beyond the subtleties of these two approaches, here we will stress their commonality – namely, the fact that wanting (to gamble, to use the drug) and seeking behaviour, once a person meets criteria for addictive disorder, have little to do with the hedonic properties of drug use/gambling consequences. Craving is thus best defined as a multifaceted construct, manifested by the urge to engage in the addictive behaviour, automatic hijacking of attention and cognitive resources by cues reminding or signalling the availability of the object of desire and imperative approach responses to such cues. With regard to its proximal and distal causes, there is also convincing evidence that craving is cue-driven and acquired through exposure to the addictive agent (Sayette, 2016).

In keeping with the importance of craving in substance use disorders (SUDs; Kober & Mell, 2015) considerable efforts have been made to prove the existence of gambling craving (Ashrafioun & Rosenberg, 2012). Additionally, recent evidence suggests that craving may involve a common brain circuitry, with an important hub in the insula, independently of the type of addictive disorder (Garavan, 2010; Limbrick-Oldfield et al., 2017). The association between this area and cravings accords with its status as an important node in interoceptive representation and the use of such information in decision making (Garavan, 2010).

From a practical point of view, however, the key question is how gambling *becomes* compulsive, and wanting detaches from hedonic value. A leading model in accounting for drug craving acquisition is the *incentive sensitisation* (IS) hypothesis. The IS model posits that all addictive drugs directly or indirectly sensitise dopamine release in the mesolimbic system, which is responsible for attributing *incentive salience* to cues signalling the availability of reward (Robinson & Berridge, 1993).

Incentive salience is hypothesised to be the inner engine of craving acquisition. In normal circumstances, when an unexpected reward is encountered, a mismatch between predicted and experienced utility generates error signals in the mesocorticolimbic system, and particularly in the ventral striatum (VS; Humphrey & Richard, 2014). However, rewards become more predictable as instrumental learning progresses, so the magnitude of error signals decreases, and incentive salience reaches asymptote. Drugs of abuse alter this system by producing supra-threshold stimulation and precluding habituation, and thus causing "irrationally strong motivation urges that are not justified by any memories of previous reward values (and without distorting associative predictions)" (Berridge, 2012, p. 1124). In other words, substance use disorders (SUDs) are normally accompanied by a subjective and behavioural dissociation between *liking* and *wanting* the drug (Pool, Sennwald, Delplanque, Brosch, & Sander, 2016).

56 Juan F. Navas et al.

In view of the success of the IS hypothesis to account for some of the seemingly irrational features of people in treatment for SUDs behaviour, the question arises whether the hypothesis can be also tested in behavioural addictions (Rømer Thomsen, Fjorback, Møller, & Lou, 2014). That is, in the absence of an external chemical agent, what misleads dopaminergic error signals?

This question can be addressed by revisiting the literature on reinforcement schedules. According to recent analyses, most gambling behaviours are under random ratio (RR) schedules (Haw, 2008). These are characterised by intermittent reward, such that the probability of reward in any single trial does not depend on the previous density of rewards. Uncertainty in RR schedules is irreducible, and the rates of responding they generate are particularly stable and free of breaks after reward (Schoenfeld, Cumming, & Hearst, 1956).

Irreducible uncertainty in gambling scenarios can be regarded as a constant source of prediction error for the mesocorticolimbic dopaminergic system to feed incentive salience. Supporting that hypothesis, Anselme, Robinson, and Berridge (2013) have indeed shown that increasing the uncertainty level in the relationship between a cue and a reward enhances incentive salience of this cue, as measured by a sign-tracking response. Further evidence supports the involvement of the incentive salience dopamine system in the effect of uncertainty on the ability of contextual cues to behave as motivational magnets (Anselme & Robinson, 2013).

Sources of heterogeneity in gambling disorder

Differences in gambling disorder vulnerability

If IS resulting from RR schedules is the main learning mechanism underlying gambling conditioning, any factors fuelling this mechanism will contribute to GD vulnerability. More specifically, any factors increasing exposure to gambling or its rewarding properties will facilitate transition from recreational to problematic gambling. Accordingly, research shows that early wins have a particularly strong effect on behaviour under RR schedules and in gambling scenarios (Haw, 2008).

Complementarily, people differ in the degree to which they are sensitive to the various appetitive and aversive properties of different types of events. Gray's (1994) psychobiological model of personality proposes reward sensitivity (RS) and punishment sensitivity (PS) (the overt manifestations of two biological systems referred to as behavioural activation and behavioural inhibitions systems) as the main foundation of motivation and personality. In the framework we are starting to sketch here, RS and PS easily enter the equation as individual differences that modulate IS. However, reinforcement-related sources of individual vulnerability could be less general than PS and RS traits and more circumscribed to the types of rewards that occur in gambling scenarios.

There is evidence, for instance, that some people who gamble experience gambling-triggered arousal or uncertainty as intrinsically rewarding (Megias et al., 2017; Sharpe, Tarrier, Schotte, & Spence, 1995), a result that converges with studies on the biological basis of individual differences in risk proneness in animals (Fiorillo, 2011). Complementarily, individuals presenting high levels of neuroticism and punishment sensitivity, or proneness towards negative mood, are more likely to use gambling to cope with psychological distress (Balodis, Thomas, & Moore, 2014).

The role of basic emotion regulation mechanisms

A growing corpus of evidence suggests that craving management, that is, succeeding in keeping IS below a given threshold, can be viewed as an instance of emotional regulation (Loewenstein, 1996) that can be implemented at different levels is subject to influences from same-level learning mechanisms (e.g., extinction, counter-conditioning, cue-interaction; Kober et al., 2010). Etkin, Büchel, and Gross (2015) have recently proposed that, at this level, emotion regulation proceeds in a model-free, automatic manner. This could be the case for loss-related learning processes necessary to compensate IS. Supporting this idea, a recent study has shown that people who gamble at casinos underestimate how much money they spend on gambling in the long run, and that their gambling expenditures could be reduced just by providing them with a player account indicating their personal expenditure (Wohl, Davis, & Hollingshead, 2017). Interestingly, behaviour changed with limited or no awareness. Accordingly, manipulations that reduce awareness of losses lead to increased wagering in a similar, almost automatic way (Monaghan, 2009).

Etkin and colleagues (2015) have identified the ventromedial prefrontal cortex (vmPFC) and the ventral anterior cingulate (vACC) as the main regions in the circuit for model-free emotion regulation, although their review mostly focuses on fear regulation, and it is unclear whether these would also constitute the most important structures for craving regulation. A discussion on the exact brain implementation of model-free emotion regulation goes beyond the scope of the present chapter. Medial and ventral parts of the PFC, the insula and their connections with the amygdala and the VS are, however, the most frequently mentioned structures (Phillips, Ladouceur, & Drevets, 2008).

With regard to the model-free regulation of craving in GD, the evidence to date remains indirect. For example, Contreras-Rodríguez et al. (2016) found a common pattern of hyperconnectivity in PGD and cocaine-dependent individuals, mostly between the orbitofrontal cortex (OFC) and VS, and between the insula and the amygdala. Complementary evidence comes from studies showing that PGD perform worse than controls on the Iowa Gambling Task, in which successful performance is known to depend on balanced emotion-driven learning (Buelow & Suhr, 2009).

Malfunctioning of basic, model-free emotion regulation will be subjectively experienced as a pervasive influence of craving on behaviour, and if such malfunctioning is extensive enough, as a disproportionate impact of emotions in other areas of decision and action. This resonates with similar findings in the SUDs literature that craving correlates with negative urgency (NU), namely the tendency to act rashly under the influence of strong negative emotions (Cyders et al., 2014; Doran, Cook, McChargue, & Spring, 2009).

58 Juan F. Navas et al.

Higher-order emotion regulation mechanisms

Model-free emotion regulation is complemented by model-based emotion regulation strategies. These form a category of learned goal-directed responses through which people act upon their own emotional processes. Not surprisingly, then, specific cerebral areas involved in this type of emotion regulation (lateral PFC, presupplementary and supplementary motor areas [pSMA, SMA] and parts of the parietal cortex) overlap with those involved in model-based instrumental behaviour (O'Doherty, Cockburn, & Pauli, 2017).

Emotion regulation strategies are varied. The emotion regulation questionnaire (ERQ; Gross & John, 2003) distinguishes between *expressive suppression* (suppressing the external manifestations of emotion) and *reappraisal* (reprocessing of the causes of the emotion), with use of the latter being considered adaptive and the former maladaptive. The more comprehensive cognitive emotion regulation questionnaire (CERQ, Garnefski & Kraaij, 2007) identifies nine cognitive strategies to deal with negative affect (*blaming oneself, blaming others, acceptance, rumination, positive refocusing, refocus on planning, positive reappraisal, putting into perspective* and *catastrophising*).

In psychobiological terms, reappraisal has been shown to downregulate the activity of the VS and the amygdala, altering the balance in favour of either continuing or interrupting gambling (Kober et al., 2010; Sokol-Hessner et al., 2009). Accordingly, studies on craving regulation have focused on this cognitive strategy (Giuliani & Berkman, 2015) and have observed that successful downregulation of craving is associated with increased activity of the lateral and dorsomedial PFC and dampened activity of the ventral striatum, subgenual cingulate, amygdala and ventral tegmental area (Kober et al., 2010).

GD can progress with malfunctioning of the basic mechanisms necessary to regulate craving and other undesirable emotions, and this can have an influence on how model-based strategies operate. In a recent study, we tested the hypothesis that regulation of negative emotions in PGD imposes an extra burden on cognitive control mechanisms, relative to healthy controls (Navas et al., 2017b). Downregulation of emotions triggered by negative pictorial stimuli activated the control network in controls and PGD, but the latter showed further hyperactivation of an area comprising parts of the premotor cortex and the dlPFC. Additionally, activation of dlPFC correlated with NU. In a separate sample, NU significantly correlated with the proneness to use expressive suppression as a (maladaptive) strategy to regulate negative affect.

The Gambling Space Model

So far, we have suggested a number of psychobiological processes 1) to account for the transition from recreational to problem gambling, 2) to facilitate that transition and contribute to GD vulnerability and 3) to underlie individual differences in PGD. In the next section these constructs are integrated into a coherent model (Table 6.1), and their contribution to the behavioural manifestations and clinical implications of disordered gambling are explicated.

The first construct in the Gambling Space Model (*sensitivity to appetitive properties of gambling*) is related to reward sensitivity. The relationship between RS and gambling

Neurocognitive components of gambling disorder **59**

TABLE 6.1 The Gambling Space Model

Construct	Sensitivity to positively reinforcing properties of gambling	Sensitivity to negatively reinforcing properties of gambling	Generalised affect dysregulation	Cognitive elaboration and self-deception
Psychobiological basis	Reward system, uncertainty-sensitive dopaminergic projections	Fronto-amygdalar systems of escape and avoidance	Model-free emotion regulation systems	Model-based emotion regulation system, cognitive control structures
Behavioural manifestations	Positive motives for gambling, reward seeking	Negative motives, poor mood, neuroticism, boredom	Affect-driven impulsivity, disinhibition, deficits in decision making	Exaggerated expectancies, interpretative biases, motivated reasoning
Clinical implications	Vulnerability to risk gambling, low motivation to quit gambling, dropout risk	Emotional vulnerability, internalising comorbidity, risk of relapse	Low problem awareness, externalising comorbidity, dropout risk	Cognitive distortions, preference for skill-based games, low change motivation, treatment reluctance
Common construct	*Incentive sensitisation driven by random ratio schedules*			

has been lingering in the literature for decades, yet it has been difficult to identify it as a strong and independent predictor of disordered gambling behaviour (Goudriaan, van Holst, Veltman, & van den Brink, 2013). More consistently, people who gamble have been found to differ from nongamblers in how they respond to the different sources of reward present in gambling scenarios (Sescousse, Barbalat, Domenech, & Dreher, 2013). Still, reward sensitivity can interact with gambling features in shaping individual gambling preferences. In a recent article, Navas et al. (2017a) found that people with recreational and disordered gambling who prefer card, skill and casino games show higher RS scores than those preferring slot machines, lotteries and bingo. These individuals are more strongly motivated by positive reinforcers and also more sensitive to the positive features of the gambling experience.

The second putative construct relies on the *negatively reinforcing properties of gambling*. Negative trait emotions can interact with sensitivity to the mood-modifying properties of gambling. In practical terms, gambling-to-cope has been observed to correlate with comorbid depression and relapse risk (Ledgerwood & Petry, 2006; Lister, Milosevic, & Ledgerwood, 2015)

The third construct, *generalised emotional dysregulation*, captures deterioration of model-free emotion regulation mechanisms. Weakness of low-level regulation mechanisms necessary to limit gambling conditioning are hypothesised to characterise all people with disordered gambling. However, extensive malfunctioning of basic emotion regulation mechanisms is likely to be responsible for differences amongst PGD. Unfortunately, to date, there is a dearth of reliable and psychometrically sound neurobehavioural tasks that could be used as tools to assess the extent and severity of this type of dysregulation. Provisionally, we propose NU as the most promising available proxy to evaluate it across disorders (Berg, Latzman, Bliwise, & Lilienfeld, 2015).

Finally, the fourth construct has to do with the use of strategic, model-based emotion regulation. Recent evidence shows the existence of a subgroup of PGD who effectively use putatively adaptive forms of emotion regulation (Navas, Verdejo-García, López-Gómez, Maldonado, & Perales, 2016). However, amongst these individuals, such strategies correlate *directly* with gambling severity and gambling-related cognitive distortions. In a similarly counterintuitive fashion, people who gamble with high dispositional optimism have been found to be more prone to maintaining positive expectations and remain motivated to gamble after negative outcomes (Gibson & Sanbonmatsu, 2004). In our model, individuals' use of model-based emotion regulation strategies in combination with certain gambling-related cognitive distortions forms part of a *self-deceptive reasoning style.* This ego-protective mechanism has been established as a factor contributing to drug use perseverance, and to reluctance to treatment (Martínez-González, Vilar López, Becoña Iglesias, & Verdejo-García, 2016). Here, we posit that self-deception has an emotional regulation function, in line with models of motivated reasoning (Kunda, 1990).

According to the present model, certain types of cognitive distortions thus reflect *spared* cognitive control, rather than cognitive dysfunction. Indeed, cognitive distortions are more frequently encountered in young, educated people who gamble using skill-games (Myrseth, Brunborg, & Eidem, 2010). Furthermore, and importantly, they are not systematically accompanied by signs of cognitive/non-planning impulsivity or lack of conscientiousness (Navas et al., 2017a). This relationship between elaborate distorted cognitions and planning abilities could partially account for the inconsistency of findings regarding the link between GD and executive tasks (Goudriaan, Yücel, & van Holst, 2014). In people who gamble self-deceptively, preserved executive function would contribute to false mastery, whereas for people in treatment who have less elaborated gambling beliefs, weaker executive functions would contribute to inflexible behaviour and unconscientious gambling.

It is worth noting that there are important connections between our Gambling Space Model and the *Pathways Model* (Blaszczynski & Nower, 2002). Figure 6.1 displays a simplified depiction of the mapping of the Pathways Model onto the Gambling Space Model. In this space, all PGD are *conditioned gamblers*, and subtypes would arise from the combination of conditioning processes with sources of heterogeneity. In individuals with high levels of neuroticism, poor mood or susceptibility to boredom, the negatively reinforcing properties of gambling would give rise to

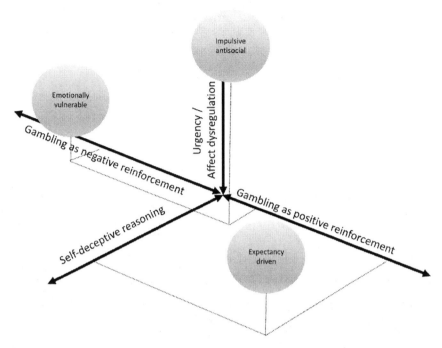

FIGURE 6.1 A simplified depiction of the mapping of gamblers subtypes onto a dimensional model

the *emotionally vulnerable gambler*, whereas in cognitively spared individuals, motivated reasoning and elaborated emotion regulation could give rise to *self-deceptive gamblers*. The latter are not specifically considered in the Pathways Model but are easily identifiable in emerging profiles (Griffiths, Wardle, Orford, Sproston, & Erens, 2009).

With regard to the *impulsive-antisocial gambler* type, our model depicts a slightly more complex scenario. Given the partial overlap between RS and impulsivity (Knezevic-Budisin, Pedden, White, Miller, & Hoaken, 2015), people in treatment who have reward-sensitive GD have remained partially confounded with impulsive-antisocial ones. RS, however, reflects the hyperreactivity of the behavioural activation system to potential sources, whereas other relevant aspects of emotion-driven impulsivity reflect a more generalised regulatory dysfunction. Hence, it would be possible to distinguish between predominantly reward- or sensation-seeking impulsive individuals who gamble, and those with high levels of urgency, with the latter presenting a higher incidence of problematic behaviours (Vachon & Bagby, 2009).

Summary and implications: What has neuroscience ever done for us?

According to a recent opinion article by Markowitz (2016), "*there is such a thing as too much neuroscience*" in psychopathology and psychotherapy research. In the context of GD research, it is true that clear-cut biomarkers are still lacking, and drug

62 Juan F. Navas et al.

trials have yielded inconclusive, mixed or unspecific results (Alexandris, Smith, & Bowden-Jones, 2015; Yip & Potenza, 2014), and other manipulations of the brain (e.g., transcranial magnetic stimulation, neurofeedback) are still matters of ongoing research (Goudriaan et al., 2014). Still, neuroscientific research has contributed to change the way we conceptualise GD, and such a change is having consequences on the way we deal with it.

Implications of conceptualising gambling disorder as an addictive disorder

Conceptualising GD as an addictive disorder implies endorsing the dissociation between wanting to gamble and liking gambling, and thus the view of gambling as economically inconsistent. Individuals with nicotine use disorder, for example, can invest considerable effort and money in purchasing tobacco *and* trying to quit smoking (Reith, 2007). The liking/wanting dissociation thus provides ethical ground for some degree of political paternalism. Given that *likes* also belong to individuals, consideration of likes beyond and above *wants* actually sanctions what has been called liberal paternalism (Camerer, 2006).

In other words, understanding the centrality of IS, its key role in the development of craving, and how loss-based learning fails to compensate it, justifies product- and offer-centred interventions regarding pervasiveness of gambling-triggering cues, and product design aimed at reducing features that enhance their addictive potential (Parke, Parke, & Blaszczynski, 2016). And the other way around, if evidence does not support the consideration of a putative addictive disorder as a genuine one, there would be less ethical ground to justify intervention. If we adopt the same "addiction" model for hypersexuality, dysregulated food intake or excessive video gaming, there would be no reason not to implement similar rules in those markets. Previous attempts to define addictive disorders based on the analogy between the excessive behaviour in question and a previously accepted addictive disorder, based on the application of DSM diagnostic criteria to the new putative "addictions", has led to overdiagnosis and overtreatment. As stated by Billieux, Schimmenti, Khazaal, Maurage, and Heeren (2015), behavioural addiction research should shift "from a mere criteria-based approach towards an approach focusing on the psychological processes involved" (p. 119). As reviewed in this chapter, neuroscience definitely has a role in defining such processes.

Implications of a psychobiological approach to heterogeneity amongst people in treatment who have a gambling disorder

Complementarily to the coexisting ways in which heterogeneity amongst people who gamble has been approached, to date, neuroscientific work can already provide a set of core dimensional constructs with practical use.

Individual treatments are likely to benefit from the reviewed evidence. First, in accordance with the Gambling Space Model, gambling motives should be assessed in order to draw a profile of the reinforcement sources that people receiving treatment find in gambling, which could become targets of intervention. The identification of reinforcement sources linked to gambling could be useful to implement individual and process-oriented psychological interventions aimed, for instance, at developing skills to cope with high relapse-risk situations (anxiety, low mood, money-related thoughts, or boredom; Ledgerwood & Petry, 2006). Second, individuals who gamble and have deficits in basic emotional dysregulation have been found as especially refractory to treatment attempts. For these cases, a better prospect is provided by studies in which mindfulness-based training has shown promising results in comorbid addictive and emotion disorders (Hoppes, 2006) and positive effects on decision-making neuropsychological tasks linked with basic emotion regulation (Alfonso, Caracuel, Delgado-Pastor, & Verdejo-García, 2011). Third, intervening on planning executive functions is likely to benefit people at the low end of the elaboration-self-deception continuum (as it has been shown with people receiving treatment who have SUDs, Verdejo-Garcia, 2016), whereas people in the high end would probably benefit more from metacognitive training skills aimed at making them aware of the connection between their dysfunctional beliefs and their motives to gamble (see Lindberg, Fernie, & Spada, 2011).

Complementarily, secondary prevention efforts in community populations could also be enriched with this dimensional-psychobiological vision, through the implementation of screening techniques aimed at identifying high-risk profiles (although we are aware that extra measures must be taken to avoid stigmatisation and stereotyping; O'Leary-Barrett et al., 2013). Neurobiologically informed risk profiling has already gone a step further than traditional personality profiling, in delineating a common vulnerability factor for externalising problems in early adolescence and dissociating it from other factors with differential loadings in separate disorders (Castellanos-Ryan et al., 2014). Prevention programmes could thus be directed to individuals in general populations (not necessarily those currently gambling) identified to have poorer basic emotion regulation. These individuals could benefit from interventions aimed at improving general emotional regulation and self-control, and thus see their risk of externalising problems, including disordered gambling, reduced.

Final remarks

The sociodemographic and behavioural map of gambling is changing rapidly. New gambling opportunities and media (e.g., mobile gambling) are generating new player profiles, so understanding the mechanisms that generate the evolving variability of vulnerabilities, symptoms, and outcomes is necessary to be proactive at providing the best possible clinical and political response to eventually diminish the public health burden of disordered gambling.

As depicted in the current chapter, a combined psychobiological and behavioural-cognitive framework has shown some capacity to capture at least some of these sources of variability. The four proposed constructs are not necessarily exhaustive

64 Juan F. Navas et al.

but are grounded in sufficient evidence to have clear implications for policy, prevention and psychological interventions. Still, further evidence should be gathered to help delineate or reconfigure this set of dimensions and evaluate its predictive power.

In parallel, it is important to acknowledge that theories of psychopathology have important, and potentially negative, consequences in real life. Biological approaches to psychopathology are often accused of crystallising abnormal behaviours that would be better understood as dynamically evolving and distributed in a continuum. As we have tried to illustrate here, psychobiological models can be learning-based and dimensional and, simultaneously, able to incorporate biological factors. At the same time, such models must be discriminative enough to allow identifying genuine addictive disorders. So, the risk of overpathologisation and psychiatrisation actually exists, in particular for many putative behavioural addictions. Most likely, misleading and overinclusive definitions are already creating more harm than good.

References

Alexandris, A., Smith, N., & Bowden-Jones, H. (2015). Understanding and managing gambling disorder: An overview of recent evidence and current practices. *Research and Advances in Psychiatry, 2*, 36–47.

Alfonso, J. P., Caracuel, A., Delgado-Pastor, L. C., & Verdejo-García, A. (2011). Combined goal management training and mindfulness meditation improve executive functions and decision-making performance in abstinent polysubstance abusers. *Drug and Alcohol Dependence, 117*, 78–81.

American Psychiatric Association. (2013). *Diagnostic and Statistical Manual of Mental Disorders (DSM-5)* (5th ed.). Arlington, VA: American Psychiatric Association.

Anselme, P., & Robinson, M. J. F. (2013). What motivates gambling behavior? Insight into dopamine's role. *Frontiers in Behavioral Neuroscience, 7*, 182.

Anselme, P., Robinson, M. J. F., & Berridge, K. C. (2013). Reward uncertainty enhances incentive salience attribution as sign-tracking. *Behavioural Brain Research, 238*, 53–61.

Ashrafioun, L., & Rosenberg, H. (2012). Methods of assessing craving to gamble: A narrative review. *Psychology of Addictive Behaviors, 26*, 536–549.

Balodis, S. R. S., Thomas, A. C., & Moore, S. M. (2014). Sensitivity to reward and punishment: Horse race and EGM gamblers compared. *Personality and Individual Differences, 56*, 29–33.

Berg, J. M., Latzman, R. D., Bliwise, N. G., & Lilienfeld, S. O. (2015). Parsing the heterogeneity of impulsivity: A meta-analytic review of the behavioral implications of the UPPS for psychopathology. *Psychological Assessment, 27*, 1129–1146.

Berridge, K. C. (2012). From prediction error to incentive salience: Mesolimbic computation of reward motivation. *European Journal of Neuroscience, 35*, 1124–1143.

Billieux, J., Schimmenti, A., Khazaal, Y., Maurage, P., & Heeren, A. (2015). Are we over-pathologizing everyday life? A tenable blueprint for behavioral addiction research. *Journal of Behavioral Addictions, 4*, 119–123.

Blaszczynski, A., & Nower, L. (2002). A pathways model of problem and pathological gambling. *Addiction, 97*, 487–499.

Buelow, M. T., & Suhr, J. A. (2009). Construct validity of the Iowa Gambling Task. *Neuropsychology Review, 19*, 102–114.

Camerer, C. (2006). Wanting, liking, and learning: Neuroscience and paternalism. *The University of Chicago Law Review, 73,* 87–110.

Castellanos-Ryan, N., Struve, M., Whelan, R., Banaschewski, T., Barker, G. J., Bokde, A. L. W., . . . IMAGEN Consortium. (2014). Neural and cognitive correlates of the common and specific variance across externalizing problems in young adolescence. *The American Journal of Psychiatry, 171,* 1310–1319.

Contreras-Rodríguez, O., Albein-Urios, N., Vilar-López, R., Perales, J. C., Martínez-Gonzalez, J. M., Fernández-Serrano, M. J., . . . Verdejo-García, A. (2016). Increased corticolimbic connectivity in cocaine dependence versus pathological gambling is associated with drug severity and emotion-related impulsivity. *Addiction Biology, 21,* 709–718.

Cyders, M. A., Dzemidzic, M., Eiler, W. J., Coskunpinar, A., Karyadi, K., & Kareken, D. A. (2014). Negative urgency and ventromedial prefrontal cortex responses to alcohol cues: fMRI evidence of emotion-based impulsivity. *Alcoholism: Clinical and Experimental Research, 38,* 409–417.

Doran, N., Cook, J., McChargue, D., & Spring, B. (2009). Impulsivity and cigarette craving: Differences across subtypes. *Psychopharmacology, 207,* 365–373.

Etkin, A., Büchel, C., & Gross, J. J. (2015). The neural bases of emotion regulation. *Nature Reviews, 63,* 693–700.

Everitt, B. J., & Robbins, T. W. (2016). Drug addiction: Updating actions to habits to compulsions ten years on. *Annual Review of Psychology, 67,* 23–50.

Fiorillo, C. (2011). Transient activation of midbrain dopamine neurons by reward risk. *Neuroscience, 197,* 162–171.

Garavan, H. (2010). Insula and drug cravings. *Brain Structure and Function, 214,* 593–601.

Garnefski, N., & Kraaij, V. (2007). The cognitive emotion regulation questionnaire. *European Journal of Psychological Assessment, 23,* 141–149.

Gibson, B., & Sanbonmatsu, D. M. (2004). Optimism, pessimism, and gambling: The downside of optimism. *Personality & Social Psychology Bulletin, 30,* 149–160.

Giuliani, N. R., & Berkman, E. T. (2015). Craving is an affective state and its regulation can be understood in terms of the extended process model of emotion regulation. *Psychological Inquiry, 26,* 48–53.

Goudriaan, A. E., van Holst, R. J., Veltman, D. J., & van den Brink, W. (2013). Contributions from neuroscience and neuropsychology. In D. C. Richards, A. Blaszczynski, & L. Nower (Eds.), *The Wiley-Blackwell Handbook of Disordered Gambling* (pp. 49–70). Oxford: John Wiley & Sons, Inc.

Goudriaan, A. E., Yücel, M., & van Holst, R. J. (2014). Getting a grip on problem gambling: What can neuroscience tell us? *Frontiers in Behavioral Neuroscience, 8,* 141.

Gray, J. A. (1994). Framework for a taxonomy of psychiatric disorder. In H. Van Goozen, N. Van De Poll, & J. Sergeant (Eds.), *Emotions: Essays on Emotion Theory* (pp. 29–59). Hillsdalle, NJ: Lawrence Erlbaum.

Griffiths, M., Wardle, H., Orford, J., Sproston, K., & Erens, B. (2009). Sociodemographic correlates of internet gambling: Findings from the 2007 British Gambling Prevalence Survey. *Cyberpsychology & Behavior, 12,* 199–202.

Gross, J. J., & John, O. P. (2003). Individual differences in two emotion regulation processes: Implications for affect, relationships, and well-being. *Journal of Personality and Social Psychology, 85,* 348–362.

Haw, J. (2008). Random-ratio schedules of reinforcement: The role of early wins and unreinforced trials. *Journal of Gambling Issues, 21,* 56–67.

Hoppes, K. (2006). The application of mindfulness-based cognitive interventions in the treatment of co-occurring addictive and mood disorders. *CNS Spectrums, 11,* 829–851.

66 Juan F. Navas et al.

Humphrey, J., & Richard, D. (2014). Dopamine and learning: Brain-behavior interactions in disordered gambling. In D. C. Richards, A. Blaszczynski, & L. Nower (Eds.), *The Wiley-Blackwell Handbook of Disordered Gambling* (pp. 98–116). Oxford: John Wiley & Sons, Inc.

Knezevic-Budisin, B., Pedden, V., White, A., Miller, C. J., & Hoaken, P. N. S. (2015). A multifactorial conceptualization of impulsivity. *Journal of Individual Differences, 36*, 191–198.

Kober, H., & Mell, M. M. (2015). Craving and the regulation of craving. In S. J. Wilson (Ed.), *The Wiley Handbook on the Cognitive Neuroscience of Addiction* (pp. 195–218). Oxford: John Wiley & Sons, Inc.

Kober, H., Mende-Siedlecki, P., Kross, E. F., Weber, J., Mischel, W., Hart, C. L., & Ochsner, K. N. (2010). Prefrontal-striatal pathway underlies cognitive regulation of craving. *Proceedings of the National Academy of Sciences of the United States of America, 107*, 14811–14816.

Kunda, Z. (1990). The case for motivated reasoning. *Psychological Bulletin, 108*, 480–498.

Ledgerwood, D. M., & Petry, N. M. (2006). What do we know about relapse in pathological gambling? *Clinical Psychology Review, 26*, 216–228.

Limbrick-Oldfield, E. H., Mick, I., Cocks, R. E., McGonigle, J., Sharman, S. P., Goldstone, A. P., . . . Clark, L. (2017). Neural substrates of cue reactivity and craving in gambling disorder. *Translational Psychiatry, 7*, e992.

Lindberg, A., Fernie, B. A., & Spada, M. M. (2011). Metacognitions in problem gambling. *Journal of Gambling Studies, 27*, 73–81.

Lister, J. J., Milosevic, A., & Ledgerwood, D. M. (2015). Psychological characteristics of problem gamblers with and without mood disorder. *Canadian Journal of Psychiatry, 60*, 369–376.

Loewenstein, G. (1996). Out of control: Visceral influences on behavior. *Organizational Behavior and Human Decision Processes, 65*, 272–292.

Markowitz, J. C. (2016). There's such a thing as too much neuroscience. *The New York Times*. Retrieved from www.nytimes.com/2016/10/15/opinion/theres-such-a-thing-as-too-much-neuroscience.html?_r=0

Martínez-González, J. M., Vilar López, R., Becoña Iglesias, E., & Verdejo-García, A. (2016). Self-deception as a mechanism for the maintenance of drug addiction. *Psicothema, 28*, 13–19.

Megias, A., Navas, J. F., Perandrés-Gómez, A., Maldonado, A., Catena, A., & Perales, J. C. (2017). Electroencephalographic evidence of abnormal anticipatory uncertainty processing in gambling disorder patients. *Journal of Gambling Studies, 34*, 321–338.

Monaghan, S. (2009). Responsible gambling strategies for Internet gambling: The theoretical and empirical base of using pop-up messages to encourage self-awareness. *Computers in Human Behavior, 25*, 202–207.

Myrseth, H., Brunborg, G. S., & Eidem, M. (2010). Differences in cognitive distortions between pathological and non-pathological gamblers with preferences for chance or skill games. *Journal of Gambling Studies, 26*, 561–569.

Navas, J. F., Billieux, J., Perandrés-Gómez, A., Lopez-Torrecillas, F., Cándido, A., & Perales, J. C. (2017a). Impulsivity traits and gambling cognitions associated with gambling preferences and clinical status. *International Gambling Studies, 17*, 102–124.

Navas, J. F., Contreras-Rodríguez, O., Verdejo-Román, J., Perandrés-Gómez, A., Albein-Urios, N., Verdejo-García, A., & Perales, J. C. (2017b). Trait and neurobiological underpinnings of negative emotion regulation in gambling disorder. *Addiction, 112*, 1086–1094.

Navas, J. F., Verdejo-García, A., López-Gómez, M., Maldonado, A., & Perales, J. C. (2016). Gambling with rose-tinted glasses on: Use of emotion-regulation strategies correlates with dysfunctional cognitions in gambling disorder patients. *Journal of Behavioral Addictions, 5*, 271–281.

O'Doherty, J. P., Cockburn, J., & Pauli, W. M. (2017). Learning, reward, and decision making. *Annual Review of Psychology, 68*, 73–100.

O'Leary-Barrett, M., Topper, L., Al-Khudhairy, N., Pihl, R. O., Castellanos-Ryan, N., Mackie, C. J., & Conrod, P. J. (2013). Two-year impact of personality-targeted, teacher-delivered interventions on youth internalizing and externalizing problems: A cluster-randomized trial. *Journal of the American Academy of Child and Adolescent Psychiatry, 52*, 911–920.

Parke, J., Parke, A., & Blaszczynski, A. (2016). *Key Issues in Product-Based Harm Minimization: Examining Theory, Evidence and Policy Issues Relevant in Great Britain*, London: Responsible Gambling Trust.

Phillips, M. L., Ladouceur, C. D., & Drevets, W. C. (2008). A neural model of voluntary and automatic emotion regulation: Implications for understanding the pathophysiology and neurodevelopment of bipolar disorder. *Molecular Psychiatry, 13*, 833–857.

Pool, E., Sennwald, V., Delplanque, S., Brosch, T., & Sander, D. (2016). Measuring wanting and liking from animals to humans: A systematic review. *Neuroscience & Biobehavioral Reviews, 63*, 124–142.

Reith, G. (2007). Gambling and the contradictions of consumption: A genealogy of the pathological subject. *American Behavioral Scientist, 51*, 33–55.

Robinson, T. E., & Berridge, K. C. (1993). The neural basis of drug craving: An incentive-sensitization theory of addiction. *Brain Research Reviews, 18*, 247–291.

Rømer Thomsen, K., Fjorback, L. O., Møller, A., & Lou, H. C. (2014). Applying incentive sensitization models to behavioral addiction. *Neuroscience & Biobehavioral Reviews, 45*, 343–349.

Sayette, M. A. (2016). The role of craving in substance use disorders: Theoretical and methodological issues. *Annual Review of Clinical Psychology, 12*, 407–433.

Schoenfeld, W. N., Cumming, W. W., & Hearst, E. (1956). On the classification of reinforcement schedules. *Proceedings of the National Academy of Sciences of the United States of America, 42*, 563–570.

Sescousse, G., Barbalat, G., Domenech, P., & Dreher, J. C. (2013). Imbalance in the sensitivity to different types of rewards in pathological gambling. *Brain, 136*, 2527–2538.

Sharpe, L., Tarrier, N., Schotte, D., & Spence, S. H. (1995). The role of autonomic arousal in problem gambling. *Addiction, 90*, 1529–1540.

Skinner, M. D., & Aubin, H. J. (2010). Craving's place in addiction theory: Contributions of the major models. *Neuroscience & Biobehavioral Reviews, 34*, 606–623.

Sokol-Hessner, P., Hsu, M., Curley, N. G., Delgado, M. R., Camerer, C. F., & Phelps, E. A. (2009). Thinking like a trader selectively reduces individuals' loss aversion. *Proceedings of the National Academy of Sciences of the United States of America, 106*, 5035–5040.

Vachon, D. D., & Bagby, R. M. (2009). Pathological gambling subtypes. *Psychological Assessment, 21*, 608–615.

Verdejo-Garcia, A. (2016). Cognitive training for substance use disorders: Neuroscientific mechanisms. *Neuroscience & Biobehavioral Reviews, 68*, 270–281.

Wohl, M. J., Davis, C. G., & Hollingshead, S. J. (2017). How much have you won or lost? Personalized behavioral feedback about gambling expenditures regulates play. *Computers in Human Behavior, 70*, 437–445.

Yip, S. W., & Potenza, M. N. (2014). Treatment of gambling disorders. *Current Treatment Options in Psychiatry, 1*, 189–203.

SECTION II

Harm reduction models and initiatives

7

DEFINING HARM REDUCTION AS PART OF A PUBLIC HEALTH APPROACH TOWARDS GAMBLING

Olivier Simon, Jean-Félix Savary, Gabriel Guarrasi and Cheryl Dickson

If the concept of "harm reduction" (HR) is as old as the hippocratic principle "primum non nocere", its application to the field of addictive behaviours is recent. The HR premise is found in institutional texts from the 1970s (World Health Organisation, WHO, 1974). At this time, harm reduction was restricted to local initiatives by street workers and people using substances, as an attempt to reduce the adverse consequences of psychoactive substance consumption. At the end of the twentieth century, the HIV epidemic brought about a focus on intravenous non-medical use of substances, in particular, heroin and cocaine. The harm reduction perspective was able to respond to this crisis, where traditional treatment-oriented services could do very little. Two measures were found to be especially effective: the provision of injecting equipment and broad access to methadone by prescription, which has been practiced since the end of the 1960s through a very restrictive framework. These two emergency measures represented a radical questioning of previous practices. The "war on drugs" prioritised the criminalisation of their use and injunctions relating to abstinence (Chappard, Couteron, & Morel, 2012). It was therefore crucial to identify a generic name for these heterogeneous and controversial measures, highlighting a series of democratic duties, other than international conventions prohibiting the nonmedical use of substances. These obligations include the right to life, prevention of discrimination, prohibition of torture, human rights and the right to health.[1] Thus, the concept of HR pragmatically emerged, putting the user at the centre of the right to support and to survival, as the person "does not want to, or has not yet been able to give up" the nonmedical use of substances.

This original political and polemic of the concept of HR highlights the lack of consensus, to accept a scientifically and legally established public health definition. If there is a significant body of publications relating to the keyword "harm reduction" applied to controlled substances,[2] it will be quite different from other themes that may be associated with development of addictive behaviours. We can cite, for example,

72 Olivier Simon et al.

therapeutic programmes aiming to control alcohol (Cournoyer, Simoneau, Landry, Tremblay, & Patenaude, 2010), vaping instead of cigarette consumption (Etter & Bullen, 2011) or even measures to limit expenses during gambling sessions (Blaszczynski, Ladouceur, & Nower, 2007). Aren't these measures indeed from HR? This is far from obvious, especially when it comes to regulation or therapeutic measures which are not in line with the HR concept. Can we speak of HR measures or policies applied to the field of gambling? Can corporate social responsibility measures for businesses, proposed by gambling operators, be considered – under certain conditions – as HR measures? In this chapter, we will revisit the scientific meaning of the term "harm reduction" within the field of substances. We will review the main areas of controversy related to definition efforts, and we will finish with the specific requirements of a public health definition of HR that is compatible with the gambling field.

From the "political" definition of HR to definitions used in the scientific community

The first HR definitions are illustrated in institutional and regulatory documents of support services for individuals using psychoactive substances. Reference is made to the people who are not ready – or according to certain formulations "may not yet be ready" – to give up the use of these substances (Lenton & Single, 1998). From this perspective, HR concerns any policy or programme to improve the health or social status of individuals consuming substances, without aiming to reduce consumption. It acknowledges the fact that some people are not in a situation where they could stop consuming but sometimes fails to see the human rights perspective, that takes into account the "choice" of the person. The concept of HR stipulates that user responsibility is at its centre, so it is not only a question of "being able" to reduce or stop consumption but also a matter of whether the person wishes to do so. Restricting HR to the clinical perspective that someone may not yet be ready to change, fails to provide this dimension of choice. This approach is, however, essential from a human rights perspective and a "non-judgmental" position that respects users. The harsh political context explains how the narrow vision of HR, has been presented as a solution for those who "cannot" stop. The human rights approach advocates, however, for a broader vision of HR, to be seen as a service for all people who use substances, without judgment of their practices. According to Lenton and Single (1998), the main criticism of this historical definition lies in the dichotomy that it creates in relation to measures either to reduce the supply or reduce the demand. On one side are the "pragmatists" aiming to improve health *here* and *now* and, on the other, the "idealists" for whom abstinence or reduced consumption would be a non-negotiable goal. The evolution of public policies, which have been in developed in Europe from the 1990s onwards, suggests that fears over the impact of this dichotomy have not been realised.

In opposition to these definitions, which focus on the target audience rather than on public processes or outcomes, different health actors have proposed to focus on the ultimate goal of HR. Thus, Wodak and Sanders (1995, p. 269) have proposed that the term HR could cover "the employment of any means to reduce the harm resulting from illicit drugs". This offers the advantage of going beyond the previously arising dichotomy. The authors note, however, that there is a risk of confusion here.

Therefore, this raises a question about the measurable nature of harm, and the scientific methods for calculating the "net gain or loss for a given policy or programme" and "those which display a net gain are said to be harm-reducing" (Lenton & Single, 1998, p. 215). We understand that this wish to give an empirical anchor to the concept of HR raises new questions, relating to the limits of knowledge and assessment methods for public policies. If methods exist which enable measurement of the social costs or the loss of quality of life and basic rights, in practice, they rely on studies, which are costly and limited by the standard monitoring framework. Such constraints ultimately face a political agenda in a democratic environment. Beauchet and Morel (2010) distinguish three phases in the development of the HR approach: the first generation had the prevention of HIV/AIDS as their objective, including access to sterile syringes and availability of methadone and other opioid agonist treatment; the second generation aimed to reduce harm due to use in party settings, by providing drug checking and relevant information; and the third generation aimed to broaden the focus by including other addictive behaviours (particularly alcohol and tobacco but also possibly behavioural addictions). We should also add that the traditional HR advocates have always stressed the need for "social" harm reduction that goes beyond pure health issues to involve, for example, housing, employment and social inclusion.

Today, in scientific publications, two definitions are particularly mentioned: the WHO-European Monitoring Centre for Drugs and Drug Addiction (EMCDDA)-UNAIDS reference document (2014), and that of Harm Reduction International (International Harm Reduction Association, 2010). These two definitions illustrate two trends: on the one hand there are definitions arising from a consensus developed under the aegis of intergovernmental bodies, which do not call into question the international treaties on the control of substances; on the other hand there are definitions proposed by nongovernmental organisations, which benefit from being more centred on the basic needs of the individual and their community. The latter point more towards the inherent conflict between fundamental rights and the treaties relating to substances.

Example of a definition from the UN and the EU

Here, the approach is to define HR by structural elements rather than processes or goals. In this case nine groups of interventions are combined to address the HIV risk for people injecting substances. This narrow perspective is often linked to controversy over the HR concept, itself. By naming the measures and not the concept, it allows multilateral bodies to endorse some measures, without making explicit reference to HR. It should, therefore, be seen as a lack of support for the HR concept on the part of these large organisations. Moreover, it demonstrates the need to

74 Olivier Simon et al.

continue advocacy efforts in order to finally achieve a legitimate HR concept. The definition is therefore only based on measures that have proven effective, according to scientific knowledge:

> A *Comprehensive Package* of interventions for the prevention, treatment and care of HIV amongst people who inject drugs has been endorsed widely, by WHO, UNAIDS, United Nations Office on Drugs and Crime (UNODC), the UN General Assembly, the Economic and Social Council, the UN Commission on Narcotic Drugs, the UNAIDS Programme Coordinating Board, the Global Fund and the President's Emergency Plan for Aids Relief. The Comprehensive Package (WHO, 2012, p. 10) includes:
>
> - Needle and syringe programmes
> - Opioid substitution therapy and other evidence-based drug dependence treatment
> - HIV testing and counselling
> - Antiretroviral therapy
> - Prevention and treatment of sexually transmitted infections
> - Condom programmes for people who inject drugs and their sexual partners
> - Targeted information, education and communication for people who inject drugs and their sexual partners
> - Prevention, vaccination, diagnosis and treatment for viral hepatitis
> - Prevention, diagnosis and treatment of tuberculosis.

Definition from the civil society: Harm reduction international

Here, the approach puts at its forefront human rights, the person and the community and the reduction of negative consequences, not only for health but also at the wider societal level.

The definition proposed by the International Harm Reduction Association (IHRA, a society which has since become Harm Reduction International) is that

> HR refers to policies, programmes and practices that aim primarily to reduce the adverse health, social and economic consequences of the use of legal and illegal psychoactive drugs without necessarily reducing drug consumption. HR benefits people who use drugs, their families and the community. [. . .] The HR approach to drugs is based on a strong commitment to public health and human rights.
>
> *(International Harm Reduction Association, 2010, p. 1)*

Main controversies from a "gambling" perspective

These historical definitions highlight the main controversies that animate the actors in the field of addictions. We will briefly look at the questions and implications relating the nature of HR (measures, policies, concept), to its different components (person-centred prevention, structural prevention, consumption reduction) and finally to its links with public health (human rights links, bottom up person-centred approach, evaluation and research) (Langham et al., 2015; see also Chapter 1, Chapter 2, Chapter 8).

Does HR refer to a concept, as has always been advocated by specialised HR groups, or to measures that can be considered separately, as often imposed by government agencies, or even to public policies that are based, above all, on the combined character of the measures? This is a significant debate, where gambling is concerned. If HR is a "concept", let alone a simple "measure", then it could be susceptible to including "harm minimisation" measures, developed by the industry (Blaszczynski, 2001). This could lead to a marketing approach, for which the net result is an increase in supply, and subsequently an increase in global burden, at a community level.

In order to pursue HR goals, it is possible to implement a set of co-ordinated approaches. It is important that these measures are combined in a balanced way and subject to both pre and post set-up evaluations (Simon, Blaser, Müller, & Waelchli, 2013). The very nature of these combined measures can be varied (for example strategies addressing stigma, measures to encourage those who consume substances to participate in public debates, access to specialised support). Such an approach invites us to answer the question of whether structural prevention measures (e.g., an increase in taxes or protection against passive smoking) form part of HR (Chaloupka, Straif, & Leon, 2011). We see that there is a big risk of confusion over the concepts of prevention and HR, which should be avoided. The big difference between the two is that one addresses the decision to consume (prevention), and the other the consequences of the consumption, for which the decision has already been taken (HR). Moreover, prevention enforces social norms, whilst HR implies a non-judgmental position. Both can be articulated but should not be confused. Another controversial point is the place of risk-related information or even the promotion of low-risk consumption, if commercial interests are involved.

Ultimately is HR considered to be a public health approach based mainly on epidemiological methods? Or is it, above all, an ethical stance towards wider public policy, typically including actors from public safety and the economic sphere? We note that a modern public health approach can hardly be conceived, without an analysis of stakeholders (Brugha & Varvasovszky, 2000), making this opposition somewhat theoretical. The right to the highest possible standard of health, as a fundamental right to access a collective set of services but also the right to have control over one's own body are inseparable from other human rights including the prohibition of discrimination, the prohibition of inhuman and degrading treatment, the right of access to fair legal proceedings and the right to participate in political life (UN Human Rights Council (HRC), 2010). It is the responsibly of the individual to make the right choice for themselves. But it is the responsibility of the collective, and society, to give access to opportunities that enable them to reduce the risks associated with addictive behaviour, whether or not the latter meet the threshold for a "disorder", according to standard diagnostic criteria.

76 Olivier Simon et al.

Towards a definition of HR for gambling?

In conclusion, the widening of HR definitions to include addictive behaviours without substances, such as gambling-related disorders, seems to make professional and ethical sense. Whilst it is premature to fix a definition, it is nevertheless possible to outline a precise way forward.

First, for gambling as for other disorders, HR should place the person, their choice and their community at its centre. This requires the State to consider the person and their relatives, both from the perspective of protection and the promotion of fundamental rights. HR should be a "bottom up" approach and should not judge people who gamble.

Second, a definition of HR which incorporates gambling should include the notion that the ultimate outcome is not problem gambling prevalence but burden of disease and loss of quality of life. A person presenting with excessive gambling can cause considerable socio-professional harms in jurisdiction A, with well-developed offers and opportunities to reduce the consequences of their gambling. However, in jurisdiction B, providing a better framework to support the practices of people who gamble, someone with the same diagnosis will manage their gambling behaviour to a level that limits harm to those around them. It follows that the target of HR gambling policy must include relatives and the community (see Chapter 5). The multiple effects of losing money causes a loss in quality of life to those surrounding the person with problematic gambling behaviours. This is even more significant than for behaviours related to substance dependence.

Third, the definition of a HR approach for gambling should include regulation measures, in relation to the operating conditions (e.g., certification of the least dangerous games) and/or positive obligations, relating to player protection, which are imposed by the State upon operators (e.g., identification of problematic sessions, self-exclusion, plans to manage conflicts of interest).

Finally, HR should be carefully monitored, based on a system of structural, process, and outcome indicators. This involves qualitative and quantitative approaches to describe and measure harm due to gambling in the broadest sense. If HR is a process for which the *primum movens* is participation, then the State's commitment is essential to achieving this, due to the inherent conflict of interest between public health, economy and public order. Ultimately, people who gamble, those close to them and the community at large, should be able to verify *a posteriori*, in an independent and transparent way, that the goals of harm reduction are actually achieved.

Notes

1 In the UN sense of the right of every person to achieve the best possible health. For a more complete definition from article 12, see general comment No. 14 (UN Committee on Economic, Social and Cultural Rights; CESCR, 2000); for the link between the right to health and risk reduction, see UN Human Rights Council (HRC) (2010).
2 For further information, see the comprehensive monograph published by the EMCDDA (Rhodes & Hedrich, 2010).

References

Beauchet, A., & Morel, L.-A. (2010). Réduction des risques. In A. Morel, J.-P. Couteron, & P. Fouilland (Eds.), *L'aide-mémoire d'addictologie*. Paris: Dunod.

Blaszczynski, A. (2001). *Harm Minimization Strategies in Gambling: An Overview of International Initiatives and Interventions*. Melbourne: Australian Gaming Council.

Blaszczynski, A., Ladouceur, R., & Nower, L. (2007). Self-exclusion: A proposed gateway to treatment model. *International Gambling Studies, 7*(1), 59–71.

Brugha, R., & Varvasovszky, Z. (2000). Stakeholder analysis: A review. *Health Policy and Planning, 15*(3), 239–246.

Chaloupka, F. J., Straif, K., & Leon, M. E. (2011). Effectiveness of tax and price policies in tobacco control. *Tobacco Control, 20*(3), 235–238.

Chappard, P., & Couteron, J. P., & Morel, A. (2012). Origine et histoire de la réduction des risques. In A., Morel, P. Chappard, & J. P. Couteron (Eds.), *L'aide-mémoire de la réduction des risques en addictologie: en 22 fiches* (pp. 8–18). Malakoff, France: Dunod.

Cournoyer, L. G., Simoneau, H., Landry, M., Tremblay, J., & Patenaude, C. (2010). Évaluation d'implantation du programme Alcochoix+. *Drogues, santé et société, 9*(2), 75–114.

Etter, J. F., & Bullen, C. (2011). Electronic cigarette: Users profile, utilization, satisfaction and perceived efficacy. *Addiction, 106*(11), 2017–2028.

International Harm Reduction Association. (2010). *What is harm reduction? A position statement from the International Harm Reduction Association*. London, UK: IHRA.

Langham, E., Thorne, H., Browne, M., Donaldson, P., Rose, J., & Rockloff, M. (2015). Understanding gambling related harm: A proposed definition, conceptual framework, and taxonomy of harms. *BMC Public Health, 16*(1), 80.

Lenton, S., & Single, E. (1998). The definition of harm reduction. *Drug and Alcohol Review, 17*(2), 213–219.

Rhodes, T., & Hedrich, D. (Eds.). (2010). *Harm Reduction: Evidence, Impacts and Challenges*. Luxembourg: Publications Office of the European Union.

Simon, O., Blaser, J., Müller, S., & Waelchli, M. (2013). Réduction des risques et jeux d'argent. Questions ouvertes par la révision du dispositif suisse. *Drogues, santé et société, 12*(2), 66–89.

UNAIDS. (2014). *Harm Reduction Works: Examples from around the World*. Retrieved from www.unaids.org/en/resources/documents/2014/20140318_JC2613_HarmReduction

UN Committee on Economic, Social and Cultural Rights (CESCR). (2000). *General Comment No. 14: The Right to the Highest Attainable Standard of Health (Art. 12 of the Covenant)*. Retrieved from www.refworld.org/docid/4538838d0.html

UN Human Rights Council (HRC). (2010). *Report of the Special Rapporteur on the Right of Everyone to the Enjoyment of the Highest Attainable Standard of Physical and Mental Health*. Retrieved from www.refworld.org/docid/4c0770ee2.html

WHO (World Health Organization). (1974). *Expert Committee on Drug Dependence: Twentieth Report*. Technical Report Series 551. Geneva: World Health Organization.

WHO (World Health Organization). (2012). *WHO, UNODC, UNAIDS technical guide for countries to set targets for universal access to HIV prevention, treatment and care for injecting drug users – 2012 revision*. Geneva: World Health Organization.

Wodak, A., & Sanders, B. (1995). Harm reduction means what I choose it to mean. *Drug and Alcohol Review, 14*(3), 269–271.

8

EFFECTIVE HARM MINIMISATION PRACTICES

Public health implications

Darren R. Christensen

Background

The following chapter on effective harm minimisation practices is based on the report by Williams, R.J., West, B.L., & Simpson, R.I. (2012). *Prevention of Problem Gambling: A Comprehensive Review of the Evidence, and Identified Best Practices.* Report prepared for the Ontario Problem Gambling Research Centre and the Ontario Ministry of Health and Long Term Care. The current chapter updates the previous report with studies since 2012.

Introduction

This chapter is a review of the core features of gambling harm minimisation practices. These include examining the effectiveness of educational, public and problem gambling awareness campaigns, specific gambling policy initiatives (i.e., gambling availability, venues, activities and participation) and aspects of gambling delivery (i.e., gambling parameters, pre-commitment, staff training and the gambling environment). Although these are prominent features, there are others that also influence harm minimisation, and for a full discussion please read the Williams et al. (2012) report. Nevertheless, this chapter summarises the existing harm minimisation literature, indicating areas of success and caveats for policymakers. Consequently, effective policy will require a sensitive understanding of the mechanisms of each harm minimisation feature and the necessity for government regulation and policing.

Educational initiatives

Child and adolescent programmes

Early childhood experiences are typically thought to significantly influence the development of problematic behaviour later in life. Accordingly, family focused programmes are often used to reduce adolescent problem behaviours and also serve to reduce problems at later ages (Foxcroft, Ireland, Lowe, & Breen, 2011). For example, family-based programmes are often effective for the primary prevention of other addictive behaviours such as alcohol and drug use by young people (Foxcroft et al., 2011). Similarly, exposure to well socialised peer groups and supportive teachers are thought to have beneficial effects on the prevention of problem gambling as it does on the prevention of other problematic behaviours (Toumbourou, Williams, Waters, & Patton, 2005). However, the research examining the effectiveness of programmes designed to influence adolescent gambling show inconsistent results. Although most research examining child and adolescent gambling prevention show improvements in correcting gambling misconceptions, gambling behaviour is typically an unmeasured variable or does not statistically reduce (for a review see Oh, Ong, & Loo, 2017). For example, St-Pierre, Derevensky, Temcheff, Gupta, and Martin-Story (2017) investigated the efficacy of targeting negative anticipated emotion related to gambling and found their video presentation was not effective at either reducing negative anticipated emotion or the frequency of gambling behaviour.

Information and awareness campaigns

Most problem gambling prevention programmes are information campaigns targeted specifically at gambling. These are typically known as "information/awareness campaigns", "mass media campaigns" or "social marketing". These initiatives are directed at the public and usually include one or more of the following elements (e.g., Jackson, Thomas, Thomason, & Ho, 2002):

- Motivational statements to "know your limits" or "gamble responsibly".
- Warnings about the potential addictive nature of gambling.
- Identification of the signs/symptoms of problem gambling.
- Information about where people can go for help or more information on problem gambling (i.e., treatment agencies; 24-hour telephone helplines).
- Notices reporting the mathematical odds of various gambling activities.
- Attempts to dispel common gambling fallacies and erroneous cognitions.
- Provision of guidelines and suggestions for problem-free gambling.

These initiatives are usually developed and delivered by governmental health or social service agencies, schools or commercial gambling providers. The information is provided through:

- Gambling products (e.g., odds printed on the back of lottery tickets, "responsible gambling messages" on electronic gambling machines).
- Posters and pamphlets at gambling venues and elsewhere throughout the community.
- Public service announcements on radio, television and newspapers.
- Presentations, plays or videos (most often presented in educational settings).
- CDs, websites and computer applications.
- Terminals in the gambling venue (e.g., "Player Awareness Terminal").

80 Darren R. Christensen

Early consumer protection initiatives focused on the responsible provision of gambling by gambling operators and regulators to provide safe gambling environments (Hing, 2002). However, recent approaches have re-directed the emphasis of responsible gambling to place the onus of responsible gambling on the person who gambles. The consumer is thought to act in a responsible manner by self-regulating their behaviours through rational thought based on informed and far-sighted decision-making (Bickel et al., 2011; Reith, 2007). However, this approach is now attracting criticism as the *exclusive focus* of responsible gambling policy because it avoids an examination of the potential harmful effects of gambling accessibility and electronic gambling machine design (Hancock, Schellinck, & Schrans, 2008; Vasiliadis, Jackson, Christensen, Francis, & Thomas, 2013).

Although there are significant efforts by industry and governments to promote responsible gambling, research on the effectiveness of these campaigns is relatively sparse. However, recently, studies have shown differences between gambling severity groups in their knowledge and use of responsible gambling measures. Thomas, Lewis, and Westberg (2012) conducted a qualitative analysis of gambling advertising and reported that most people who gamble recalled the main messages in social marketing campaigns. They found that lower severity gamblers took less notice when they saw advertisements for problem gambling services, whilst many moderate risk and problem gamblers found it difficult to identify with or act on responsible gambling messages. Further, most gamblers reported that the responsible gambling messages had less power to "cut-through" the positive messages from the gambling industry. Moreover, the responsible gambling messages seemed to reinforce the perspective that problem gambling was caused by poor decision making and lack of control, and people who gamble preferred messages that were related to the harms associated with different gambling products rather than inferring individual responsibility. Further, the responsible gambling messages were thought to impede help-seeking and reinforce perceptions of shame, secrecy and stigma.

In addition, awareness of specific harm minimisation measures, policies and procedures designed to reduce the negative consequences of gambling are even less well-known. A notable exception is the study by Jackson, Christensen, Francis, and Dowling (2016) who reported relatively low awareness of various responsible gambling harm minimisation measures (e.g., ban on Automated Teller Machines [ATMs], limits on Electronic Gaming Machine [EGM] numbers, etc.) across gambling severities, especially for specific venue (15.4%, limit of hours) and machine characteristics (13.8%, reduction in number of lines). However, the ban on smoking in a gambling venue was widely known across all severities (95.8%).

Further, evaluations of specific gambling awareness campaigns show limited recall by the public for responsible gambling advertising (8%, Najavits, Grymala, & George, 2003; 34%, Turner, Wiebe, Falkowski-Ham, Kelly, & Skinner, 2005). However, responsible gambling campaigns appear to increase knowledge of problem gambling for those who are aware of the campaigns (72%, Najavits et al., 2003). Public awareness campaigns can also result in changes to help-seeking behaviours and associated relationships. For example, Jackson et al. (2002) evaluated a multimedia

Effective harm minimisation practices **81**

gambling awareness advertising campaign and found the programme increased the number of callers to gambling helplines and new clients entering treatment and greater collaboration between treatment services and staff at gambling venues.

Specific educational interventions have shown some promise. Wohl, Christie, Matheson, and Anisman (2010) evaluated the effectiveness of a short video informing viewers on EGMs, setting limits and responsible gambling strategies. Participants who gambled and were assigned to the video condition were significantly more likely to stay within preselected spending limits, have fewer erroneous cognitions and endorse responsible gambling strategies. However, the next day, there were no differences in the money spent between the video and control conditions, and by day 30 the only effect that persisted was the decrease in erroneous cognitions. By contrast, Doiron and Nicki (2007) delivered a two-session responsible gambling education programme to "at-risk" gamblers and found the programme resulted in significant decreases in erroneous gambling beliefs and gambling behaviour one month later.

Responsible Gambling Information Centres

Responsible Gambling Information Centres (RGIC) located in gambling venues provide, on gambling patron request, information and education about the risks of gambling (e.g., odds of winning and losing; demonstrations/tutorials about slot machine design/random number generation). Staff at these centres also attempt to identify, support and refer gambling patrons with problems to treatment services. Immediate interventions and counselling may be provided onsite, but typically counselling services are not usually included at these centres. These information centres are sometimes staffed by casino employees and sometimes by employees of treatment or government regulation agencies.

RGIC utilisation rates appear lower than gambling venue patron utilisation standards but appear higher by treatment provider standards. Williams et al. (2012) reported approximately 61,400 people visited one of Ontario's RGIC from 2005 to 2009 compared to an estimated 200 million visitors to Ontario's casinos. Further, Williams et al., (2012) reported approximately 8,000 customers accessed Manitoba's RGIC between 2003 and 2006; 75% were for information only, 10% for support and referral and 15% for other reasons. By comparison, approximately 10,000 people visit Manitoba's casinos every day. Evaluations of RGIC found most gambling patrons were aware of the centres, with higher rates for casino staff (Osborne Group, 2008). However, only a minority of casino staff referred patrons to these centres, and only 9% of counselling referrals contacted counselling services (Osborne Group, 2008).

Responsible gambling messages during EGM play

Recently, specific responsible gambling messages have been incorporated into EGM designs as warnings or responsible gambling messages. Gainsbury, Aro, Ball, Tobar, and Russell (2015) investigated the effects of messaging on EGM screens and found

82 Darren R. Christensen

messages in the middle of the screen were recalled more often than messages on the periphery. However, when responsible gambling messages were part of a suite of other measures the effects were less powerful. In addition, Blaszczynski, Gainsbury, and Karlov (2014) found that although most participants were aware of at least one responsible gambling feature, very few used any of them. Approximately 22% of participants noticed the onscreen EGM responsible gambling messages, where 7% reported these messages made them stop and think about their gambling, and only 4.2% thought the messages influenced their gambling behaviour. Therefore, although these approaches appear to have some value, there appears to be limited evidence to support their efficacy. Nonetheless, as they are part of the gambling experience, they have the potential to immediately influence gambling behaviour.

Gambling policy initiatives

Gambling availability

Increases in the general availability of a product usually results in greater use and harms. For example, alcohol availability is positively associated with higher levels of consumption, which is correlated with higher levels of alcohol-related problems (Babor, Caetano, Caswell, et al., 2010). Similar relationships exist for illegal drugs (Babor, Caulkins, Edwards, et al., 2010) and gun ownership (Ajdacid-Gross et al., 2006). Nonetheless, these relationships are not fixed and can change over time depending on the environment, government policies, experience and competing activities. Although there is data to support a relationship between the introduction of greater gambling availability and greater gambling harms (Williams, Belanger, & Arthur, 2011), there also is evidence for an adaptation process; despite the increasing availability of gambling opportunity, rates of gambling participation have declined since the early 2000s (Williams, Volberg, & Stevens, 2012). In addition, significant heterogeneity exists in these reports, where accessibility appears multidimensional, including physical dimensions of proximity and density (Vasiliadis et al., 2013; see also McMillen & Doran, 2006), number of gambling formats (Williams et al., 2012), socioeconomic and demographic factors (Mason, 2008), employment factors (Hing & Nisbet, 2009), expenditure (Marshall, McMillen, Niemeyer, & Doran, 2004), travelling time (Doran, Marshall, & McMillen, 2007) and gambling venue type (Pearce, Mason, Hiscock, & Day, 2008). This complexity implies significant constraints on the efficacy of managing gambling availability as a *singular avenue* for reducing problem gambling rates.

Gambling venues

Gambling can occur in specialised gambling venues, such as casinos, horse racing tracks, and dedicated bingo halls. However, the purchase of lottery and instant tickets are typically available across a range of retail outlets, including supermarkets, local convenience stores and gas stations. Further, non-regulated gambling activities between peers occurs in a variety of locations including private dwellings, public places and in nongambling designated areas. Although, most legislation is focused on the placement of EGMs and casinos. Research suggests the closer the physical distance between a residence and a casino the greater the likelihood of engaging in gambling, regular gambling and problem gambling (Welte, Barnes, Tidwell, Hoffman, & Wieczorek, 2016). Further, this relationship appears to have dose-response characteristics where higher numbers of proximal casinos were related to higher probabilities of gambling problematically. Consequently, proximity analyses appear to be a key factor for determining the relative harm on a community and are often included in "community impact reports" in some Australian jurisdictions.

Gambling activities

Conventional wisdom suggests continuous forms of gambling; activities that can be played quite rapidly and provide a high frequency of reinforcement are thought to be a riskier form of gambling (Parke & Griffiths, 2007). This is analogous to substance abuse, where the speed of the drug effect and duration of the drug half-life are potent determinants of the dependency-forming potential of different substances (Nutt, King, Saulsbury, & Blakemore, 2007).

EGMs, slot machines and video lottery terminals (North America), fixed odds betting terminals and fruit machines (U.K.), pokies (Australia) and pachinko (Japan) provide the fastest gambling forms and are often identified by people who gamble problematically, treatment agencies and gambling researchers as creating the most problems (e.g., Williams et al., 2012).

Two other forms of continuous gambling with high theoretical propensities for addictive behaviour are "continuous" lotteries and casino table games. "Continuous lotteries" have a draw every few minutes (e.g., "electronic keno", "Rapido"), providing heightened gambling experiences compared to traditional lotteries. Casino table games (e.g., baccarat, blackjack, roulette, craps) are gambling activities with quick play and a high frequency of reinforcement. These games (particularly baccarat) are often identified as the most problematic form of gambling in Asian countries and also have higher rates of gambling harms in Western countries (Williams et al., 2012). Consequently, continuous forms are the most heavily regulated gambling activity.

Gambling participation

Regulated forms of gambling participation typically restrict gambling participation to the legal age of adulthood. However, some countries have no age restrictions for some gambling activities. For example, no age restrictions exist for lotteries and instant win tickets in Poland (Dzik, 2009), non-casino gambling in Slovenia (Macur, Makarovic, & Roncevic, 2009), and electronic gambling machine ("fruit machine") play with low prize limits in the United Kingdom, amongst other jurisdictions. In general, policing of gambling tends to be more rigorous in regulated adult-only venues (e.g., casinos, bars/clubs/lounges), and less so where gambling is available in public locations. Nevertheless, despite restrictions on under-age gambling, past year problem gambling by youths is typically higher than adult rates (Williams et al., 2012) and appears related to greater impulsivity in the under-age group (Temcheff, St-Pierre, & Derevensky, 2014). Protective factors for adolescents appear to be associated to family and school connectedness, parental modelling, problem focused coping skills and the availability of school guidance counsellors.

Some jurisdictions place gambling restrictions on gambling participation. These include restrictions on residents or nonresidents, availability of terrestrial and online gambling formats and limits based on socioeconomic status. For example, Australia does not permit residents to gamble on Australian online casinos although it does permit its citizens to wager money on Australian online sports, race books and lottery sites provided they are associated with a terrestrial business (Williams et al., 2012). Similarly, the 2018 Singapore Casino Control Act requires citizens or permanent residents to pay the casino operator a $100 daily fee or a $2,000 annual membership. Williams et al. (2012) report this policy and associated measures to limit or otherwise contain gambling expenditures to higher economic groups may have some utility in preventing gambling harms.

Self-exclusion is a common harm minimisation measure. Casinos and jurisdictions around the world have adopted self-exclusion programmes (Responsible Gambling Council, 2008), including Internet gambling sites (Griffiths, 2012). Typically, people are enrolled in self-exclusion programmes when gambling losses or gambling behaviour becomes problematic (Meyer & Hayer, 2007). However, research suggests that self-exclusion programmes are underutilised by people who gamble problematically and are not completely effective in preventing individuals from gambling in venues from which they are excluded, or on other forms (Gainsbury, 2014). For example, Williams et al. (2007) investigated the self-exclusion data from seven Canadian provinces with casinos and reported between 0.6 and 7.0% of problem gamblers signed up to self-exclude themselves from gambling venues. Nonetheless, self-report evidence suggest that self-excluders generally experience benefits from programmes including decreased gambling (Kotter, Kräplin, & Bühringer, 2017) and increased psychological well-being and overall functioning (Gainsbury, 2014). Generally, self-exclusion is thought to be an important component in a suite of public health strategies to reduce gambling harms (Gainsbury, 2014), although better player tracking is required for self-exclusion to be universally effective.

Gambling delivery

Gambling parameters

Several empirical analyses of EGM design suggest gambling parameters influence gambling behaviour. Typically, these studies have identified the effects of random ratio schedules and variable reinforcement patterns, resulting in greater gambling persistence. For example, Dixon and Schreiber (2002) found that the speed of play increased as the number of non-reinforced trials (i.e., without wins) increased. Similarly, some evidence suggests that reductions in the delay between gambles, and therefore gambling payouts, resulted in significantly more gambles and more money spent compared to slower games (Ladouceur & Sévigny, 2006). Also, people who gamble prefer numerous pay-lines and the possibility of greater payouts (Walker, 2001), resulting in an increase in the number of gambles and time spent gambling compared to single line gambling (Delfabbro, Falzon, & Ingram, 2005). Further, proposed reductions in maximum bet lines differentially reduced proposed gambling expenditure by problem gamblers compared to non-problem gamblers (Jackson et al., 2016). Additionally, the incidence of "near misses", or situations where a loss occurs but appears visually close to a win, results in longer gambling sessions (Giroux & Ladouceur, 2006) and extended gambling sessions in laboratory settings (Côté, Caron, Aubert, Desrochers, & Ladouceur, 2003). Moreover, "losses disguised as wins", or machines signalling the outcome of "winning" a smaller amount of money than the money lost from the gamble, appears to increase the likelihood of gambling persistence, although perhaps less so than actual wins (Leino et al., 2016). Consequently, prudent public health approaches need to continually monitor gambling parameters as new machine designs are constantly appearing with novel features designed to prompt continual play.

Pre-commitment

"Pre-commitment" is an often studied and considered concept in public health approaches to minimise gambling harm. Pre-commitment refers to an individual setting a limit on the amount of gambling time, frequency or money spent prior to the start of play. The rationale for the effectiveness of pre-commitment is that from an extended temporal distance people can make decisions that incorporate their long-term interests to a greater degree than when faced with the immediate possibility of gambling. The assumption is that pre-commitments, or limits on gambling play and/or expenditure, will stop gambling before problematic gambling begins. Although intuitively appealing, and with evidence to support the efficacy of pre-commitment, the issues with pre-commitment are based on the use of prophylactic limits and whether these limits can be negated. For example, time limits on gambling play can protect against extended gambling sessions, the likelihood of significant losses, and the return to other less harmful activities. Research suggests that people who gamble problematically are more likely to set a time limit compared to non-problem gamblers (Wiebe, Mun, & Kauffman, 2006) but were also more likely to exceed time limits (Wood & Griffiths, 2014). Similarly, loss limits are often a concrete way of reducing gambling spend, where all gambling severities appear to set some sort of loss limit (Drawson, Tanner, Mushquash, Mushquash, & Mazmanian, 2017), although people who gamble problematically appear to set higher loss limits (Lalande & Ladouceur, 2011) and are more likely to exceed self-imposed loss limits (Blaszczynski et al., 2014). Other pre-commitment strategies include limits on the frequency of play and pre-commitments for all or some gambling activities. Notably, pre-commitment is particularly well-suited for online gambling as the implementation of these features is electronically linked to an identifiable individual, although like terrestrial gambling, these features can be circumvented by gambling on other gambling sites (Williams et al., 2012). Therefore, the utility of pre-commitment is related to the implementation of these strategies, whether limit setting is mandatory or voluntary, whether limits can be exceeded and the availability of pre-commitment features on other gambling activities (Thomas et al., 2016).

Staff training

Staff training regarding responsible gambling is now a common jurisdictional requirement. Typically, gambling venue staff receive problem gambling awareness training, with the purpose to direct individuals with possible issues to appropriate resources including gambling information centres, responsible gambling staff and treatment resources. Although gambling venue staff often receive training in the jurisdictional requirements for the provision of gambling activities, very little research has been conducted on staff training. Notably, there appears some disparity between staff and consumer ratings of problem gambler severity amongst gambling patrons. For example, Delfabbro, Borgas, and King (2012) reported that 22 participants who gamble were assessed as meeting the Problem Gambling Severity Index (PGSI: Ferris & Wynne, 2001) criteria for problem gambling, although the venue staff only correctly identified one person as a problem gambler, from this group. Furthermore, venue staff identified 15 people as moderate or problem gamblers, but patron responses on the PGSI indicated they were either at no risk or at a low-risk for problem gambling. Similarly, Rintoul, Deblaquiere, and Thomas (2017) found gambling venue staff made isolated supportive interactions with people who gamble to address gambling harm and concluded staff are failing to meet their gambling codes of conduct responsibilities. One possibility that might explain these inconsistencies between stated venue intentions to protect those who gamble and the behaviour by staff is the lack of ease workers have in approaching people about their problem gambling behaviours. Hing and Nuske (2012) interviewed venue staff regarding their interactions with patrons and found staff reported feeling awkward when discussing personal issues because they were embarrassed about the situation. They also reported difficulties because they were uncertain whether an individual was having problems and other issues relating to privacy and interfering with personal relationships. Consequently, staff training and regular evaluation of adherence to responsible gambling requirements, possibly related to greater staff confidence about speaking with patrons about their problematic gambling, appears to be an issue where jurisdictions and venues can improve their delivery of responsible gambling training.

Gambling environment

People who gamble often choose to frequent commercial gambling venues that are attractive, have a variety of gambling opportunities and offer the highest level of service (Williams et al., 2012). Casinos are typically constructed to create an engaging experience: absence of clocks, maze-like interiors, low ambient lighting punctuated by bright colourful EGM lights (Griffiths, 2009). Although these features are likely to encourage an immersive experience, the research on these factors is sparse. However, one notable gambling venue characteristic implied in the immersive experience, the lack of visible clocks, does show some promise as a possible characteristic related to gambling severity. Jackson et al. (2016) found that problem gamblers thought the introduction of visible clocks would result in greater expected decreases in gambling expenditure compared to non-problem gamblers. Other features related to the gambling environment, such as the availability of automatic teller machines and smoking bans also differentially influenced the perceptions of non-problem and problem gamblers. Consequently, the gambling environment is a potential area for reducing gambling harm.

Summary

This review of the core features of the provision of gambling suggests several potential public health policy initiatives for harm minimisation. Although all have some value, the efficacy of each feature relies on how the policy is implemented and whether people who gamble can avoid, exceed or delay the adherence to harm minimisation initiatives. Importantly, government regulation and policing of the industry appears a necessary component for the provision of responsible gambling. Consequently, a broad range of harm minimisation initiatives and effective policing of these regulations are necessary to meet population needs and achieve government goals.

References

Ajdacic-Gross, V., Killias, M., Hepp, U., Gadola, E., Bopp, M., Lauber, C., et al. (2006). Changing times: A longitudinal analysis of international firearm suicide data. *American Journal of Public Health, 96*(10), 1752–1755.

Babor, T., Caetano, R., Casswell, S., Edwards, G., Giesbrecht, N., Graham, K., . . . Rossow, I. (2010). *Alcohol: No Ordinary Commodity: Research and Public Policy* (2nd ed.). Oxford: Oxford University Press.

Babor, T., Caulkins, J., Edwards, G., Fischer, B., Foxcroft, D., Humphreys, K., . . . Strang, J. (2010). *Drug Policy and the Public Good*. Oxford: Oxford University Press.

Bickel, W. K., Landes, R. D., Christensen, D. R., Jackson, L., Jones, B. A., Kurth-Nelson, Z., & Redish, D. A. (2011). Single- and cross-commodity discounting among cocaine addicts: The commodity and its temporal location determine discounting rate. *Psychopharmacology, 217*(2), 177–187.

Blaszczynski, A., Gainsbury, S., & Karlov, L. (2014). Blue gum gaming machine: An evaluation of responsible gambling features. *Journal of Gambling Studies, 30*(3), 697–712.

Côté, D., Caron, A., Aubert, J., Desrochers, V., & Ladouceur, R. (2003). Near wins prolong gambling on a video lottery terminal. *Journal of Gambling Studies, 19*(4), 433–438.

Delfabbro, P., Borgas, M., & King, D. (2012). Venue staff knowledge of their patrons' gambling and problem gambling. *Journal of Gambling Studies, 28*(2), 155–169.

Delfabbro, P., Falzon, K., & Ingram, T. (2005). The effects of parameter variations in electronic gambling simulations: Results of a laboratory-based pilot investigation. *Gambling Research, 17*(1), 7–25.

88 Darren R. Christensen

Dixon, M. R., & Schreiber, J. B. (2002). Utilizing a computerized video poker simulation for the collection of data on gambling behaviour. *Psychological Record*, *52*(4), 417–428.

Doiron, J. P., & Nicki, R. M. (2007). Prevention of pathological gambling: A randomized controlled trial. *Cognitive Behaviour Therapy*, *36*(2), 74–84.

Doran, B. J., Marshall, D. C., & McMillen, J. (2007). A GIS-based investigation of gaming venue catchments. *Transactions in GIS*, *11*(4), 575–595. doi: 10.1111/j.1467-9671.2007. 01061.x

Drawson, A. S., Tanner, J., Mushquash, C. J., Mushquash, A. R., & Mazmanian, D. (2017). The use of protective behavioural strategies in gambling: A systematic review. *International Journal of Mental Health and Addiction*, *15*(6), 1302–1319.

Dzik, B. (2009). Poland. In G. Meyer, T., Hayer, & M. Griffiths (Eds.), *Problem Gambling in Europe: Challenges, Prevention, and Interventions* (pp. 219–227). New York: Springer Science & Business Media.

Ferris, J., & Wynne, H. (2001). *The Canadian Problem Gambling Index: Final Report*. Ottawa, ON: Canadian Centre on Substance Abuse.

Foxcroft, D., Ireland, D., Lowe, G., & Breen, R. (2011). Primary prevention for alcohol misuse in young people. *Cochrane Database of Systematic Reviews*, *9*. doi:10.1002/14651858. CD003024.pub2

Gainsbury, S. M. (2014). Review of self-exclusion from gambling venues as an intervention for problem gambling. *Journal of Gambling Studies*, *30*(2), 229–251.

Gainsbury, S. M., Aro, D., Ball, D., Tobar, C., & Russell, A. (2015). Determining optimal placement for pop-up messages: Evaluation of a live trial of dynamic warning messages for electronic gaming machines. *International Gambling Studies*, *15*(1), 141–158.

Giroux, I., & Ladouceur, R. (2006). The effect of near wins on the choice of a video lottery terminal. *Gambling Research*, *18*(1), 69–75.

Griffiths, M. D. (2009). Casino design: Understanding gaming floor influences on player behaviour. *Casino and Gaming International*, *5*(1), 21–26.

Griffiths, M. D. (2012). Internet gambling, player protection, and social responsibility. In R. J. Williams, R. Wood, & J. Parke (Eds.), *Routledge International Handbook of Internet Gambling* (pp. 227–249). London: Routledge.

Hancock, L., Schellinck, T., & Schrans, T. (2008). Gambling and Corporate Social Responsibility (CSR): Re-defining industry and state roles on duty of care, host responsibility and risk management. *Policy and Society*, *27*(1), 55–68.

Hing, N. (2002). The emergence of problem gambling as a corporate social issue in Australia. *International Gambling Studies*, *2*(1), 101–122.

Hing, N., & Nisbet, S. (2009). *Testing the Link between Accessibility and Gambling Problems: Gambling and Problem Gambling Amongst Gaming Venue Staff*. Melbourne and New South Wales, Australia: Office of Gaming and Racing, Victorian Department of Justice.

Hing, N., & Nuske, E. (2012). Responding to problem gamblers in the venue: Role conflict, role ambiguity, and challenges for hospitality staff. *Journal of Human Resources in Hospitality & Tourism*, *11*(2), 146–164.

Jackson, A. C., Christensen, D. R., Francis, K. L., & Dowling, N. A. (2016). Consumer perspectives on gambling harm minimisation measures in an Australian jurisdiction. *Journal of Gambling Studies*, *32*(2), 801–822.

Jackson, A. C., Thomas, S. A., Thomason, N., & Ho, W. (2002). *Longitudinal Evaluation of the Effectiveness of Problem Gambling Counselling Services, Community Education Strategies and Information Products, Volume 3: Community Education Strategies and Information Products*. Melbourne, Australia: Victorian Department of Human Services.

Kotter, R., Kräplin, A., & Bühringer, G. (2017). Casino self- and forced excluders' gambling behaviour before and after exclusion. *Journal of Gambling Studies*, *34*(2), 597–615.

Ladouceur, R., & Sévigny, S. (2006). The impact of video lottery game speed on gamblers. *Journal of Gambling Issues, 17*.

Lalande, D. R., & Ladouceur, R. (2011). Can cybernetics inspire gambling research? A limit-based conceptualization of self-control. *International Gambling Studies, 11*(2), 237–252. doi: 10.1080/14459795.2011.598540

Leino, T., Torsheim, T., Pallesen, S., Blaszczynski, A., Sagoe, D., & Molde, H. (2016). An empirical real-world study of losses disguised as wins in electronic gaming machines. *International Gambling Studies, 16*(3), 470–480.

Macur, M., Makarovic, M., & Roncevic, B. (2009). Slovenia. In G. Meyer, T., Hayer, & M. Griffiths (Eds.), *Problem Gambling in Europe: Challenges, Prevention, and Interventions* (pp. 265–279). New York: Springer Science & Business Media.

Marshall, D., McMillen, J., Niemeyer, S., & Doran, B. (2004). *Gaming Machine Accessibility and Use in Suburban Canberra: A Detailed Analysis of the Tuggeranong Valley*. Canberra, Australia: ACT Gambling and Racing Commission.

Mason, K. (2008). *Raising the Odds? Gambling Behaviour and Neighbourhood Access to Gambling Venues in New Zealand*. Wellington, New Zealand: New Zealand Ministry of Health.

McMillen, J., & Doran, B. (2006). Problem gambling and gaming machine density: Socio-spatial analysis of three Victorian localities. *International Gambling Studies, 6*(1), 5–29. doi:10.1080/14459790600644093

Meyer, G., & Hayer, T. (2007). Die Spielsperre des Glücksspielers – Eine Bestandsaufnahme [The exclusion of gamblers: The current situation]. *Sucht, 53*(3), 160–168.

Najavits, L. M., Grymala, L. D., & George, B. (2003). Can advertising increase awareness of problem gambling? A Statewide survey of impact. *Psychology of Addictive Behaviors, 17*(4), 324–327.

Nutt, D., King, L. A., Saulsbury, W., & Blakemore, C. (2007). Development of a rational scale to assess the harm of drugs of potential misuse. *The Lancet, 369*(9566), 1047–1053.

Oh, C. B., Ong, Y. J., & Loo, J. M. Y. (2017). A review of educational-based gambling prevention programs for adolescents. *Asian Journal of Gambling Issues and Public Health, 7*(1), 4.

Osborne Group. (2008). *Responsible Gaming Information Centres: 2007 Evaluation*. Retrieved from www.responsiblegambling.org/rg-news-research/rgc-centre/published-research/docs/research-reports/responsible-gaming-information-centres-2007-evaluation

Parke, J., & Griffiths, M. (2007). The role of structural characteristics in gambling. In G. Smith, D. C. Hodgins, & R. J. Williams (Eds.), *Research and Measurement Issues in Gambling Studies* (pp. 217–249). Burlington, MA: Elsevier.

Pearce, J., Mason, K., Hiscock, R., & Day, P. (2008). A national study of neighbourhood access to gambling opportunities and individual gambling behaviours. *Journal of Epidemiology and Community Health, 62*, 862–868.

Reith, G. (2007). Gambling and the contradictions of consumption: A genealogy of the "pathological" subject. *American Behavioral Scientist, 51*(1), 33–55.

Responsible Gambling Council. (2008). *From Enforcement to Assistance: Evolving Best Practices in Self-Exclusion*. Toronto: Responsible Gambling Council.

Rintoul, A., Deblaquiere, J., & Thomas, A. (2017). Responsible gambling codes of conduct: Lack of harm minimisation intervention in the context of venue self-regulation. *Addiction Research & Theory, 25*(6), 451–461.

St-Pierre, R. A., Derevensky, J. L., Temcheff, C. E., Gupta, R., & Martin-Story, A. (2017). Evaluation of a school-based gambling prevention program for adolescents: Efficacy of using the theory of planned behaviour. *Journal of Gambling Issues, 36*, 113–137.

Temcheff, C. E., St-Pierre, R. A., Derevensky, J. L. (2014). Gambling among teens, college students and youth. In D. C. S. Richard, A. Blaszczynski, & L. Nower (Eds), *The*

Wiley-Blackwell Handbook of Disordered Gambling (pp. 306–326). NJ, New York: John Wiley & Sons.

Thomas, S. L., Lewis, S., & Westberg, K. (2012). "You just change the channel if you don't like what you're going to hear": Gamblers' attitudes towards, and interactions with, social marketing campaigns. *Health Expectations, 18*(1), 124–136.

Thomas, A., Christensen, D., Deblaquiere, J., Armstrong, A., Moore, S., Carson, R., & Rintoul, A. (2016). *Review of electronic gaming machine pre-commitment features: Limit setting.* Melbourne: Australian Institute of Family Studies.

Toumbourou, J. W., Williams, J., Waters, E., & Patton, G. (2005). What do we know about preventing drug-related harm through social developmental intervention with children and young people? In T. Stockwell, P. J. Gruenewald, J. W. Toumbourou, & W. Loxley (Eds.), *Preventing Harmful Substance Use: The Evidence Base for Policy and Practice* (pp. 87–100). New York: John Wiley & Sons.

Turner, N., Wiebe, J., Falkowski-Ham, A., Kelly, J., & Skinner, W. (2005). Public awareness of responsible gambling and gambling behaviours in Ontario. *International Gambling Studies, 5*(1), 95–112.

Vasiliadis, S., Jackson, A. C., Christensen, D. R., Francis, K. L., & Thomas, S. A. (2013). Physical accessibility of gaming opportunity and its relationship to gaming involvement and problem gambling: A systematic review. *Journal of Gambling Issues, 28*, 1–46.

Walker, M. B. (2001). Strategies for winning on poker machines. In A. Blaszczynski (Ed.), *Culture and the Gambling Phenomenon: Proceedings of the 12th Annual Conference of the National Association for Gambling Studies* (pp. 391–396). Sydney, AU: National Association for Gambling Studies.

Welte, J. W., Barnes, G. M., Tidwell, M.-O. O., Hoffman, J. H., & Wieczorek, W. F. (2016). The relationship between distance from gambling venues and gambling participation and problem gambling among US adults. *Journal of Gambling Studies, 32*(4), 1055–1063.

Wiebe, J., Mun, P., & Kauffman, N. (2006). *Gambling and Problem Gambling in Ontario 2005.* Retrieved from Responsible Gambling Council Website www.responsiblegambling.org/docs/researchreports/gambling-and-problem-gambling-in-ontario- 2005.pdf?sfvrsn=12

Williams, R. J., Belanger, Y. D., & Arthur, J. N. (2011). *Gambling in Alberta: History, Current Status, and Socioeconomic Impacts.* Final Report for the Alberta Gaming Research Institute. Retrieved from http://hdl.handle.net/1880/48495

Williams, R. J., Volberg, R. A., & Stevens, R. (2012). *The Population Prevalence of Problem Gambling: Methodological Influences, Standardized, Rates, Jurisdictional Differences, and Worldwide Trends.* Report prepared for the Ontario Problem Gambling Research Centre and the Ontario Ministry of Health and Long Term Care. Retrieved from http://hdl.handle.net/10133/3068

Williams, R. J., West, B. L., & Simpson, R. I. (2007). *Prevention of Problem Gambling: A Comprehensive Review of the Evidence.* Guelph: Ontario Problem Gambling Research Centre.

Williams, R. J., West, B. L., & Simpson, R. I. (2012). *Prevention of Problem Gambling: A Comprehensive Review of the Evidence, and Identified Best Practices.* Report Prepared for the Ontario Problem Gambling Research Centre and the Ontario Ministry of Health and Long Term Care. Retrieved from http://hdl.handle.net/10133/3121

Wohl, M. J. A., Christie, K.-L., Matheson, K., & Anisman, H. (2010). Animation-based education as a gambling prevention tool: Correcting erroneous cognitions and reducing the frequency of exceeding limits among slots players. *Journal of Gambling Studies, 26*(3), 469–486.

Wood, R. T., & Griffiths, M. D. (2014). Understanding positive play: An exploration of playing experiences and responsible gambling practices. *Journal of Gambling Studies, 31*(4), 1715–1734. doi:10.1007/s10899-014-9489-7

9

HARM PREVENTION AND REDUCTION EFFORTS IN GAMBLING DISORDER

An international perspective

Charles Livingstone

Prevention of gambling-related harm

There is significant evidence that strategies for prevention of harm derived from gambling have been substantially misdirected for many years. This is largely a result of gambling industry interference in selection of research priorities. The consequence of this is that post-hoc gambling harm minimisation (important as it is) has often been the sole focus of efforts to curtail gambling-related harms. The *prevention* of gambling-related harms has been greatly neglected, despite significant experience in other public health fields, (e.g., tobacco control and motor vehicle injury reduction) that prevention is not only possible but highly effective and of significant benefit to individuals and populations.

The philosophy and logic of public health derived harm prevention and minimisation differs significantly from traditional, non-evidence based, "responsible gambling" discourse and its focus on the "problem gambler".

The nature and extent of gambling-related harm

For each person experiencing high levels of gambling-related harm, multiple others are harmed (Goodwin, Browne, Rockloff, & Rose, 2017). These involve family, including partners, children, friends, employers and the broader society. These harms are not insignificant and concern family breakdown and separation, mental health problems, financial ruin and loss of assets, criminal activities including heightened rates of intimate partner violence, the neglect of children and in some cases suicide. Gambling-related harm is very widespread and affects many more people than previously considered, even those at low and moderate risk of gambling-related harm (Browne et al., 2016).

Further, the costs of such harm are believed to significantly exceed previous estimates (Browne et al., 2017).

Considerable resources, in fact, have been devoted to measuring "problem gambling", without necessarily pursuing an understanding of its nature, or what to do about it. Prevalence studies seeking to measure the extent of "problem gambling" have been a popular (Markham & Young, 2016) technique for maintaining the status quo. Such studies allow industry and authorities to argue that those affected by "problem gambling" are proportionately few and underplay the significance of other harm categories. This is a welcome message for the gambling industry, which argues that it cares about "problem gambling" but asserts repeatedly that it is a problem for individuals (see, for example, Clubs Australia, ND).

Central to "responsible gambling" discourse has been the "problem gambler". This category is derived from the notion that the population can be accurately divided into gambling harm categories. Undoubtedly, individuals experience harms of differing severity from addictive disorders. However, the concept of "problem gambling" has been effectively used as a device to conflate gambling-related harm into a simplistic category representing a small proportion of the population. Further, "responsible gambling" discourse transfers responsibility for harm to these "flawed" individuals, to whom it also devolves responsibility for changing their behaviour (Livingstone & Woolley, 2007; Miller & Thomas, 2018).

The discourse of responsible gambling

"Responsible gambling" had its origins in the gambling industry's concern that emerging evidence of harm would lead to more effective regulation of their business (Blaszczynski et al., 2011). "Responsible gambling" purports to defend the individual's right to make poor choices. In reality, it protects the industry's right to exploit those who gamble too much.

As a strategy to stymie the development of effective harm prevention, "responsible gambling" has been very successful (Livingstone & Adams, 2011). Academic research and gambling regulation have been focused on the topic for decades (Hancock & Hao, 2016; Ladouceur, Shaffer, Blaszczynski, & Shaffer, 2017).

The well-known "Reno model" (Blaszczynski, Ladouceur, & Shaffer, 2004) provides an excellent example of the theorisation of "responsible gambling". It is presented as a "science-based" "public health" approach to the minimisation of gambling-related harm. Yet it fails to take account of the significantly distinct effects of different gambling modes, accepting that high impact gambling forms (such as electronic gambling machines, or EGMs) are immutable and cannot be modified. This is the equivalent of arguing that water supplies polluted by pathogens cannot be disinfected, and that the most effective way to treat the disease arising is via distribution of antibiotics as required. Treatment is important, but it is, obviously, not prevention.

Further, it argues that individuals can be classified into various categories of gambling risk, and that these categories should form the focus of harm minimisation efforts. This is at odds with population health approaches – a cornerstone of public health – which are most likely to be effective in preventing the development of harm (Rose, Khaw, & Marmot, 2008).

It is reasonable that prevention, rather than mitigation, of harms should be a major priority. Yet in the Reno model such considerations are absent. This is characteristic of the "responsible gambling" discourse. Most interventions associated with "responsible gambling" are not based in evidence (Livingstone, Rintoul, & Francis, 2014), and, in some cases, are focused on "detection" of the person who gambles by means of observation (Thomas, Delfabbro, & Armstrong, 2014). Further, "responsible gambling" argues that collaboration with industry is desirable (see Hancock & Smith, 2017).

The role of gambling research in maintaining gambling-related harm

Considerable effort has been expended by the gambling industry to influence academic research. This includes establishment of "charities" and suchlike organisations, effectively Social Aspect Public Relations Organisations (or SAPROs), similar to those established by the tobacco and alcohol industries (Miller, de Groot, McKenzie, & Droste, 2011). Such activities maintain the focus on individuals, and regularly fund initiatives to provide counselling and research individual factors that may "predispose" certain individuals to gambling harm. In Britain, GambleAware (previously the Responsibility in Gambling Trust) has been the key funder of gambling research for many years (GambleAware, 2018). In the United States, the National Centre for Responsible Gaming (sic) has funded researchers for many years, allocating millions annually to "responsible gambling" initiatives (NCRG, 2018). These are industry funded organisations. Although they claim to focus on minimising harm, it is arguable that their major priority is minimising the potential impact of regulation.

Gambling actors also directly fund their own research on "responsible gambling", involving senior gambling researchers, which in at least one case is seen as an "investment" by industry (Clubs NSW, 2017).

Available evidence from gambling and other fields (Adams, 2007, 2016; Babor et al., 2010; Cassidy, Loussouarn, & Pisac. 2014; Miller, Babor, McGovern, Obot, & Bühringer, 2008; Oreskes & Conway, 2011), tell us that industry engagement leads to delays, confusion as to goals, misdirection of research efforts, inadequate evidence bases, pseudo-academic argument about the insuperability of harms and the sowing of doubt, particularly around the widespread nature of harm, and their product-driven nature (Petticrew et al., 2017). This effort has regularly involved the enrolment of researchers.

Recently, in the face of growing criticism (Cassidy et al., 2014; Livingstone & Adams, 2016), some researchers have argued that industry does not affect outcomes or directions. Why this would be so in the gambling field, but not fields such as alcohol or tobacco, is unexplained (Blaszczynski & Gainsbury, 2014; Wohl & Wood, 2015).

The research field is also debased by significant industry influence in research conferences, the spaces where researchers gather for discussion, reflection and engagement on issues of moment (Livingstone, 2018a). The close association of the gambling industry with gambling researchers is part of a strategy utilised by harmful consumption industries to influence public policy via control of the research agenda, whether to misdirect priorities or contest emerging consensus. This influence has impeded the development of effective preventive measures for gambling-related harm. It has done this by misdirection of priorities, co-option of researchers and diversion of research effort into the cul-de-sac of "responsible gambling", where prevention of harm is not a priority and where evidence is poor or non-existent.

"Responsible gambling" codes and practices

"Responsible gambling" codes of conduct are the principal manifestation of the discourse of responsible gambling (Williams, West, & Simpson, 2012). These codes assert that the worst excesses of gambling-related harm can be reduced by displaying warning signs, providing information about gambling games to inform users of risks, and via slogans such as "Gamble Responsibly". Codes generally require gambling operators to allow people to ban themselves (or sometimes, relatives) from using gambling services (self-exclusion). These measures are most effective where identification is required to enter gambling venues. In the absence of such a requirement, self-exclusion is regularly breached (Livingstone et al., 2014).

Some jurisdictions also require gambling operators to intervene if a person who gambles displays visible signs of distress or exhibits behaviours characteristic of gambling-related harm. Such behaviours have been catalogued and verified, and are likely indicative of high-level harms (Thomas et al., 2014). However, as with other manifestations of "responsible gambling", the evidence for efficacy of interventions is poor. Indeed, there is no evidence that such interventions even occur. In practice, gambling operators appear focused on encouraging people who gamble to keep spending (FCA, 2015; Rintoul, Deblaquiere, & Thomas, 2017; Schüll, 2012).

The conclusion to be drawn from this is that "responsible gambling" is ineffective in reducing harm, let alone preventing it. It is a project without a goal (Livingstone & Woolley, 2007), other than to provide cover for an industry whose aim is to maximise revenue and minimise its own responsibility.

Gambling forms – severity and distribution of revenues

Gambling does not come as a single commodity form. There is considerable difference between the harmful potential of ubiquitous high intensity slot machines and a weekly lottery. That is not to suggest that lotteries are harm-free. However, people who gamble regularly in some gambling forms experience rates of harm well above those of alternatives. For example, a long-running longitudinal survey in Australia found that harm rates amongst people who regularly gamble using the lottery were at the population average, whereas 41% of regular slot machine users incurred harms at some level (Livingstone, 2017a; Wilkins, 2016).

The Australian situation is informative. Australia is notorious for its widespread and regressive (Rintoul, Livingstone, Mellor, & Jolley, 2013) distribution of electronic gambling machines (EGMs), known as "pokies". As Schüll (2012) has observed, Australian-style pokies are high-intensity, complex and have set the pattern for EGMs in many other jurisdictions. Because of the widespread availability of pokies, most Australian gambling revenue derives from their use. This is why Australia continues to lead the world in terms of per capita gambling expenditure (The Economist, 2017). Of the AU\$23.7 billion spent in Australia on gambling in 2016–17, AU\$12.1 billion was spent on pokies in pubs and clubs, with another AU\$2.5 billion spent on pokies in casinos. Around 60% of Australian gambling losses are on pokies, of which there were more than 196,000 in 2015–16 (QGSO, 2018).

Recent developments in the UK, where EGMs known as Fixed Odds Betting Terminals (Davies, 2017), or the United States, where slots dominate casino revenue (Schüll, 2012), suggest a similar pattern. Not all gambling is equal in its potential for harm production.

The importance of game design and characteristics

As recognition of the dangers of high intensity gambling forms has developed so has a literature on the mechanisms of gambling-related harm. As Schüll (2012) demonstrates, addictive behaviour is the goal of EGM design. The mechanism for this behaviour, via the well-articulated psychological principles of operant and classical conditioning, is likely the striatal dopamine system (Yücel, Carter, Harrigan, van Holst, & Livingstone, 2018; see also Clark, Boileau, & Zack, 2018). Put bluntly, gambling incorporating high event frequencies will "hijack" the dopamine system and may induce an addictive disorder, with an increased likelihood of this occurring in stressed populations. This is exacerbated, and made possible, by the circumstances in which gambling is made available and marketed (Yücel et al., 2018; see also Chapter 6).

Research has now demonstrated the significance of some key aspects of the structural characteristics of gambling forms. Event frequency is a key factor. The schedule of reinforcement available on an EGM is a major element in the addictive potential of the device. Given EGMs' digital nature, this can be modified to produce a range of differing schedules (Livingstone, 2017b). Reinforcement can be boosted significantly by utilising "losses disguised as wins", available on multiline games where 50 or more lines can be wagered at once. This provides the potential for a modest reward on one or more of the multiple lines, although the net effect is an overall loss. However, the device provides audio-visual reinforcement of this. The effect of this can be to double the reinforcement rate, at no cost to the operator. Such reinforcement appears to have similar physiological and neurological effects as an actual win (Harrigan, Maclaren, Brown, Dixon, & Livingstone, 2014). The same is true of "near misses" (Harrigan, 2008), which can be engineered via virtual reels of differing "length", and different numbers of winning symbols (Livingstone, 2017b). Jackpots, particularly "linked jackpots", are a reward much sought after

96 Charles Livingstone

by people who gamble (Browne et al., 2015; Rockloff & Hing, 2013). "Features", which provide "free spins" or "bonus rounds" with increased prizes are similar (Harrigan, Dixon, & Brown, 2015; Livingstone, Woolley, Zazryn, Bakacs, & Shami, 2008). All of these characteristics enhance reinforcement and thus addictive potential. All can be modified to reduce harmful potential.

Different jurisdictions have taken varying approaches to the emerging concern about, and evidence of, high rates of gambling-related harm, by modifying game characteristics and otherwise. In the Australian state of New South Wales, EGMs are permitted a "load up" (the maximum credit amount) of AU$7,500, with bets of AU$D10 every three seconds. However, other Australian jurisdictions have introduced important harm prevention measures. In Queensland and Tasmania, "losses disguised as wins" are prohibited. Maximum bets in most Australian jurisdictions are now AU$5 per "spin". In New Zealand, they are NZ$2.50 (Livingstone, 2018b). Automatic Teller Machines (ATMs) are prohibited in gambling venues in Victoria (Thomas et al., 2013).

The British Government, faced with growing concern about the harmful potential of Fixed Odds Betting Terminals (FOBTs), recently announced that maximum bets would be reduced from £100 to £2 per "spin", and this will occur in 2019 (Davies, 2018).

The Australian government recently announced a package of consumer protection measures addressing online wagering (Australian Government, 2018). These include prohibitions on credit betting, availability of a voluntary pre-commitment system, "one button" self-exclusion, and limits on gambling advertising during sporting broadcasts.

A more adventurous Australian government attempt to introduce a universal pre-commitment system in 2010 failed after opposition from the gambling industry. Political activity by gambling industry operators is effective and well-resourced (Panichi, 2013). This appears common where industry is private and licensed. Scandinavian countries have had more success in restraining the excesses of gambling operators.

In Norway, concern about the proliferation of gambling machines operated on behalf of charities lead first to their nationalisation in 2003. In 2006, bank note acceptors were removed. In 2007, EGMs were withdrawn from operation, and replaced in 2009 by newly designed multiuse terminals, imposing a statutory limit on expenditure using an account-based system. The harm prevention effects of this were significant (Lund, 2009; Rossow & Hansen, 2016).

As evidence of the effects of structure in gambling games has grown, and experience of reform has expanded, so too has the potential for effective harm prevention. Modifying the characteristics of gambling forms, or the circumstances of their availability, can be effective in preventing or minimising harm.

Advancing harm prevention

Tobacco control provides an excellent example of successful harm prevention. The tobacco industry fought to discredit evidence-based reforms (Oreskes & Conway, 2011). The gambling industry has learned from this. However, incremental change to the marketing, pricing and availability of tobacco, and the circumstances of its consumption, have produced remarkable changes to smoking behaviour (Borland & Yong, 2018). Motor vehicle mortality and injury has also been reduced in many jurisdictions by adopting an approach incorporating understanding of the multiple causes of injury. As with tobacco, incremental change has led to success in reducing mortality and morbidity from vehicle collisions (World Health Organisation, 2015).

An effective preventive public health approach would emulate the approach taken in tobacco control and motor vehicle injury reduction. Behaviour change is achieved by changes in the circumstances in which the product is offered and/ or by changes to the product. Lessons can also be learnt from other public health fields, such as prevention of blood borne viruses, where success in limiting disease-transmission was supported by engaging those affected, actively reducing stigma (Bowtell, 2005). Encouraging participation by those affected by harmful gambling in the design of harm prevention interventions will reduce barriers to help seeking and improving interventions. At present, those affected by harmful gambling often experience stigma and shame (Miller & Thomas, 2018), which effectively silences them.

The range of regulatory changes that will allow populations to make better choices about the consumption of dangerous gambling products is extensive. It includes, but is certainly not limited to, the following:

- Reduction in accessibility of gambling opportunities, particularly the most dangerous products, particularly in areas of social stress.
- Modifications to the structural characteristics of gambling games.
- Restriction on advertising of gambling, and sports sponsorship by gambling operators, notably where young people are likely to be affected.
- Use of universal and binding pre-commitment systems to permit people who gamble to set and adhere to predetermined limits across a jurisdiction.
- Reducing easy accessibility of cash in gambling venues, and prohibition on use of credit cards or provision of other forms of credit for gambling.
- Encouraging effective programmes to de-stigmatise gambling-related harms, including abandonment of the "responsible gambling" slogan and the use of the term "problem gambler".
- Reducing the reliance of researchers on gambling industry funding and providing incentives for researchers to avoid industry-sponsored research forums.
- Requiring gambling operators to provide de-identified data for research purposes and facilitate recruitment of people who gamble for research purposes.

There is little doubt that shifting from a "responsible gambling" frame to a public health-oriented harm prevention and minimisation frame will reduce gambling-related harm. As gambling grows and new forms emerge, effective harm prevention will become more and more pressing a priority. We know what needs to be done. It is time to do it.

98 Charles Livingstone

References

Adams, P. J. (2007). *Gambling, Freedom and Democracy: Routledge Studies in Social and Political Thought.* New York: Routledge Falmer.

Adams, P. J. (2016). *Moral Jeopardy: Risks of Accepting Money from the Alcohol, Tobacco and Gambling Industries.* Cambridge: Cambridge University Press.

Australian Government, Department of Social Services. (2018). *Gambling.* Retrieved from www.dss.gov.au/communities-and-vulnerable-people/programmes-services/gambling

Babor, T. F., Babor, T., Caetano, R., Casswell, S., Edwards, G., & Giesbrecht, N. (2010). *Alcohol: No Ordinary Commodity: Research and Public Policy.* Oxford: Oxford University Press.

Blaszczynski, A., Collins, P., Fong, D., Ladouceur, R., Nower, L., Shaffer, H., . . . Venisse, J.-L. (2011). Responsible gambling: General principles and minimal requirements. *Journal of Gambling Studies, 27*(4), 565–573.

Blaszczynski, A., & Gainsbury, S. (2014). Editor's notes. *International Gambling Studies, 14,* 354–356.

Blaszczynski, A., Ladouceur, R., & Shaffer, H. J. (2004). A science-based framework for responsible gambling: The Reno model. *Journal of Gambling Studies, 20*(3), 301–317.

Borland, R., & Yong, H. H. (2018). Tobacco control: Preventing smoking and facilitating cessation. In E. Fisher et al. (Eds.), *Principles and Concepts of Behavioral Medicine* (pp. 771–805). New York, NY: Springer.

Bowtell, W. (2005). *Australia's Response to HIV/AIDS 1982–2005.* Sydney, Australia: Lowy Institute for International Policy.

Browne, M., Greer, N., Armstrong, T., Doran, C., Kinchin, I., Langham, E., & Rockloff, M. (2017). *The Social Cost of Gambling to Victoria.* Melbourne: Victorian Responsible Gambling Foundation. Retrieved from https://responsiblegambling.vic.gov.au/resources/publications/the-social-cost-of-gambling-to-victoria-121/

Browne, M., Langham, E., Rawat, V., Greer, N., Li, E., Rose, J., . . . Best, T. (2016). *Assessing Gambling-Related Harm in Victoria: A Public Health Perspective.* Melbourne: Victorian Responsible Gambling Foundation. Retrieved from https://responsiblegambling.vic.gov.au/documents/69/Research-report-assessing-gambling-related-harm-in-vic.pdf

Browne, M., Langham, E., Rockloff, M. J., Li, E., Donaldson, P., & Goodwin, B. (2015). EGM jackpots and player behaviour: An in-venue shadowing study. *Journal of Gambling Studies, 31*(4), 1695–1714.

Cassidy, R., Loussouarn, C., & Pisac, A. (2014). *Fair Game: Producing Gambling Research.* Goldsmiths: University of London.

Clark, L., Boileau, I., & Zack, M. (2018). Neuroimaging of reward mechanism in gambling disorder: An integrative review. *Molecular Psychiatry, 1.* doi:10.1038/s41380-018-0230-2

Clubs Australia. (ND). *Responsible Gambling (Webpage).* Retrieved from www.clubsaustralia.com.au/advocacy/policy-centre/responsible-gambling

Clubs NSW. (2017). *Annual Report.* Retrieved from www.clubsnsw.com.au/sites/default/files/2018-08/clubsnsw-2017-annual-report.pdf

Davies, R. (2017, May). UK gamblers lose record £13.8bn as industry braces for FOBT crackdown. *The Guardian.* Retrieved from www.theguardian.com/society/2017/may/25/uk-gamblers-fobt-dcms-losses

Davies, R. (2018, May). Maximum stake for fixed-odds betting terminals cut to £2. *The Guardian.* Retrieved from www.theguardian.com/uk-news/2018/may/17/maximum-stake-for-fixed-odds-betting-terminals-cut-to-2

The Economist. (2017, February 9). The world's biggest gamblers. Retrieved from www.economist.com/graphic-detail/2017/02/09/the-worlds-biggest-gamblers

Financial Counselling Australia. (2015, August). *Duds, Mugs, and the A-List: The Impact of Uncontrolled Sports Betting.* Melbourne: Financial Counselling Australia. Retrieved from www.financialcounsellingaustralia.org.au/getattachment/Corporate/Home/FINAL-PDF-Duds,-Mugs-and-the-A-List-The-Impact-of-Uncontrolled-Sports-Betting-low-res.pdf

GambleAware. (2018). *About Gamble Aware (Webpage)*. Retrieved from https://about.gambleaware.org/fundraising/

Goodwin, B., Browne, M., Rockloff, M., & Rose, J. (2017). A typical problem gambler affects six others. *International Gambling Studies, 17*(2), 276–289.

Hancock, L., & Hao, Z. (2016). Gambling regulatory regimes and the framing of "responsible gambling" by transnational casino corporations: Asia-Pacific regimes in comparative perspective. *Asia Pacific Journal of Public Administration, 38*(3), 139–153.

Hancock, L., & Smith, G. (2017). Critiquing the Reno Model I-IV International influence on Regulators and Governments (2004–2015): The distorted reality of "responsible gambling". *International Journal of Mental Health and Addiction, 15*(6), 1151–1176.

Harrigan, K. A. (2008). Slot machine structural characteristics: Creating near misses using high award symbol ratios. *International Journal of Mental Health and Addiction, 6*(3), 353–368.

Harrigan, K. A., Dixon, M., & Brown, D. (2015). Modern multi-line slot machine games: The effect of lines Wagered on winners, losers, bonuses, and losses disguised as wins. *Journal of Gambling Studies, 31*(2), 423–439.

Harrigan, K. A., Maclaren, V., Brown, D., Dixon, M. J., & Livingstone, C. (2014). Games of chance or masters of illusion: Multiline slots design may promote cognitive distortions. *International Gambling Studies, 14*(2), 301–317.

Ladouceur, R., Shaffer, P., Blaszczynski, A., & Shaffer, H. J. (2017). Responsible gambling: A synthesis of the empirical evidence. *Addiction Research & Theory, 25*(3), 225–235.

Livingstone, C. (2017a). Pokies, sports and racing harm 41% of regular gamblers. *The Conversation*. Retrieved from https://theconversation.com/pokies-sport-and-racing-harm-41-of-monthly-gamblers-survey-81486

Livingstone, C. (2017b). *How Electronic Gambling Machines Work*. AGRC Discussion Paper 8. Melbourne: Australian Gambling Research Centre, Australian Institute of Family Studies. Retrieved from https://aifs.gov.au/agrc/publications/how-electronic-gambling-machineswork

Livingstone, C. (2018a). A case for clean conferences in gambling research. *Drug and Alcohol Review, 37*(5), 683–686.

Livingstone, C. (2018b). *A Blueprint for Preventing and Minimising Harm from Electronic Gambling Machines in the ACT*. Canberra: Canberra Alliance for Gambling Reform. Retrieved from www.anglicare.com.au/wp-content/uploads/2018/10/A-blueprint-for-preventing-and-minimising-harm-from-EGMs-in-the-ACT-Final-2Oct2018128288.pdf

Livingstone, C., & Adams, P. J. (2011). Harm promotion: Observations on the symbiosis between government and private industries for the development of highly accessible gambling markets. *Addiction, 106*(1), 13–14.

Livingstone, C., & Adams, P. J. (2016). Clear principles are needed for integrity in gambling research. *Addiction, 111*(1), 5–10.

Livingstone, C., Rintoul, A., & Francis, L. (2014). What is the evidence for harm minimisation measures in gambling venues? *Evidence Base, 2*, 1–24.

Livingstone, C., & Woolley, R. (2007). Risky business: A few provocations on the regulation of electronic gaming machines. *International Gambling Studies, 7*(3), 361–376.

Livingstone, C. H., Woolley, R., Zazryn, T. R., Bakacs, L., & Shami, R. G. (2008). *The Relevance and Role of Gaming Machine Games and Game Features on the Play of Problem Gamblers*. South Australia: Independent Gambling Authority. doi:10.13140/rg.2.1.3070.2249

Lund, I. (2009). Gambling behaviour and the prevalence of gambling problems in adult EGM gamblers when EGMs are banned: A natural experiment. *Journal of Gambling Studies, 25*(2), 215–225.

Markham, F., & Young, M. (2016). Commentary on Dowling et al (2016): Is it time to stop conducting problem gambling prevalence studies? *Addiction, 111*(3), 436–437.

Miller, H. E., & Thomas, S. L. (2018). The problem with "responsible gambling": Impact of government and industry discourses on feelings of felt and enacted stigma in people who experience problems with gambling. *Addiction Research & Theory, 26*(2), 85–94.

Miller, P. G., Babor, T. F., McGovern, T., Obot, I., & Bühringer, G. (2008). Relationships with the alcoholic-beverage industry, pharmaceutical companies, and other funding agencies: Holy Grail or poisoned chalice? *Publishing Addiction Science: A Guide for the Perplexed*, 190–212.

Miller, P. G., de Groot, F., McKenzie, S., & Droste, N. (2011). Vested interests in addiction research and policy: Alcohol industry use of social aspect public relations organizations against preventative health measures. *Addiction, 106*(9), 1560–1567.

National Center for Responsible Gaming. (2018). *About NCRG (Webpage)*. Retrieved from www.ncrg.org/about-ncrg

Oreskes, N., & Conway, E. M. (2011). *Merchants of Doubt: How a Handful of Scientists Obscured the Truth on Issues from Tobacco Smoke to Global Warming*. New York: Bloomsbury Publishing USA.

Panichi, J. (2013). The lobby group that got much more bang for its buck. *Inside Story*. Retrieved from inside.org.au/the-lobby-group-that-got-much-more-bang-for-its-buck

Petticrew, M., Katikireddi, S. V., Knai, C., Cassidy, R., Hessari, N. M., Thomas, J., & Weishaar, H. (2017). Nothing can be done until everything is done: The use of complexity arguments by food, beverage, alcohol and gambling industries. *Journal of Epidemiology and Community Health, 71*(11), 1078–1083.

Queensland Government Statistician's Office. (2018). *Australian Gambling Statistics 1987–88 to 2016–17*. Retrieved from www.qgso.qld.gov.au/products/reports/aus-gambling-stats/

Rintoul, A., Deblaquiere, J., & Thomas, A. (2017). Responsible gambling codes of conduct: Lack of harm minimisation intervention in the context of venue self-regulation. *Addiction Research & Theory, 25*(6), 451–461.

Rintoul, A., Livingstone, C., Mellor, A., & Jolley, D. (2013). Modelling vulnerability to gambling related harm: How disadvantage predicts gambling losses. *Addiction Research & Theory, 21*(4), 329–338.

Rockloff, M. J., & Hing, N. (2013). The impact of jackpots on EGM gambling behavior: A review. *Journal of Gambling Studies, 29*(4), 775–790.

Rose, G., Khaw, K. T., & Marmot, M. (2008). *Rose's Strategy of Preventive Medicine: The Complete Original Text*. Oxford: Oxford University Press.

Rossow, I., & Hansen, M. B. (2016). Gambling and gambling policy in Norway: An exceptional case. *Addiction, 111*(4), 593–598.

Schüll, N. D. (2012). *Addiction by Design: Machine Gambling in Las Vegas*. Princeton, NJ: Princeton University Press.

Thomas, A., Delfabbro, P., & Armstrong, A. (2014). *Validation Study of In-Venue Problem Gambling Indicators*. Gambling Research Australia. Retrieved from www.gamblingresearch.org.au/resources/85c394ee-bfcd-48ea-a507-992555401eaa/validation_study_of_invenue_problem_gambler_indicatorsv2.pdf

Thomas, A., Pfeifer, J., Moore, S., Meyer, D., Yap, L., & Armstrong, A. (2013). *Evaluation of the Removal of ATMs from Gaming Venues in Victoria, Australia: Final Report*. Victoria: Department of Justice, Office of Liquor, Gaming and Racing.

Wilkins, R. (2016). *The Household, Income and Labour Dynamics in Australia Survey: Selected Findings from Waves 1 to 15*. Melbourne, Victoria: Melbourne Institute of Applied Economic and Social Research. Retrieved from https://melbourneinstitute.unimelb.edu.au/__data/assets/pdf_file/0010/2437426/HILDA-SR-med-res.pdf

Williams, R. J., West, B. L., & Simpson, R. I. (2012). *Prevention of Problem Gambling: A Comprehensive Review of the Evidence and Identified Best Practices*. Toronto: Ontario Problem Gambling Research Centre and the Ontario Ministry of Health and Long Term Care.

Wohl, M. J., & Wood, R. T. (2015). Is gambling industry-funded research necessarily a conflict of interest? A reply to Cassidy (2014). *International Gambling Studies, 15*(1), 12–14.

World Health Organisation. (2015). *Global Status Report on Road Safety 2015*. WHO Geneva.

Yücel, M., Carter, A., Harrigan, K., van Holst, R. J., & Livingstone, C. (2018). Hooked on gambling: A problem of human or machine design? *The Lancet Psychiatry, 5*(1), 20–21.

10

THE ROLE OF TREATMENT IN REDUCING GAMBLING-RELATED HARM

David C. Hodgins and Magdalen Schluter

Introduction

A successful public health approach to gambling, in addition to having prevention and consumer protection components, must include a range of intervention options for individuals who develop mild to severe gambling-related problems. There is a growing body of literature evaluating the efficacy and effectiveness of specific treatment interventions (Petry, Ginley, & Rash, 2017; Yakovenko & Hodgins, 2016), and many jurisdictions provide formal treatment programmes for individuals with severe problems. However, even when available, only 10–20% of individuals experiencing problems seek formal treatment (Cunningham, 2005; Petry et al., 2017; Slutske, 2010). Providing telephone and online helplines and gambling venue services to link individuals to treatment is a very common approach to increasing treatment uptake. However, the effectiveness of linkage and outreach efforts, such as helplines, on promoting treatment uptake are not often evaluated. Nonetheless, we are beginning to have some understanding of the large non-treatment-seeking population and their reluctance to seek treatment. Some individuals actively reject formal treatment but are amenable to briefer, self-directed activities to reduce harm or to stop gambling. Others prioritise and seek treatment for other comorbid mental health problems (e.g., depression, anxiety) or social concerns (e.g., family conflict). Stepped-care-type models, adapted from other areas of mental health and addictive disorders, have been developed to describe the required elements of a coordinated response. In this chapter, we present an expanded stepped care model that incorporates a broader public health orientation recognising a diverse array of pathways to recovery, including but not limited to formal treatment. This chapter reviews what we have learned about non-treatment-assisted recovery pathways from gambling problems, and then provides the public health integrated stepped care model. Finally, we identify gaps for further research and development.

Treatment versus non-treatment-assisted change

It has been documented for over 30 years that, like recovery from substance use disorders, the most common pathway to recovery from gambling problems is self-directed (Hodgins & el-Guebaly, 2000; Hodgins, Wynne & Makarchuk, 1999). Examination of the processes of recovery in gambling samples has yielded some insight into who does and does not choose the assistance of treatment, and some of the reasons for their choice. For example, it has been demonstrated in both samples of convenience and representative community samples that the likelihood of individuals seeking treatment increases along with their problem severity (Slutske, Blaszczynski, & Martin, 2009; Toneatto et al., 2008). Although individuals with the greatest level of problem severity are still relatively unlikely to attend treatment, those with lower severity very rarely do. For example, in a large Australia twin sample (Slutske et al., 2009), the relationship between the number of DSM-IV symptoms (0–10) and the likelihood of seeking gambling treatment was moderately strong ($r = 0.42$). Only 70% of individuals meeting criteria for pathological gambling with five symptoms reported treatment-seeking compared with 92% of individuals reporting nine or ten symptoms.

One explanation for the seeming reluctance of individuals with gambling problems to seek treatment is that treatment seeking requires that an individual acknowledges to themselves and others that they have a gambling problem. This acknowledgement represents an existential shift in identity or self-concept. Studies examining the ordinal onset of various gambling-related symptoms (such as DSM criteria) or items from rating scales such as the South Oaks Gambling Screen (SOGS; Lesieur & Blume, 1987) and Problem Gambling Severity Index (PGSI; Currie, Hodgins, & Casey, 2013) show that endorsement of an item such as "I have a gambling problem" is a later-stage development (e.g., Slutske et al., 2009; Toce-Gerstein, Gerstein, & Volberg, 2003). Individuals acknowledge many significant negative consequences (gambling too much, chasing losses, family and financial impacts) at a much earlier stage than they label themselves as having a "gambling problem". Moreover, such individuals often tackle these issues well before they see themselves as having a problem. In short, it appears that much self-directed change occurs in individuals who don't really see themselves as being a problem gambler or needing treatment, although they see themselves as frequently gambling in a problematic fashion.

The importance of self-concept is underscored by interviews with individuals with past disordered gambling about what precipitated their recoveries. Viewing their problem gambling as "incompatible with their self-image" is frequently offered as a major precipitant for beginning to address the problem (Hodgins & el-Guebaly, 2000; Toneatto et al., 2008). In a prospective study, Kim, Salmon, and Santesso (2017) also identified that feelings of self-discontinuity (i.e., feeling that gambling has fundamentally changed the person from their past self) at baseline amongst a sample of Americans who gamble problematically increased the likelihood of engaging in self-directed change throughout a subsequent six-month follow-up (Kim et al., 2017).

104 David C. Hodgins and Magdalen Schluter

Consistent with the observation that efforts to change can precede problem acknowledgement is the finding that "wanting to handle the problem on my own" is the most frequently reported reason for not seeking treatment (Hodgins, 2005). In a review of the available literature on perceived barriers to seeking treatment, Suurvali, Hodgins, Toneatto, and Cunningham (2009) identified 19 studies conducted across five countries that asked individuals with gambling problems directly about why they did not seek treatment. The most frequently cited reason across these diverse samples was a "desire to handle problems themselves" and/or the belief that they could do so. The second most frequent reason was feelings of shame, embarrassment, and fear of stigma, followed by lack of acknowledgement or minimisation of the problem. Treatment availability and other treatment-related concerns were also cited but relatively less frequency.

Another important observation about the recovery process from gambling problems is that almost all people who do ultimately seek treatment describe having made attempts to change on their own or by using information gleaned from websites or other media (Suurvali et al., 2008). This change strategy is consistent with the stepped care model where the least intensive or intrusive option is the first step for individuals. Failure at self-recovery helps people acknowledge the seriousness of the problem and promotes willingness to seek treatment. In this sense, it appears that individuals are essentially making appropriate decisions for themselves, both when attempting self-recovery and when they seek treatment if it becomes necessary. Support for this is found in a recent prospective study of a group of Canadians with DSM-5 disordered gambling. A quarter of the participants sought treatment in the following 12 months and three factors were robust predictors of treatment seeking: higher severity of gambling problems, greater readiness to change, and greater attention to public awareness information (Kowatch & Hodgins, 2015). Importantly, the gambling outcomes of those seeking treatment were similar to those who used informal or no supports, consistent with the idea that individuals make sensible decisions about their needs.

This study also points to the important role that public awareness most likely plays in facilitating treatment seeking. Unfortunately, formal evaluations of public health awareness initiatives appear to be rare. Awareness campaigns are associated with increased calls to problem gambling helplines (Productivity Commission, 2010), which suggests that people attend to and are most receptive to the information when they are ready to hear it. They may also serve the important function of reducing the shame and fear of stigmatisation that limits treatment-seeking (Horch & Hodgins, 2015). By targeting public misperceptions that contribute to the stigmatisation of problem gambling, awareness campaigns can potentially reduce this stigma and its deleterious effects on healthcare service utilisation (Hing, Russell, & Gainsbury, 2016). A general population survey in Ontario, Canada, reported that of individuals who screened positively for past year gambling problems, 62% indicated that they had seen advertisements for telephone helpline services for gambling problems, 66% were able to name a service and 89% were able to describe a strategy for finding treatment if they wanted to do so (Suurvali et al., 2008). This survey was not associated with a specific campaign in Ontario, although it occurred during a period of heightened media attention.

Another factor that may affect the rate of problem gambling treatment-seeking is the high rate of mental health and substance use disorder comorbidity in gambling disorder. A recent scoping review revealed several systematic reviews of comorbidity prevalence in both general population and clinical samples of disordered gambling (Yakovenko & Hodgins, 2017). Gambling problems are associated with many mental health disorders including anxiety and mood disorders, substance use, personality disorders, as well as psychotic spectrum disorders, and they are more the norm than the exception. Given these high rates, surprisingly little attention has been paid to the implications of comorbidity on the course and treatment of gambling disorder (Yakovenko & Hodgins, 2017). Treatment outcome studies generally neither address the comorbid mental health and substance use disorder issues of their clients directly nor assess the impact of comorbidity on gambling outcomes.

Interestingly, overall prevalence of mental health and substance use disorder comorbidity in general population gambling disorder samples (e.g., Lorains, Cowlishaw, & Thomas, 2011) is as high as the prevalence in clinical gambling disorder samples (Dowling et al., 2015). Typically, for other mental health disorders, clinical samples have much higher rates of comorbidity because comorbidity drives people to treatment (Berkson, 1946). One explanation for this unusual finding in the gambling literature may be that many people with gambling disorder and comorbidities choose to seek treatment for their comorbid disorder rather than their gambling disorder (i.e., they are not represented in clinical gambling disorder samples). In fact, studies of the prevalence of gambling disorder in other clinical samples do show high rates (Yakovenko & Hodgins, 2017). The comorbid disorder may be perceived as more pressing, or treatment for the comorbid disorder might be perceived as more available or less stigmatised. If true, then treatment systems for anxiety, depression, substance use and other mental health disorders need to be able to identify and address gambling-related issues. Similarly, systems that service individuals with housing needs, family problems or family violence, all of which have been linked to gambling problems, need also to be capable of identifying and responding to gambling problems.

Although some jurisdictions have funded initiatives to promote gambling disorder literacy in other service sectors, the details and successes are rarely documented for dissemination. One exception is a recent report from an effort to promote cross sector collaboration in Victoria, Australia (Martyres & Townsend, 2016). Funding was provided for outreach by gambling treatment services to other health and welfare services already engaged with clients. Qualitative evaluation found that some outreach efforts were relatively more successful (training staff in these agencies to address gambling problems, providing secondary case consultation, increasing screening for gambling problems) and other strategies were more challenging (colocating gambling counsellors at the other agencies, providing single sessions at the other agency). The report includes some practical principles for successful implementation.

106 David C. Hodgins and Magdalen Schluter

In summary, a comprehensive treatment system needs to include both specialist gambling services as well as incorporating gambling focus into related service systems. The role of natural recovery and self-change as both a developmental phase (an effort that fails but helps the person be ready to seek more formal help) and as a recovery pathway also needs to be recognised and promoted. In the following section, we outline such a model and discuss its components.

Expanded stepped care model

Figure 10.1 outlines a comprehensive heuristic for the conceptualisation of ideal intervention components in a public health framework. As shown, individuals with gambling problems are influenced by both gambling availability and a range of harm-reduction features from the local environment, including availability of pre-commitment, various electronic gaming machine (EGM) structural features, low-risk gambling promotion, etc. (see Chapters 11 and 13). Individuals can be broadly conceptualised as either experiencing their gambling problem as a primary issue or as less immediately disruptive than some other health or social issue (secondary issue). For individuals accessing services for these other issues, including mental health, addictive disorders, primary care and social services, a variety of interventions are potentially helpful in motivating them to be ready to change their gambling as well. These interventions include awareness messages, brief screening by the involved clinicians and web-based advice. Several trials of brief advice with populations such as people in medical treatment and college students have been reported with modest but positive results (Yakovenko & Hodgins, 2016).

Similarly, within the population of individuals that are experiencing gambling as their primary concern, most will not be ready to change. Interventions aimed at moving such individuals into being ready to change include public awareness campaigns, online gambling and venue interventions, family support interventions and screening customers seeking financial services. Given our understanding of the process of change, public awareness messages that are likely to be effective are ones that promote optimism towards changing behaviour and the idea that treatment can help. In contrast, messages suggesting that certain behaviours indicate that a person gambles problematically are less likely to be effective. In terms of online gambling and venue interventions, these are increasingly available. In Canada, for example, casinos routinely have information services available either staffed or through interactive technology. These services vary in terms of how proactive they are, with some available only if contact is initiated by customers and other models in which at-risk customers are approached based upon some "red flag" in their behaviour. Online gambling sites similarly have begun to provide links to information and support with some sites proactively identifying high-risk players and other sites through more passive links. Individuals with gambling problems can also be encouraged to address their gambling issues by their family members and interventions have been designed to provide assistance to families for this purpose (Dowling, Rodda, Lubman, & Jackson, 2014).

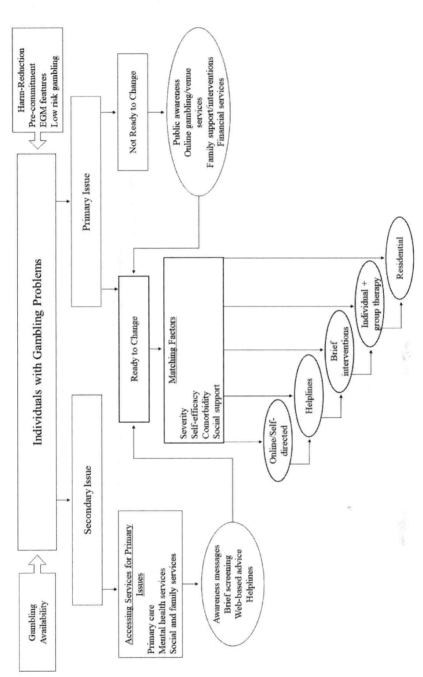

FIGURE 10.1 Expanded stepped care model addressing gambling problems

108 David C. Hodgins and Magdalen Schluter

The goal of these interventions is to motivate people towards change and to provide a gateway to treatment when needed. Given that people who gamble problematically represent a heterogeneous group of individuals, a range of intervention possibilities of different intensities is ideal, as outlined in Figure 10.1. Moreover, many empirically supported treatments show comparable efficacy at reducing symptom severity and frequency of gambling (Petry et al., 2017; Yakovenko & Hodgins, 2016). A stepped-care approach may enhance the provision of treatment for disordered gambling by matching individuals to an appropriate level of intervention based on personal characteristics; individuals are matched to the least intensive and intrusive level of intervention that is likely to be effective, based on characteristics such as severity of gambling behaviour, comorbid mental health problems, level of social support and personal goals. A range of interventions is outlined in the following section. In some jurisdictions, gambling services are free-standing, and in others they are imbedded in either addiction or mental health services.

Online/Self-directed treatments are the least intensive or intrusive. These typically incorporate principles from traditional therapies into a workbook or web-based format. They are relatively inexpensive, easily accessible and may be particularly helpful to individuals who live in areas without access to many resources (Gainsbury & Blaszczynski, 2011; Petry et al., 2017). Self-help workbooks based upon cognitive behavioural principles have shown reasonable efficacy and web-based treatments for disordered gambling show promising results across cognitive-behavioural and brief treatment modalities (Yakovenko & Hodgins, 2016).

Voluntary self-exclusion programmes are increasingly available in both casinos and online. Such programmes are useful at increasing an individual's perception of control and reducing gambling behaviour (Ladouceur et al., 2007). Although these programmes are often used alone, they may be used concurrently with other treatments.

Helplines are easily accessible and are of low cost to the individual. Traditionally intended to only provide information and resources, they are increasingly providing additional support to callers, and some now offer telephone counselling (Clifford, 2008). However, helpline services are time-limited, necessitating brief intervention and problem-focused strategies (Shandley & Moore, 2008). As such, they may be particularly useful for helping individuals in acute crisis and provide opportunities to help sustain motivation for change.

Brief interventions such as Motivational Interviewing (MI) are design to facilitate behaviour change with less extensive assessments and of shorter duration than traditional therapies. MI can produce reductions in diagnostic symptoms and frequency of gambling behaviour similar to that of more extensive Cognitive Behavioural Treatment/Therapy (CBT) (Yakovenko & Hodgins, 2016). Brief interventions may be particularly useful in areas without enough staff to meet the demand and can be provided in public health contexts to individuals not seeking treatment (Petry et al., 2017). They may also be used as an adjunct to other types of intervention, including self-directed or individual therapy to improve outcomes.

The role of treatment in reducing harm   **109**

Individual and group therapies such as CBT or exposure therapy require greater time commitment and are typically used only in traditional treatment settings. CBT may be delivered to individuals or in group situations, with similar effectiveness between the two modes of delivery (Oei, Raylu, & Casey, 2010).

Finally, *inpatient programmes* represent the most intensive intervention. As such, they should be recommended for the most severe and/or complex cases for which less intervention is unlikely to be effective.

Conclusions

A range of prevention, consumer protection components and intervention options is necessary for a successful approach to problem gambling. The expanded stepped-care model described here is a comprehensive heuristic for the conceptualisation of ideal intervention components imbedded within a public health framework. This approach has been adapted from other areas of mental health and addictive disorders but remains inchoate with problem gambling. Although many of the individual components are offered in numerous jurisdictions, they have not yet been systematically linked. Moreover, even where offered, many components are not comprehensively evaluated. Many questions have yet to be answered, including the impact of service information utilisation within casinos on treatment seeking, the long-term effect of many less intensive interventions and how many intervention components may be most effectively combined. Implementation of a stepped-care approach will provide opportunities to evaluate many of these questions.

References

Berkson, J. (1946). Limitations of the application of fourfold table analysis to hospital data. *Biometrics, 2*(3), 47–53.

Clifford G. (2008). The Evolution of Problem Gambling Helplines. In M. Zangeneh, A. Blaszczynski, N. E. Turner (Eds.), *The Pursuit of Winning* (pp. 291–312). Boston, MA: Springer.

Cunningham, J. A. (2005). Little use of treatment among problem gamblers. *Psychiatric Services, 56*(8), 1024–1025. doi:10.1176/appi.ps.56.8.1024

Currie, S. R., Hodgins, D. C., & Casey, D. M. (2013). Validity of the problem gambling severity index interpretive categories. *Journal of Gambling Studies, 29*(2), 311–327. doi:10.1007/s10899-012-9300-6

Dowling, N. A., Cowlishaw, S., Jackson, A. C., Merkouris, S. S., Francis, K. L., & Christensen, D. R. (2015). Prevalence of psychiatric co-morbidity in treatment-seeking problem gamblers: A systematic review and meta-analysis. *Australian and New Zealand Journal of Psychiatry, 49*(6), 519–539. doi:10.1177/0004867415575774

Dowling, N. A., Rodda, S. N., Lubman, D. I., & Jackson, A. C. (2014). The impacts of problem gambling on concerned significant others accessing web-based counselling. *Addictive Behaviors, 39*(8), 1253–1257.

Gainsbury, S., & Blaszczynski, A. (2011). A systematic review of internet-based therapy for the treatment of addictions. *Clinical Psychology Review, 31*(3), 490–498.

Hing, N., Russell, A. M., & Gainsbury, S. M. (2016). Unpacking the public stigma of problem gambling: The process of stigma creation and predictors of social distancing. *Journal of Behavioural Addiction, 5*(3), 448–456. doi:10.1556/2006.5.2016.057

Hodgins, D. C. (2005). Implications of a brief intervention trial for problem gambling for future outcome research. *Journal of Gambling Studies, 21*(1), 13–19. doi:10.1007/s10899-004-1917-7

Hodgins, D. C., & el-Guebaly, N. (2000). Natural and treatment-assisted recovery from gambling problems: A comparison of resolved and active gamblers. *Addiction, 95*(5), 777–789.

Hodgins, D. C., Wynne, H., & Makarchuk, K. (1999). Pathways to recovery from gambling problems: Follow-up from a general population survey. *Journal of Gambling Studies, 15*, 93–104.

Horch, J. D., & Hodgins, D. C. (2015). Self-stigma coping and treatment-seeking in problem gambling. *International Gambling Studies, 15*(3), 470–488. doi:10.1080/14459795.2015.1078392

Kim, H. S. M. J., Salmon, M., & Santesso, D. (2017). When do gamblers help themselves? Self-discontinuity increases self-directed change over time. *Addictive Behaviors, 64*, 148–153. doi:10.1016/j.addbeh.2016.08.037

Kowatch, K. R., & Hodgins, D. C. (2015). Predictors of help-seeking for gambling disorder from the transtheoretical model perspective. *International Gambling Studies, 15*(3), 450–469. doi:10.1080/14459795.2015.1078391

Ladouceur, R., Sylvain, C., & Gosselin, P. (2007). Self-exclusion program: A longitudinal evaluation study. *Journal of Gambling Studies, 23*(1), 85–94.

Lesieur, H. R., & Blume, S. B. (1987). The South Oaks Gambling Screen (SOGS): A new instrument for the identification of pathological gamblers. *American Journal of Psychiatry, 144*(9), 1184–1188. doi:10.1176/ajp.144.9.1184

Lorains, F. K., Cowlishaw, S., & Thomas, S. A. (2011). Prevalence of comorbid disorders in problem and pathological gambling: Systematic review and meta-analysis of population surveys. *Addiction, 106*(3), 490–498. doi:10.1111/j.1360-0443.2010.03300.x

Martyres, K., & Townsend, P. (2016). Addressing the needs of problem gamblers with co-morbid issues: Policy and service delivery approaches. *Journal of Gambling Issues, 33*(2), 68–81.

Oei, T. P., Raylu, N., & Casey, L. M. (2010). Effectiveness of group and individual formats of a combined motivational interviewing and cognitive behavioral treatment program for problem gambling: A randomized controlled trial. *Behavioural and Cognitive Psychotherapy, 38*(2), 233–238.

Petry, N. M., Ginley, M. K., & Rash, C. J. (2017). A systematic review of treatments for problem gambling. *Psychology of Addictive Behaviors, 31*(8), 951–961.

Productivity Commission, P. (2010). *Gambling.* Canberra: Productivity Commission.

Shandley, K., & Moore, S. (2008). Evaluation of gambler's helpline: A consumer perspective. *International Gambling Studies, 8*(3), 315–330.

Slutske, W. S. (2010). Why is natural recovery so common for addictive disorders? *Addiction, 105*(9), 1520–1521; discussion 1524. doi:10.1111/j.1360-0443.2010.03035.x

Slutske, W. S., Blaszczynski, A., & Martin, N. G. (2009). Sex differences in the rates of recovery, treatment-seeking, and natural recovery in pathological gambling: Results from an Australian community-based twin survey. *Twin Res Hum Genet, 12*(5), 425–432. doi:10.1375/twin.12.5.425

Suurvali, H., Cordingley, J., Hodgins, D. C., & Cunningham, J. (2009). Barriers to seeking help for gambling problems: A review of the empirical literature. *Journal of Gambling Studies, 25*(3), 407–424. doi:10.1007/s10899-009-9129-9

Suurvali, H., Hodgins, D., Toneatto, T., & Cunningham, J. (2008). Treatment seeking among Ontario problem gamblers: Results of a population survey. *Psychiatric Services, 59*(11), 1343–1346. doi:10.1176/ps.2008.59.11.1343

Toce-Gerstein, M., Gerstein, D. R., & Volberg, R. A. (2003). A hierarchy of gambling disorders in the community. *Addiction, 98*(12), 1661–1672. doi:10.1111/j.1360-0443.2003.00545.x

Toneatto, T., Cunningham, J., Hodgins, D., Adams, M., Turner, N., & Koski-Jannes, A. (2008). Recovery from problem gambling without formal treatment. *Addiction Research & Theory, 16*(2), 111–120. doi:10.1080/16066350801923638

Yakovenko, I., & Hodgins, D. C. (2016). Latest developments in treatment for disordered gambling: Review and critical evaluation of outcome studies. *Current Addiction Reports, 3*(3), 299–306.

Yakovenko, I., & Hodgins, D. C. (2017). A scoping review of co-morbidity in individuals with disordered gambling. *International Gambling Studies, 18*(1), 143–172. doi:10.1080/14459795.2017.1364400

11

PUBLIC HEALTH AND GAMBLING

The potential of *nudge* policies

Magaly Brodeur

In recent decades, gambling has significantly grown in popularity. However, whilst for a large part of the population gambling is a hobby, certain individuals are faced with problematic gambling. Excessive gambling represents a major public health problem. Unfortunately, the measures currently used in many jurisdictions do not appear to have a significant effect. Indeed, despite the measures put in place, the prevalence of problem gambling remains stable (Brodeur, 2015; Kairouz et Nadeau, 2011; Ladouceur, Jacques, Chevalier, Hamel, & Allard, 2004; Ladouceur, 1991; Shaffer & Korn, 2002; Kallick, Suits, Dielman, & Hybels, 1976; Billieux et al., 2016). The public are becoming more and more aware of the problem (Bélanger, Boisvert, Papineau, & Vétéré, 2003). However, unfortunately problematic players appear to be relatively unaffected by the awareness campaigns implemented in many countries.[1]

In such a context, what can be done to better reach problematic players? How can we reduce harm in the gambling sector? Over recent years, *nudge* approaches have significantly grown in popularity and their effectiveness has been demonstrated in many areas (Thaler & Sunstein, 2008). These approaches are intended to encourage and not compel individuals to adopt a specific behaviour.

The aim of this chapter is therefore to demonstrate the potential of *nudge* approaches in the gambling sector. This chapter is divided into three sections. In the first section, we present *nudge* approaches. In the second section, we review the issue of excessive gambling in the province of Quebec, Canada, and finally, in the third section, we present ways to improve the effectiveness of public policies for harm reduction in the gambling sector.

Nudge approaches

What is a *nudge*? A *nudge* represents a "gentle push"; a form of encouragement to adopt a specific behaviour. The main characteristic of a *nudge* is that it involves no coercion or constraint.

Richard Thaler, Professor of Economics and Behavioural Science at the University of Chicago, and Cass Sunstein, a Professor of Law at Harvard University, are the thinkers behind the *nudge* concept (Thaler & Sunstein, 2008). In observing individuals' behaviour, they came to the following conclusion: people regularly make "bad" decisions and do so in many areas (health, personal finance, activities of daily living, etc.). As these decisions can have a significant impact on individuals, their families and society, those close to them offer a way to influence individuals' behaviour by adopting a form of "soft" paternalism, called libertarian paternalism.

Libertarian paternalism aims to guide individuals in directions likely to increase their well-being or reduce the economic and social costs associated with their behaviour. It does this whilst respecting the individual's freedom, and they are therefore free from constraints.

To better illustrate a *nudge,* we will look at two examples. The first concerns Amsterdam airport (Thaler & Sunstein, 2010). A few years ago, Amsterdam airport was faced with high cleaning costs, especially for the men's toilets. The main issue was splashes around the urinals that caused odour problems and required an increase in the frequency of the cleaning.

Amsterdam airport had tried several approaches to tackle this problem. However, nothing worked. Classic prevention measures such as posters suggesting that men take care when using the facilities were ineffective.

To solve this problem, a simple solution was found: engraving flies in the background of the urinals. Why? By providing targets, the flies helped men to "aim better". The results were instant. It was immediately possible to observe an 80% decrease in splashes and a proportionate reduction in the associated cleaning costs (Thaler & Sunstein, 2010).

Another well-known example of *nudge* was created in the city of Chicago in the United States. The problem was this: a stretch of road called Lake Shore Drive was S shaped and very dangerous. Many accidents were reported on this stretch of road every year.

Several measures had been put in place: reduction in the speed limit, increase in speed-control measures and administering fines, etc. However, these measures proved to be ineffective, and accidents were still too frequent.

What solution was suggested? Painting lines on the floor to create an optical illusion, giving the driver the impression that their speed was much higher. The result: drivers automatically decreased their speed before entering the dangerous stretch of road, and over a period of six months, accidents decreased by 36% (Thaler & Sunstein, 2010).

These two examples highlight the potential of *nudge* approaches. In effect, by making modest changes these measures enabled the resolution of problems that resisted classic prevention measures. Could *nudge* help harm reduction in the gambling sector? This is what we believe and will attempt to demonstrate in the next two sections.

114 Magaly Brodeur

Gambling: The state of play

In recent decades, excessive gambling has been given a special position in the public arena. Indeed, during this period, excessive gambling has become an issue regularly discussed in the media and this is due, amongst other things, to the involvement of public health stakeholders.

According to data from the last prevalence survey conducted in Quebec (Kairouz & Nadeau, 2015), 98,1% of Quebecois are categorised as non-problem gamblers or at "low risk" of developing gambling problems. 1.4% of Quebecois are at "moderate risk" of developing gambling problems and 0.4% are probable "pathological" gamblers (Kairouz & Nadeau, 2015).

When we look at prevalence studies of problem gambling conducted in Quebec over the past decades, we can see that the prevalence of problem gambling has remained stable, at about 1% since 1989. This is despite a considerable increase in gambling revenue and spending on prevention efforts (Brodeur, 2015; Kairouz & Nadeau, 2011, 2015; Ladouceur et al., 2004; Ladouceur, 1991). Moreover, this phenomenon has not only been observed in Quebec. Indeed, studies conducted elsewhere in the Canada and the United States also confirm the finding (Shaffer & Korn, 2002; Kallick et al., 1976; Billieux et al., 2016).

In this context, it is necessary to question the effectiveness of current prevention measures. For example, in Quebec, various measures have been implemented to tackle excessive gambling: a decrease in the number of video lottery terminals, awareness campaigns, self-exclusion programmes at gambling venues, etc. These measures have had a considerable impact on the population by raising awareness of the issue of excessive gambling, amongst other things. However, they do not appear to help reduce the prevalence of excessive gambling.

How can we directly reach the players? How can we lead them to change their approach towards gambling? For some, the solution lies in the prohibition of certain games, particularly those with high-risk characteristics, or even the close control of all games. However, is this the solution? Is it a violation of an individual's freedom? Is it legitimate to ban certain games to protect a small percentage of the population? This problem raises many ethical issues. The prohibitionist measures implemented in many jurisdictions in the 19th and 20th centuries have largely demonstrated the ineffectiveness of such measures (Brodeur, 2010; Dixon, 1991). In such a context, what can be done?

We believe that *nudge* approaches represent an interesting possibility in the case of gambling. Alike to the problems in Chicago and Amsterdam, excessive gambling represents a persistent problem which is difficult to tackle. In the next section, we will try to demonstrate how *nudge* policies could be integrated in the gambling sector.

Gambling and *nudge* policies

In this section, we will try to highlight how *nudge* policy could be applied in the gambling sector. To do this, we will give examples of *nudge* that could be integrated into the following three fields: 1) games characteristics 2) the processes associated with gaming 3) player characteristics. It is important to note that these are only examples. Indeed, the possibilities for *nudge* are endless. Our aim here is only to highlight their potential to reduce gambling-related harm.

Game characteristics: The implementation of a stop system

The first example we present relating to the game characteristics is inspired by existing *stop* systems. What is a *stop* system? It is a measure (product, technical feature, etc.) which aims to make a product or a behaviour disagreeable in order to discourage the user from consuming the product and/or maintaining this behaviour.

The use of Disulfiram (Antabuse®), aldehyde dehydrogenase inhibitor for individuals with alcohol-related problems causes the accumulation of alcohol's main metabolite in the individual's system. This creates unpleasant symptoms such as nausea, vomiting, headaches, diaphoresis, palpitations, etc. The medication, therefore, enables individuals who have problems related to alcohol consumption to maintain abstinence. This treatment has helped and continues to help many people in their wish to stop their alcohol use (Skinner, Lahmek, Pham, & Aubin, 2014). However, it is important to note that its use is controversial within the medical community.

For its part, bitter nail polish works in a similar way to Disulfiram (Antabuse®). Bitter nail polish is a product that is applied to the nails to help individuals stop nail biting. The aim is to make the nails taste unpleasant and thus to help individuals change their behaviour. The product has helped many individuals to reduce or stop their nail biting (Thaler & Sunstein, 2008)

In relation to driving, the Nissan ECO Pedal® has the same objective to change individuals' behaviours. It is a "smart" pedal that detects rapid acceleration, etc., and makes the accelerator pedal heavier. This leads the driver to lift their foot from the accelerator and decrease their speed and acceleration, which results in fuel savings for the driver (Thaler & Sunstein, 2008).

Stop systems have a considerable potential and they could be a useful tool to potentially tackle high-risk games such as video lottery terminals (VLTs). Over recent years, many researchers have highlighted certain features of games that increase their addictive nature. For some, the solution is the prohibition of this type of game. However, as mentioned previously, history has shown that this type of measure is generally ineffective (Brodeur, 2010; Dixon, 1991).

In this context, it might be interesting to adapt the risk factors, after a certain amount of time or money spent. This could be done in various ways. For example, by slowing down the speed of the game, by reducing the colours, changing the sounds, by obliging the individual to "login" more frequently, to impose mandatory breaks for the player, by increasing the button response times or even by reducing the payout. In short, the possibilities are endless. However, the goal remains the same: make the game, at a certain threshold, unpleasant for the player and lead them to stop playing.

Game-related processes: Customer account with default "conservative" options

A second area where it is possible to intervene by applying *nudge* measures involves the process (administration, etc.) leading up to the game. The aim is to encourage people to adopt a behaviour by default.

An example of this type of *nudge* is applied in many jurisdictions in the area of organ donation by adopting a system of presumed consent. Presumed consent means to assume that individuals wish to donate their organs upon their death. But giving the opportunity to individuals who do not want to do so, to report and demonstrate their wish. It is therefore a type of consent that is diametrically opposed to the explicit consent that is currently used in many jurisdictions. Explicit consent requires the formal consent of the individuals (via a notarised act, signed organ donor card, etc.). However, despite the fact that the majority of the Canadian population (95%) wish to donate their organs upon their death (IPSOS, 2010), a small proportion take measures to do so.

Why? The intention is there. However, the situation seems to get stuck when the time comes to move from words to actions. In many cases, individuals intend to act but fail to do so due to forgetting, lacking time or becoming distracted (Brodeur, 2012). A presumed consent system to counter these factors and allow individuals to be on the list of organ donors upon their death, without having to take administrative steps, in this sense.

Such a system could be developed within the gambling sector, via all types of games that require a customer account. We might consider, at first glance, that no individual wants an account. In other words, we could consider not immediately creating an account for every citizen. However, an alternative goal is, to automatically include the "conservative" options when opening an account, i.e., options that severely limit the playing time, the amounts spent, etc. Changes to these options may be possible but only through complex administrative procedures. For example, players may have to provide statements to demonstrate their income, be obliged to meet stakeholders specialising in the area of problem gambling, at certain intervals, etc. The goal is to make the modification process unpleasant for the player and encourage them to adopt the default options.

Player characteristics: Feedback and using "big data"

Finally, it could also be interesting to intervene by using individual players' characteristics. Many games requiring an electronic platform have the capacity to gather information about the players (playing habits, etc.). The goal is to use this in order to perform personalised interventions for problematic players.

This type of approach was used, amongst other things, to promote energy conservation. In certain jurisdictions, individuals' consumption statistics were used to encourage their reduced energy consumption (Thaler & Sunstein, 2008). The strategies used were to compare their consumption to that of other users of the area, to indicate the monetary losses linked to their over-consumption, etc. In short, the goal is to lead individuals to conform to a behaviour defined as "acceptable", which is based on social norms.

In the gambling sector, this type of approach could be used to highlight peoples' behaviours. For example, by providing real-time feedback on their playing habits (gaming time, monetary losses, etc.), compare them to the average player, etc., and in order to lead them to reflect and question their playing habits. Furthermore, in order to encourage individuals to seek help, a system – the game screen, even – could allow individuals to make an instant appointment with a professional or provide a freephone number where the individual can call immediately to receive help.

We believe that these measures combined with the other ideas presented in this section could, intervene in a more direct way, within the excessive gambling sector. Of course, these measures are not miracles. They will not completely stop excessive gambling, but they could ensure better intervention for problematic playing.

Conclusion: *Nudge* approaches in the gambling sector

In this chapter, our goal was to highlight the potential of *nudge* approaches for the harm prevention gambling sector. Indeed, excessive gambling is a major public health problem that has many consequences for problematic players and those close to them. The implications are major: bankruptcy, divorce, depression, suicide, family problems, loss of employment, crime, etc.

In recent decades, many measures have been implemented in order to raise awareness of excessive gambling and attempt to minimise associated harm. However, these measures do not seem to have helped reduce the prevalence of excessive gambling in many countries.

We believe the combination of *nudge* policies to the current measures could make our interventions in this domain more effective. Indeed, *nudge* approaches have demonstrated their effectiveness in many areas. Therefore, why not to apply them to the gambling sector? This is the idea that we have tried to introduce in this chapter.

We believe that by intervening in various areas such as game characteristics, game-related processes as well as using individual players' characteristics, we will be able to guide the behaviour of individuals with gambling difficulties.

And what is especially important in all of this is that these measures respect the individuals' freedom in relation to gaming. Thus, no restrictions are imposed on recreational players having no problematic gaming habits. Indeed, the measures proposed here would only be brought about when problematic gaming behaviours are observed. In other words, all the proposed measures respect the individuals' freedom in gambling but impose a limit where systems observe the need to reduce problem gambling behaviours.

Of course, it is not a "miracle" policy. However, if they are conceptualised as an adjunct to current policies, it is certain that these measures would allow the current framework to be more effective.

118 Magaly Brodeur

In this context, it is essential to undertake research in the area of behavioural sciences for the gambling sector. Furthermore, it is important to promote the implementation of *nudge* policies as well as assessment of this type of public policy. Follow-up indicators also need to be developed. Indeed, despite their usefulness on many levels, prevalence rates mask the extent of gambling-related harm. It is therefore necessary to have more specific indicators in the gambling sector. However, to do this, researchers will need better access to industry data.

It is important to keep in mind that the implementation of *nudge* policies in the gambling sector raises many issues. First, how do we limit the use and exploitation of *nudge* measures by the industry? But also, how do we preserve individuals' freedom of choice? Are we about to intrude a little too much upon the individuals' free will? Indeed, the risks of going off track are many. It is essential to be cautious and closely observe the implementation of such policies.

Note

1 In fact, the prevalence rate of problem gambling remains stable in many jurisdictions, despite an increase in spending on prevention efforts. However, more detailed studies into the impact of prevention measures on prevalence are still needed. It is important to understand that gambling prevalence is not appropriate for estimating the public cost of problem gambling. For more information, see Chapters 1, 2 and 3.

References

Bélanger, Y., Boisvert, Y., Papineau, E., & Vétéré, H. (2003). *La responsabilité de l'État québécois en matière de jeu pathologique: La gestion des appareils de loterie vidéo.* Montréal: INRS Urbanisation, Culture et Société.

Billieux, J., Acahb, S., Savary, J. F., Simon, O., Richter, F, Zullino, D., & Khazaal, Y. (2016). Gambling and problem gambling in Switzerland. *Addiction, 111*(9), 1677–1683.

Brodeur, M. (2010). *Vice et corruption à Montréal.* Québec: Presses de l'Université du Québec.

Brodeur, M. (2012). Sauver plus de vie . . . sans effort: Repenser la politique québécoise sur les dons d'organes. *Huffington Post: Québec.* https://quebec.huffingtonpost.ca/magaly-brodeur/sauver-plus-de-viesans-ef_b_1312184.html

Brodeur, M. (2015). *Construction des problèmes publics, controverse et action publique: Santé publique et jeux de hasard et d'argent au Québec* (Thèse de doctorat (Ph.D.)), Université de Montréal, Québec (Canada).

Dixon, D. (1991). *From Prohibition to Regulation: Bookmaking, Anti-Gambling and the Law.* Oxford: Oxford University Press.

IPSOS. (2010). Views toward organ and tissue donation and transplantation. *Canadian Blood Service*, Final Report.

Kairouz, S., & Nadeau, L. (2011). *Portrait du jeu au Québec: prévalence, incidence et trajectoires sur quatre ans.* Montréal: Fonds de recherche sur la société et la culture, Université de Montréal et Université: Concordia.

Kairouz, S., & Nadeau, L. (2015). *Portrait du jeu au Québec: prévalence, incidence et trajectoires sur auqtre ans.* Fonds de recherche sur la société et la culture, Université de Montréal et Université: Concordia.

Kallick, M., Suits, D., Dielman, T., & Hybels, J. (1976). *A Survey of American Gambling Attitudes and Behavior.* Survey Research Center, Institute of Social Research. Ann Arbor: University of Michigan Press.

Ladouceur, R. (1991). Prevalence estimates of pathological gambling in Quebec. *Canadian Journal of Psychiatry, 36*(10), 732–734.

Ladouceur, R., Jacques, C., Chevalier, S., Hamel, D., & Allard, D. (2004). *Prévalence des habitudes de jeu et du jeu pathologique au Québec en 2002.* Institut national de la santé publique du Québec et Université Laval.

Shaffer, H. J., & Korn, D. A. (2002). Gambling and related mental disorders: A public health analysis. *Annual Review of Public Health, 23,* 171–212.

Skinner, M. D., Lahmek, P., Pham, H., & Aubin, H. J. (2014). Disulfiram efficacy in the treatment of alcohol dependence: A meta-analysis. *PLoS One, 9*(2). doi:10.1371/journal.pone.0087366

Thaler, R., & Sunstein, C. (2008). *Nudge: Improving Decisions about Health, Wealth and Happiness.* New Haven: Yale University Press.

Thaler, R., & Sunstein, C. (2010). *Nudge: La méthode douce pour inspirer la bonne décision.* Paris: Vuibert.

12

EARLY DETECTION OF AT-RISK GAMBLING TO REDUCE HARM

Suzanne Lischer

Introduction

Protection of people who gamble is very important in Swiss society, and few other countries have such stringent legal provisions for identifying and preventing problem gambling behaviour in casinos. Before obtaining a licence, each casino must develop a clear prevention strategy with procedures for identifying and protecting people with potentially hazardous gambling behaviours (Billieux et al., 2016). According to the Gaming Act (Swiss Federal Assembly, 2017) and its Ordinance (Swiss Federal Council, 2018), Swiss casinos must have measures in place for detecting people who gamble problematically at an early stage. More precisely, casino staff must follow guidelines and use checklists for identifying at-risk gambling behaviour, and they are required to open files on players of concern and to systematically track indicators of gambling-related problems over eight-week intervals. These measures aim to help casinos implement appropriate intervention measures in the form of imposed or voluntary exclusions. Exclusions are imposed if there is proof or a strong suspicion of an individual having excessive debts, using stakes that are disproportionate to their financial means, or otherwise disrupting the game. On the other hand, players can also ask to be self-excluded. Players who can plausibly document their financial situation and show that their gambling habits are reasonably in line with their financial means will have their early detection file closed. Under the Federal Gambling Act, casino personnel must be trained in early detection, and providers must collect data about gambling disorder. The law also stipulates that casinos must meet their social obligations by collaborating with addictive disorder treatment and prevention centres (Carlevaro, Lischer, Sani, Simon, & Tomei, 2017). To this end, casinos in Switzerland are supervised by the independent Swiss Federal Gaming Board (SFGB), which is also responsible for enforcing the Casino Act and the associated executive ordinances on mitigating the socially harmful effects of gambling by imposing social safeguards.

Early detection of at-risk gambling **121**

In January 2019, Swiss law was amended to also permit online gambling. Opening the online gambling market, however, has proved to be challenging in terms of meeting player protection objectives. In order to define appropriate Responsible Gambling (RG) measures and tools for early detection, it is necessary to first consider the expertise that terrestrial casinos have acquired in more than 15 years. On the other hand, it is also possible to apply predictive models developed for detecting at-risk players at an early stage. Lastly, it is necessary to consider best-practice models that online-gambling operators have gained through previous experience. On this basis, the chapter will review current research on instruments used for the early detection of people who gamble problematically in both terrestrial and online environments. Furthermore, it will outline the ongoing process of developing and systematically reevaluating effective safeguards for protecting people who gamble in the Swiss gambling sector.

Early detection as a way of reducing harm in problem gambling

Early detection implies that problematic developments can be systematically recorded and that structures are in place, through which the observations can be carried out, documented and analysed. The objective is to implement binding rules, develop standardised procedures and anchor the fundamental principles of early detection and early intervention in the corporate culture (Häfeli, Lischer, & Schwarz, 2011). Whilst problem gambling is a widely known phenomenon, it is important to recognise that some people who gamble occasionally, alternate between the problem and non-problem stages (Smith, Volberg, & Wynne, 1994). The challenge therefore is to identify those in the problem stage (Hancock, Schellinck, & Schrans, 2008). Being able to identify gambling-related harm is a prerequisite for promoting a layered rather than a blanket approach to regulatory controls for harm minimisation in gambling. Early detection can be used to identify individuals who are at risk of experiencing harm, to minimise harm whilst containing the negative impact on the gambling experience of people who do not gamble problematically, to evaluate the impact of harm minimisation and to communicate with players with a view to facilitating awareness and control (Blaszczynski, Parke, Parke, & Rigbye, 2014). Professional counsellors must therefore help to train casino staff in RG practices – especially customer interaction – by developing their listening and communication skills and ability to manage potentially difficult customer interaction (Hing & Nuske, 2011). Furthermore, staff members must be well trained in properly analysing the recorded data.

Identifying problem gambling in land-based venues

This field first gained attention through a review conducted with the support of the Australian Gaming Council in 2002. This included a project with compilations of submissions by various Australian and international researchers and clinical practitioners (Allcock et al., 2002). Allcock's study mainly focused on behaviour in gambling venues. In addition, a field study by Schellinck and Schrans (2004) identified combinations of behavioural, physiological and emotional responses to gambling and to helping identify problem gambling. Similarly, Häfeli and Schneider (2005) conducted qualitative interviews in Swiss casinos with a sample of 28 participants who gambled problematically, 23 casino employees and seven regular gambling patrons. Their aim was to develop indicators for identifying people who gamble problematically. The results from these interviews were analysed and classified into 39 items. A study by Delfabbro and colleagues replicated and extended Schellinck and Schrans' (2004) study by examining a wider range of cues and the practicality of using observational methods to identify problem gambling (Delfabbro, Osborn, Nevile, Skelt, & McMillen, 2007). However, the early detection indicators for terrestrial gambling as mentioned by these authors are quite similar and generally fall into the categories that Häfeli and Schneider (2005) have identified: *frequency and duration of visits, sourcing money, betting behaviour, social behaviour, gambling behaviour and reactions* and *outward appearance*. Although existing studies confirm, in theory, that valid indicators for identifying problem gambling exist, there are still some limitations, especially with respect to validation (Delfabbro, King, & Griffiths, 2012).

Häfeli and Lischer (2010) performed an empirical evaluation of the criteria applied by Swiss casino employees for the early detection of problem gambling. The authors pointed out the importance of empirical validation for early detection systems, since many of the predictors used in practice displayed low sensitivity. It should be noted that, since 2010, the early detection criteria used by Swiss casinos has been revised and the associated processes improved. Some casinos have also added automated real-time alerts to their early detection processes. These provide objective data to assist in identifying riskier gambling patterns and allow for direct interventions on the gambling floor. However, research results on the effectiveness of early detection measures are still very limited and rudimentary.

Analysing player activity

People play Electronic Gaming Machines (EGMs) in casinos and other venues, and they often gamble online. Both types of gambling rely on computerised systems that can track the activity of players over time (Delfabbro et al., 2012). This makes it possible to record the entire period of play (which is indicated by the insertion of a card into an EGM), including the frequency of visits, the time spent playing and the number of machines used (Griffiths & Wood, 2008). However, the fact that player cards are not mandatory within all jurisdictions must also be considered as players can remove their cards from an EGM at any time and continue playing without leaving any traceable record. The impact of this non-representative data (people who gamble self-select whether they would like to participate) plus the possibility that data may be incomplete must be considered in any analysis (Wardle, Seabury, Ahmed, & Coshall, 2013).

Early detection of at-risk gambling **123**

On the Internet, in contrast, information about players is even more detailed because online gambling is by definition account-based. It has been frequently noted that every transaction in online gambling leaves an identifiable audit trail that can be used for research or for player protection purposes (Gainsbury, 2011; Philander, 2014) also see chapter 12. This provides a unique opportunity to use actual playing data, making it possible to develop predictive, behaviourally precise algorithms about people who are at risk of developing gambling-related problems (Braverman, LaPlante, Nelson, & Shaffer, 2013). Records of all gambling transactions involving a specific player are saved in real time and assigned to the player's account. The following factors and trends over time could be used to indicate problem gambling: *duration and frequency of gambling activities, number and frequency of bets, size of the stakes, chasing of losses* and *lack of adaptation in gambling behaviour* (TUV, 2009). These indicators could enable operators to track and monitor gambling behaviour at relatively little expense and to identify problems at an early stage.

Over the last decade, the scientific evidence regarding the description and analysis of actual gambling behaviour has grown significantly. Empirically validated models for predicting future self-exclusion of people who gamble online, based on variables of gambling behaviour, were first put forward by Braverman and Shaffer (2010). In this study, longitudinal data and k-means clustering analysis were used to identify a small subgroup of people with high-risk gambling behaviours. The adopted behavioural parameters of players measured during their gambling activities were as follows: *frequency* captured the total number of active days for one month of betting, *intensity* indicated the average number of bets per active day, *variability* defined the variance of stakes over time and *trajectory* reflected the stake sizes over time (Braverman & Shaffer, 2010). The same indicators and clustering procedures were also used by Dragicevic, Tsogas, and Kudic (2011), who analysed two new datasets relating to online casino use and poker games. They found that the same methodology as in Braverman and Shaffer (2010) makes it possible to identify a small group of people who show markedly different gambling behaviours compared with others in their first month of activity. Furthermore, they suggest that these findings provide a basis for using behavioural analysis to educate players about the risks associated with gambling. Adami and colleagues (2013) also expand Braverman and Shaffer (2010) and found two new markers for identifying people with at-risk gambling behaviours – the *sawtooth* oscillation between increasing wager size and rapid drops and the number of games played (*gambling involvement*).

To advance the identification of behavioural markers for people who gamble problematically online, a study by Gray, LaPlante, and Shaffer (2012) examined the behavioural characteristics of subscribers to an Internet gambling provider who triggered corporate RG interventions (i.e., "responsible gambling cases") and compared these subscribers' behaviours against controls. The authors conclude that indices of gambling intensity (e.g., *total number of bets made, number of bets per betting day*) best distinguished cases from controls, particularly in the case of live-action sports betting. Considering that RG guidelines often lack quantifiable markers to guide people who gamble in wagering safely, Quilty, Avila Murati, and Bagby (2014) assessed the gambling *frequency*, *expenditure* and *duration* of 228 community members and 275 people receiving psychiatric outpatient treatment with the goal of developing a model for predicting gambling-related problems. Gambling involvement was assessed using the Diagnostic and Statistical Manual of Mental Disorders (DSM-IV) and Canadian Problem Gambling Index (CPGI), whereby 120 (24%) participants met the criteria for lifetime pathological gambling. Logistic regression analyses revealed that overall gambling frequency uniquely predicted the presence of harmful problem gambling. Furthermore, frequency indicators for ticket purchasing and casino attendance uniquely predicted the presence of both harmful and problem gambling. The thresholds for determining problem gambling therefore differed depending on the type of gambling activity being assessed, suggesting that efforts for promoting RG should be tailored to each type of gambling offered by operators.

Indicators for early detection of gambling-related problems apply only to specific types of games. Therefore, taking a closer look at payment behaviour and its inherent cross-game nature could yield risk predictors that apply universally across all types of games. An analysis of monitoring playing behaviour by Häusler (2016) used transactional data to study the extent to which it and the respective methods make it possible to differentiate between people who self-exclude and controls. The *number and amount of deposits*, the *variance of withdrawals, the amount of funds subject to reversed withdrawals* and *the use of mobile phone billing* were found to be positively associated with self-exclusion, whilst the number of active gambling months and the use of electronic wallets and prepaid cards were negatively associated. Logistic regression analyses revealed that overall gambling frequency uniquely predicted the presence of harmful and problem gambling. It must therefore be noted that the validity of the resulting predictive model derived from payment data is lower than comparable models derived from gambling data.

In contrast to using gambling transactions as predictors, Häfeli et al. (2011) do not consider behavioural elements strictly related to gaming sessions. Rather, they focus on communication-based indicators by studying the interactions between users and the customer services of gambling operators. The authors found that *frequency, urgency, tonality* and *causation of email messages* provide robust indicators that make it possible to differentiate between self-excluders and controls. A follow-up study by Häfeli, Lischer, and Häusler (2015) explores the possibility of using automated text analysis software to extract quantitative markers from written player correspondence. The authors state that the combination of automated and human assessments can streamline customer service processes to increase the validity of the prediction and reduce response delays for a given customer service backlog. However, they point out that text analysis methods are unable to replace human assessors. In line with earlier findings, Häfeli and colleagues (2015) emphasise that detecting potentially risky behaviour based on customer correspondence requires casino staff to be highly trained.

In a recently published review of the evidence of RG measures, Ladouceur, Shaffer, Blaszczynski, and Shaffer (2017) state that algorithms and diagnostic criteria are increasingly gaining attention as a means of identifying potential gambling-related problems. Yet only a few algorithms and diagnostic systems currently offered are based on empirical evidence or actual gambling behaviours.

Conclusion

In Switzerland, neither regulators nor casinos can draw on best-practice models because of the country's social protection legislation, which is unique in the world. Instead, they will have to develop their own processes as well as the corresponding systems and instruments for successfully implementing early detection in the online environment. The expertise gained by the casinos, during more than 15 years of functioning in an offline environment, is an important prerequisite. The experience of international online providers must be considered as well. Although there were no validated standards for the early detection of risky and suspicious behaviour, online gaming providers regularly perform automated data checks (Aro, Jakob, & Gainsbury, 2014). As noted by the previously mentioned researchers, using predictive models for the purposes of gambling research or harm minimisation has strong potential value. It must, however, be taken into consideration that such predictive models rely on statistics and can never be perfectly accurate, and they may therefore not always be able to predict problem gambling behaviour accurately. Consequently, such algorithms should not be used as the only basis for the decision by operators to ban or inhibit players from gambling (Auer, Littler, & Griffiths, 2015). Automated alerts are, however, very helpful for administering interventions with low impact (for example, information about preventive measures, like voluntarily setting limits).

This brief overview indicates that combining several early detection measures, such as analysing customer communication and the implementation of algorithms to predict upcoming risk events is a very promising harm-reduction strategy. Developing standardised and validated procedures for early detection, intervention and prevention of problematic gambling behaviour is essential. Moreover, conclusive evidence about integrating these algorithms and predictors within fully developed RG programmes is essential. Therefore, implementing effective safeguards for protecting people who gamble calls not only for constant evidence-based and systematic reevaluation but also for close collaboration between public and private sector stakeholders and prevention policymakers.

References

Adami, N., Benini, S., Boschetti, A., Canini, L., Maione, F., & Temporin, M. (2013). Markers of unsustainable gambling for early detection of at-risk online gamblers. *International Gambling Studies, 13*(2), 188–204.

Allcock, C., Blaszczynski, A., Dickerson, M., Earl, K., Haw, J., Ladouceur, R., & Symond, P. (2002). *Current Issues Related to Identifying the Problem Gambler in the Gambling Venue.* Current Issues: Australian Gaming Council, Melbourne, 2–7.

Aro, D., Jakob, L., & Gainsbury, S. (2014). *Use of Data Analytics for Responsible Gambling Regulatory Directives (Final Report).* Ontario Problem Gambling Research Centre (OPGRC). Retrieved from

126 Suzanne Lischer

www.greo.ca/Modules/EvidenceCentre/files/Aro%20et%20al%282014%29Use_of_
data_analytics_for_responsible_gambling_regulatory_directives.pdf

Auer, M., Littler, A., & Griffiths, M. D. (2015). Legal aspects of responsible gaming pre-commitment and personal feedback initiatives. *Gaming Law Review and Economics*, *19*(6), 444–456.

Billieux, J., Achab, S., Savary, J.-F., Simon, O., Richter, F., Zullino, D., & Khazaal, Y. (2016). Gambling and problem gambling in Switzerland. *Addiction*, *111*(9), 1677–1683.

Blaszczynski, A., Parke, A., Parke, J., & Rigbye, J. (2014). *Operator-based approaches to harm minimisation in gambling: Summary, review and future directions*. London: The Responsible Gambling Trust.

Braverman, J., LaPlante, D. A., Nelson, S. E., & Shaffer, H. J. (2013). Using cross-game behavioral markers for early identification of high-risk internet gamblers. *Psychology of Addictive Behaviors*, *27*(3), 868.

Braverman, J., & Shaffer, H. J. (2010). How do gamblers start gambling: Identifying behavioural markers for high-risk internet gambling. *The European Journal of Public Health*, *22*(2), 273–278.

Carlevaro, T., Lischer, S., Sani, A.-M., Simon, O., & Tomei, A. (2017). The inclusion of health concerns in Swiss gambling legislation: An opportunity to access industry data. *International Gambling Studies*, *17*(2), 251–258.

Delfabbro, P., King, D. L., & Griffiths, M. (2012). Behavioural profiling of problem gamblers: A summary and review. *International Gambling Studies*, *12*(3), 349–366.

Delfabbro, P., Osborn, A., Nevile, M., Skelt, L., & McMillen, J. (2007). *Identifying Problem Gamblers in Gambling Venues*. Gambling Research Australia, Melbourne.

Dragicevic, S., Tsogas, G., & Kudic, A. (2011). Analysis of casino online gambling data in relation to behavioural risk markers for high-risk gambling and player protection. *International Gambling Studies*, *11*(3), 377–391.

Gainsbury, S. (2011). Player account-based gambling: Potentials for behaviour-based research methodologies. *International Gambling Studies*, *11*(2), 153–171.

Gray, H. M., LaPlante, D. A., & Shaffer, H. J. (2012). Behavioral characteristics of Internet gamblers who trigger corporate responsible gambling interventions. *Psychology of Addictive Behaviors*, *26*(3), 527–535.

Griffiths, M., & Wood, R. (2008). Responsible gaming and best practice: How can academics help? *Casino & Gaming International*, *4*(1), 107–112.

Häfeli, J., & Lischer, S. (2010). Die Früherkennung von Problemspielern in Schweizer Kasinos. Eine repräsentative, quantitative Datenanalyse der ReGaTo-Daten 2006 [Early detection of problem gamblers in Swiss casinos: A representative quantitative analysis of the 2006 ReGaTo data]. *Prävention und Gesundheitsförderung*, *5*, 145–150.

Häfeli, J., Lischer, S., & Häusler, J. (2015). Communications-based early detection of gambling-related problems in online gambling. *International Gambling Studies*, *15*(1), 23–38.

Häfeli, J., Lischer, S., & Schwarz, J. (2011). Early detection items and responsible gambling features for online gambling. *International Gambling Studies*, *11*(3), 273–288.

Häfeli, J., & Schneider, C. (2005). *Identifikation von Problemspielern im Kasino – Ein Screeninginstrument (ID-PS)*. Luzern: Hochschule für Soziale Arbeit.

Hancock, L., Schellinck, T., & Schrans, T. (2008). Gambling and corporate social responsibility (CSR): Re-defining industry and state roles on duty of care, host responsibility and risk management. *Policy and Society*, *27*(1), 55–68.

Häusler, J. (2016). Follow the money: Using payment behaviour as predictor for future self-exclusion. *International Gambling Studies*, *16*(2), 246–262.

Hing, N., & Nuske, E. (2011). Assisting problem gamblers in the gaming venue: An assessment of practices and procedures followed by frontline hospitality staff. *International Journal of Hospitality Management*, *30*(2), 459–467.

Early detection of at-risk gambling **127**

Ladouceur, R., Shaffer, P., Blaszczynski, A., & Shaffer, H. J. (2017). Responsible gambling: A synthesis of the empirical evidence. *Addiction Research & Theory, 25*(3), 225–235.

Philander, K. S. (2014). Identifying high-risk online gamblers: A comparison of data mining procedures. *International Gambling Studies, 14*(1), 53–63.

Quilty, L. C., Avila Murati, D., & Bagby, R. M. (2014). Identifying indicators of harmful and problem gambling in a Canadian sample through receiver operating characteristic analysis. *Psychology of Addictive Behaviors, 28*(1), 229.

Schellinck, T., & Schrans, T. (2004). Identifying problem gamblers at the gambling venue: Finding combinations of high confidence indicators. *Gambling Research: Journal of the National Association for Gambling Studies (Australia), 16*(1), 8.

Smith, G. J., Volberg, R. A., & Wynne, H. J. (1994). Leisure behavior on the edge: Differences between controlled and uncontrolled gambling practices. *Loisir et Société/Society and Leisure, 17*(1), 233–248.

Swiss Federal Assembly. (2017). *The Casino Act of the 29th of September 2017.* Swiss Federal Council. Bern, Switzerland: Swiss Federal Assembly.

Swiss Federal Council. (2018). *Ordinance of the Casino Act of 7th November 2018.* Bern, Switzerland: Swiss Federal Council.

TÜV Rheinland Secure iT GmbH. (2009). *What the Internet Can Do.* Report Nr. 63002072-01-06. Köln: TÜV.

Wardle, H., Seabury, C., Ahmed, H., and Coshall, C. (2013). *Machines 3: Scoping the use of industry data on Category B gaming machines.* Responsible Gambling Trust. Available at: https://www.rgsb.org.uk/publications.html

13

BEHAVIOURAL TRACKING IN GAMBLING

The use and efficacy of online responsible gambling tools

Mark D. Griffiths

Introduction

Online gambling is a psychological and sociological phenomenon that is becoming a focus of interest for an increasing number of researchers in the social sciences. As the Internet offers a new venue for gambling, the risks for engaging in pathological behaviours are potentially increased (Griffiths, 2003). This has resulted in a large increase of empirical research into online gambling (Gainsbury, 2015; Kuss & Griffiths, 2012). At present, there are numerous different methodologies in which data about online gambling can be collected (e.g., online surveys, online experiments, online interviews and focus groups, online ethnographic methods, etc.; Griffiths, 2010). However, this chapter briefly examines one of the newer methodologies that have been utilised in the last few years by those in the gambling studies field (i.e., behavioural tracking) and briefly reviews the advantages, disadvantages and uses, as well as examining how the use of such data has been utilised to evaluate the effectiveness of various online gambling tools such as limit setting, pop-up messaging and personalised feedback.

The use of online methodologies to study gambling

Over the past decade, researchers in the gambling studies field have started to use online methods to gather their data rather than traditional offline research approaches (Griffiths, 2010; Wood & Griffiths, 2007). Psychological research that can be done online includes correlational, cross-sectional, experimental, self-report and/or observational research. A methodological review paper by Griffiths (2010) examined seven different online data collection methods used for collecting gambling and gaming data including 1) online questionnaires, 2) online forums, 3) online participant observation, 4) online secondary data, 5) online interviews, 6) online exemplar websites and 7) online evaluations (including online "mystery shopping"). He also argued in the same paper that the Internet can be a very useful medium for eliciting rich and detailed data in sensitive areas such as problem gambling.

There are a number of reasons why the online medium is a good place to conduct research with online gamblers. This is because the Internet: 1) is usually accessible to these gamblers, and they are usually proficient in using it (Wood & Griffiths, 2007); 2) allows for studies to be administered to potentially large scale samples quickly and efficiently (Buchanan, 2000, 2007; Wood, Griffiths, & Eatough, 2004); 3) can facilitate automated data inputting allowing large scale samples to be administered at a fraction of the cost and time of 'pen and paper' equivalents (Buchanan, 2007); 4) has a disinhibiting effect on users and reduces social desirability, leading to increased levels of honesty (and therefore higher validity in the case of self-report; Joinson, Paine, Buchanan, & Reips, 2008); 5) has a potentially global pool of participants, therefore researchers are able to study extreme and uncommon behaviours as well as make cross-cultural comparisons (Buchanan, 2000); 6) provides access to "socially unskilled" individuals who may not have taken part in the research if it was offline (Wood et al., 2004; Wood & Griffiths, 2007); 7) can aid participant recruitment through advertising on various bulletin boards and websites (Wysocki, 1998); and 8) can aid researchers because they do not have to be in the same geographical location as either the participants or fellow research colleagues (e.g., Whitty, 2004a, 2004b; Wood et al., 2004).

Online behavioural tracking in gambling

Over 15 years ago, Griffiths and Parke (2002) noted that one of the most potentially worrying concerns about online gambling was the way online gambling website operators could collect data about their players (i.e., those who gamble on their websites). Customer data is the lifeblood of any company and online gamblers provide tracking data that can be used to compile customer profiles. Such data can tell commercial enterprises (such as those in the gambling industry) exactly how customers are spending their time in any given financial transaction (i.e., in the case of online gambling, which games their customers are gambling on, for how long, how much money they are spending, what games are the profitable, etc.). This information can help in the retention of customers and can also link up with existing customer databases and operating loyalty schemes. Companies who have one central repository for all their customer data have an advantage. It can also be accessed by different parts of the business. Many consumers are unknowingly passing on information about themselves and are being profiled according to how they transact with service providers. Linked loyalty schemes can then track the account from the established opening date.

The technology to sift and assess vast amounts of customer information has developed substantially over the last decade. Using the latest sophisticated software, gaming companies can tailor its service to the customer's known interests. When it comes to gambling, there is a very fine line between providing what the customer

130 Mark D. Griffiths

wants and exploitation. The gaming industry sell products in much the same way that any other business sells things. They are now in the business of brand marketing, direct marketing (via mail with personalised and customised offers) and loyalty schemes (that create the illusion of awareness, recognition and loyalty).

On joining loyalty schemes, players supply lots of information including name, address, telephone number, date of birth and gender. Those who operate online gambling sites are no different. They know the gambler's favourite game and the amounts they have wagered. Basically, gambling operators can track the playing patterns of any gambler. They arguably know more about the gambler's playing behaviour than the gamblers themselves. They are able to send the gambler offers and redemption vouchers, complimentary accounts, etc. These are done to enhance customer experience (Griffiths & Wood, 2008a). Benefits and rewards to the customer can include cash, food and beverages, entertainment and general retail. However, more unscrupulous operators have the means to entice known problem gamblers back onto their premises with tailored freebies (such as the inducement of "free" bets in the case of Internet gambling). However, later papers by Griffiths and colleagues began to argue that behavioural tracking data could potentially be used to help identify problem gamblers rather than exploit them and to use behavioural tracking data for research purposes (Griffiths & Wood, 2008b; Griffiths, Wood, Parke, & Parke, 2007).

The advantages and disadvantages of behavioural tracking methods in gambling research

There have been a number of different approaches to collecting data from and about gamblers. This has traditionally included self-report methods (surveys, focus groups, interviews, etc.), experiments (in the laboratory or in gambling venues) and participant and/or nonparticipant observation. More recently (i.e., since around 2005), a number of researchers in the gambling studies field have been given direct access to gambling data collected by gaming companies from their commercial online gambling sites. These types of data (i.e., behavioural tracking data) are providing insights into gamblers' behaviour that is helping to better understand how such people act and behave online and over long periods of time.

There has been a much recent debate in the gambling studies field as to whether online gambling is more dangerous and harmful than offline gambling. Much of the debate has relied on the data collected by either behavioural tracking or survey methodologies. Griffiths and colleagues (Auer & Griffiths, 2013; 2014a; Delfabbro, King, & Griffiths, 2012; Griffiths, 2009; Griffiths & Auer, 2011; Griffiths & Whitty, 2010) have written a number of papers outlining the key differences between these two methods. These can be summarised as follows:

- Behavioural tracking data provide a totally objective record of an individual's gambling behaviour on a particular online gambling website (whereas gamblers in self-report studies may be prone to social desirability factors, unreliable memory, etc.).

Behavioural tracking in gambling **131**

- Behavioural tracking data overcome the problem of finding suitable online gambling participants as they provide an immediate data set (if access is granted by the gaming company). Participants do not even have to travel to participate in the study.
- Behavioural tracking data provide a record of events and can be revisited after the event itself has finished (whereas in general self-report studies cannot).
- Behavioural tracking data usually comprise very large sample sizes (e.g., studies by Auer & Griffiths [2013, 2014b, 2014c, 2015a, 2015b, 2016, 2017a, 2017b]; Auer, Malischnig, & Griffiths, 2014) have used databases with access to over 50,000–100,000 online gamblers) whereas self-report studies are based on much smaller sample sizes (e.g., the national *British Gambling Prevalence Surveys* typically comprise samples of around 8,000–9,000 people; e.g., Wardle et al., 2007, 2011).
- Behavioural tracking data collect data from only one gambling site and tells us nothing about the person's Internet gambling in general as Internet gamblers typically gamble on more than one site (Wardle et al., 2011).
- Behavioural tracking data always come from unrepresentative samples (i.e., the players that use one particular Internet gambling site), whereas the very best self-report studies (e.g., the *British Gambling Prevalence Surveys* in Great Britain) use random and nationally representative samples (e.g., Wardle et al., 2011).
- Behavioural tracking data do not account for the fact that more than one person can use a particular account.
- Behavioural tracking data tell us nothing about *why* people gamble (whereas self-report data can provide greater insight into motivation to gamble).
- Behavioural tracking data cannot be used for comparing online and offline gambling or for making comparisons about whether online gambling is safer or more dangerous than offline gambling as data are only collected on one group of people (i.e., online gamblers).
- Self-report methods can be used to compare two (or more) groups of gamblers and is the only method we currently have to infer to what extent one medium of gambling may or may not be more or less safe.
- Some self-report studies have the potential to use nationally representative samples of gamblers whereas behavioural tracking studies rely on self-selected samples of gamblers who use one specific online gambling website.
- Behavioural tracking data tells us nothing about the relationships between gambling and other behaviours (e.g., the relationship between gambling and alcohol or the relationship between gambling and tobacco use).
- Behavioural tracking data cannot examine problem gambling using current diagnostic criteria (whereas self-report studies can). In fact, behavioural tracking data studies cannot tell us anything about problem gambling as this is not a variable that has been examined in any of the published studies to date (except by using proxy measures of problem gamblers, such as those people who exclude themselves from the site to prevent further gambling on it).

132 Mark D. Griffiths

Research using actual gambling data began when one team of researchers affiliated to Harvard University were given access to a large behavioural tracking data set of over 47,000 online gamblers by the Austrian gaming company *bwin*. This has led to many papers examining the actual behaviour of online gamblers based on behavioural tracking data (e.g., Broda et al., 2008; LaBrie, Kaplan, LaPlante, Nelson, & Shaffer, 2008; LaPlante, Kleschinsky, LaBrie, Nelson, & Shaffer, 2009; LaBrie, LaPlante, Nelson, Schumann, & Shaffer, 2007; LaPlante, Schumann, LaBrie, & Shaffer, 2008; Xuan & Shaffer, 2009). These data have been used to make claims along the lines that online gambling is no more problematic than offline gambling.

However, comparative statements relating to whether one medium of gambling is more problematic than another can only be made if actual gambling behaviour is studied across different forms of gambling (e.g., direct comparison of Internet gambling with [say] land-based casino gambling). None of the various publications by the Harvard-affiliated research team have empirically compared different forms of gambling (e.g., Broda et al., 2008; LaBrie et al., 2008; LaPlante et al., 2009; LaBrie et al., 2007; LaPlante et al., 2008). Nor have they examined "problem gambling" as no problem gambling screens were given to any online gambler included in their studies. Therefore, conclusions about the harmfulness of online gambling in comparison to other forms of gambling cannot be drawn from these particular studies using these types of behavioural tracking data. Furthermore, none of the publications focusing on online gambling examine overall gambling behaviour. All the publications have tended to examine a single type of game (e.g., sports betting, casino games, poker).

Behavioural tracking has also been used in other innovative ways including the use of tracking data to examine the influence of structural characteristics in slot machine gambling (Leino et al., 2015), the amount of gambling behaviour engaged in when comparing gambling behaviour in alcohol and non-alcohol serving venues (Leino et al., 2017), to develop and evaluate new measures of gambling intensity (i.e., theoretical loss which is the amount of money staked by gamblers multiplied by the probability of winning on a specific gambling activity; Auer & Griffiths, 2014b, 2015c), to identify behavioural markers of high-risk online gambling (Braverman & Shaffer, 2012; Braverman et al., 2013; Gray et al., 2012), to compare online gamblers who self-exclude with those that do not (Dragicevic et al., 2015) and to test classic psychological theories such as cognitive dissonance (Auer & Griffiths, 2017b). Other studies have used tracking data to demonstrate that what money individuals say they have spent gambling is different from their actual gambling behaviour with all studies showing that the more someone gambles, the less reliable they are about estimating what they have financially spent gambling (Auer & Griffiths, 2017a; Braverman et al., 2014; Wohl, Davis, & Hollingshead, 2017).

Behavioural tracking tools

Over the past few decades, innovative social responsibility tools that track player behaviour with the aim of preventing problem gambling have been developed including *PlayScan* (developed by the Swedish gaming company *Svenska Spel*),

Observer (developed by Israeli gaming company *888.com*) and *mentor* (developed by *neccton Ltd*) (Griffiths, Wood, & Parke, 2009; Griffiths et al., 2007). These tracking tools are providing insights about problematic gambling behaviour that in turn may lead to new avenues for future research in the area. The companies who have developed these tools claim that they can detect problematic gambling behaviour through analysis of behavioural tracking data (Delfabbro et al., 2012; Griffiths et al., 2009). If problem gambling can be detected online via observational tracking data, it suggests that there are identifiable behaviours associated with online problem gambling. Given that almost all of the current validated problem gambling screens diagnose problem gambling based on many of the consequences of problem gambling (e.g., compromising job, education, hobbies and/or relationships because of gambling; committing criminal acts to fund gambling behaviour; lying to family and friends about the extent of gambling, etc.), behavioural tracking data appear to suggest that problem gambling can be identified without the need to assess the negative psychosocial consequences of problem gambling.

Behavioural tracking tools generally use a combination of behavioural science, psychology, mathematics and artificial intelligence. Some tools (such as *PlayScan*) claim to detect players at risk of developing gambling problems and offer the gamblers ways to help change their behaviour (e.g., tools that help gamblers set time and money limits on what they are prepared to lose over predetermined time periods). Unlike the conventional purpose of customer databases (i.e., to increase sales), the objective of these new tools is the opposite. They are designed to detect and help those who would benefit from playing less. Such tools have been compared to a safety belt (i.e., something you use without intending to actually make use of). The use of these systems is voluntary, but the gaming operator strongly recommends its customers to use it (Griffiths et al., 2009). These tools use many parameters from the players' behaviour from the preceding year that is then matched against a model based on behavioural characteristics for problem players. If it predicts players' behaviour as risky they get an advance warning together with advice on how they can change their patterns in order to avoid future unhealthy and/or risky gambling. Behavioural tracking data can also be used to evaluate whether the tools and advice given to gamblers can actually change (i.e., reduce) potentially problematic behaviour. These studies are briefly reviewed in the next section.

Evaluation of responsible gambling tools using tracking data

Responsible gambling tools (e.g., limit-setting tools, pop-up messages, personalised feedback, temporary self-exclusions) are a way of facilitating players to gamble in a more responsible manner (Harris & Griffiths, 2017). However, very few of these tools have been evaluated empirically in real gambling environments. Broda et al. (2008) examined the effects of player deposit limits on Internet sports betting by customers of *bwin Interactive Entertainment*. Their study examined 47,000 subscribers to *bwin* over a period of two years and compared the behaviour of players who tried to exceed their deposit limit with all other players. Deposit limit referred to the amount of money deposited into a player's spend account excluding any accumulated winnings. At the time of initial data collection in 2005, *bwin* set a mandatory deposit limit of no more than €1000 per day or €5000 per 30 days. Players could also set their own deposit limits (per 30 days) below the mandatory limits. Overall, the study found that less than 1% of the players (0.3%) attempted to exceed their deposit limit. However, Wood and Griffiths (2010) argued that the large mandatory limit may be the main reason for this finding, as LaPlante et al. (2008) noted that the majority of online gamblers never reached the maximum deposit limit. In fact, 95% of the players never deposited more than €1050 per 30 days (i.e., one-fifth of the €5000 maximum). Furthermore, LaPlante and colleagues did not distinguish between those who attempted to exceed either their own personally set deposit limits or mandatory limits. Using the same dataset, Nelson et al. (2008) examined online gamblers that voluntarily set limits on the *bwin* gambling website over an 18-month period. A total of 567 online gamblers (out of more than 47,000) used the voluntary limit-setting feature, and the findings demonstrated that limit-setting gamblers bet more heavily and played a wider variety of games prior to setting limits. After setting voluntary limits, these online gamblers reduced their gambling activity but not the amount wagered per bet.

A study by Auer and Griffiths (2013) used behavioural tracking data to evaluate whether the setting of voluntary time and money limits helped players who gambled the most (i.e., the most gambling intense individuals using "theoretical loss" [Auer et al., 2012; Auer & Griffiths, 2014b]). Data were collected from a representative random sample of 100,000 online players who gambled on the *win2day* gambling website during a three-month test period. This sample comprised 5,000 registered gamblers who chose to set themselves limits whilst playing on *win2day*. During the registration process, there was a mandatory requirement for all players to set time and cash-in limits. For instance, the player could limit the daily, weekly and/or monthly cash-in amount and the playing duration. The latter could be limited per playing session and/or per day. In the three-month test period, all voluntary limit setting behaviour by online gamblers was tracked and recorded for subsequent data analysis. Changes in gambling behaviour were analysed overall and separately for casino, lottery and poker gambling.

The results of this study clearly showed that voluntary limit setting had a specific and statistically significant effect on high intensity gamblers (i.e., voluntary limit setting had the largest effect on the most gaming intense players). More specifically, the analysis showed that (in general) gaming intense players specifically changed their behaviour in a positive way after they limited themselves with respect to both time and money spent. Voluntary spending limits had the highest significant effect on subsequent monetary spending amongst casino and lottery gamblers. Monetary spending amongst poker players significantly decreased after setting a voluntary time limit. Studies such as this highlight the advantageous way in which behavioural tracking methodologies can be used to provide results and insights that would be highly difficult to show using other more traditional methodologies.

Auer et al. (2014) investigated the effect of a pop-up message that appeared after 1,000 consecutive online slot machine games had been played by individuals during a single gambling session. The study analysed 800,000 gambling sessions (400,000 sessions before the pop-up had been introduced and 400,000 after the pop-up had been introduced comprising around 50,000 online gamblers). The study found that the pop-up message had a limited effect on a small percentage of players. More specifically, prior to the pop-up message being introduced, five gamblers ceased playing after 1,000 consecutive spins of the online slot machine within a single playing session (out of approximately 10,000 playing sessions). Following the introduction of the pop-up message, 45 gamblers ceased playing after 1,000 consecutive spins (i.e., a nine-fold increase in session cessations). In the latter case, the number of gamblers ceasing play was less than 1% of the gamblers who played 1,000 games consecutively.

In a follow-up study, Auer and Griffiths (2015a) argued that the original pop-up message was very basic and that redesigning the message using normative feedback and self-appraisal feedback may increase the efficacy of gamblers ceasing play. As in the previous study, the new enhanced pop-up message that appeared within a single session after a gambler had played 1,000 consecutive slot games. Consequently, Auer and Griffiths (2015a) examined 1.6 million playing sessions comprising two conditions (i.e., simple pop-up message [800,000 slot machine sessions] versus an enhanced pop-up message [800,000 slot machine sessions]) with approximately 70,000 online gamblers. The study found that the message with enhanced content more than doubled the number of players who ceased playing (1.39% who received the enhanced pop-up compared to 0.67% who received the simple pop-up). However, as in Auer et al.'s (2014) previous study, the enhanced pop-up only influenced a small number of gamblers to cease playing after a long continuous playing session.

Auer and Griffiths (2016) in a study of the efficacy of personalised feedback, examined whether the use of three types of information (i.e., personalised feedback, normative feedback and/or a recommendation) could enable players to gamble more responsibly as assessed using three measures of gambling behaviour, i.e., theoretical loss, amount of money wagered and gross gaming revenue (i.e., net win/loss). By manipulating the three forms of information, data from six different groups of players were analysed. The participant sample drawn from the population were those that had played at least one game for money on the *Norsk Tipping* online platform (*Instaspill*) during April 2015. A total of 17,452 players were randomly selected from 69,631 players that fulfilled the selection criteria. Gambling activity amongst the control group (who received no personalised feedback, normative feedback or no recommendation) was also compared with the other five groups that received information of some kind (personalised feedback, normative feedback and/or a recommendation). Compared to the control group, all groups that received some kind of messaging significantly reduced their gambling behaviour as assessed by theoretical loss, amount of money wagered and gross gaming revenue. The results supported the hypothesis that personalised

136 Mark D. Griffiths

behavioural feedback can enable behavioural change in gambling. However, normative feedback did not appear to change behaviour significantly more than personalised feedback.

Forsström, Hesser, and Carlbring (2016) carried out a study on the use of the behavioural tracking tool *PlayScan*. The data from a total of 9,528 players who voluntarily used the system were analysed. They found that the initial usage of the tool was high, but that repeated usage was low. Two groups of users (i.e., "self-testers" and "multi-function users") utilised the tool to a much greater extent than other groups. However, the study did not analyse changes in behaviour as a consequence of using the tool.

Wood and Wohl (2015) obtained data from 779 *Svenska Spel* online players who received behavioural feedback using *PlayScan*. Feedback to players took the form of a "traffic-light" risk rating that was created via a proprietary algorithm (red = problematic gambling, yellow = at-risk gambling and green = no gambling issues). In addition, expenditure data (i.e., amounts deposited and gambled) were collected at three time points 1) the week of *PlayScan* enrolment, 2) the week following *PlayScan* enrolment and 3) 24 weeks after *PlayScan* enrolment. The findings indicated that those players at risk (yellow gamblers) who used *PlayScan* significantly reduced the amounts of money both deposited and gambled compared to those who did not use *PlayScan*. This effect was also found the week following *PlayScan* enrolment as well as the 24-week mark. Overall, the authors concluded that informing at-risk gamblers about their gambling behaviour appeared to have a desired impact on their subsequent monetary spending.

Conclusions

This chapter has highlighted that when it comes to studying online gambling behaviour, behavioural tracking methodologies offer a number of advantages for researchers. However, it should also be noted that there are a number of disadvantages of using tracking data only when compared to other more traditional research methods (i.e., surveys), and that no single methodology is better than another in the collection of data concerning online gamblers. However, when evaluating the results of studies that make statements about whether one medium of gambling is more problematic to gamblers than another, the inherent strengths and weaknesses of the methodology used must be taken into consideration. In relation to the efficacy of online responsible gambling tools, there are some types of study (e.g., the evaluation of whether social responsibility tools actually have an effect on subsequent player behaviour) where behavioural tracking methodologies appear to be the only reliable way of collecting data to show that specific interventions have a direct effect on player behaviour. Findings to date suggest that limit setting and personalised feedback appear to be responsible gambling tools with high efficacy, but further replication studies are needed. The studies evaluating pop-up messaging are far from conclusive and suggest that on their own, pop-up messages only help a very small percentage of within-session intense gamblers.

References

Auer, M., & Griffiths, M. D. (2013). Voluntary limit setting and player choice in most intense online gamblers: An empirical study of gambling behaviour. *Journal of Gambling Studies, 29,* 647–660.

Auer, M., & Griffiths, M. D. (2014a). Personalised feedback in the promotion of responsible gambling: A brief overview. *Responsible Gambling Review, 1,* 27–36.

Auer, M., & Griffiths, M. D. (2014b). An empirical investigation of theoretical loss and gambling intensity. *Journal of Gambling Studies, 30,* 879–887.

Auer, M., & Griffiths, M. D. (2015a). Testing normative and self-appraisal feedback in an online slot-machine pop-up message in a real-world setting. *Frontiers in Psychology, 6,* 339. doi:10.3389/fpsyg.2015.00339

Auer, M., & Griffiths, M. D. (2015b). The use of personalized behavioral feedback for problematic online gamblers: An empirical study. *Frontiers in Psychology, 6,* 1406. doi:10.3389/fpsyg.2015.01406

Auer, M., & Griffiths, M. D. (2015c). Theoretical loss and gambling intensity (revisited): A response to Braverman et al (2013). *Journal of Gambling Studies, 31,* 921–931.

Auer, M., & Griffiths, M. D. (2016). Personalized behavioral feedback for online gamblers: A real world empirical study. *Frontiers in Psychology, 7,* 1875. doi:10.3389/fpsyg.2016.01875

Auer, M., & Griffiths, M. D. (2017a). Self-reported losses versus actual losses in online gambling: An empirical study. *Journal of Gambling Studies, 33,* 795–806.

Auer, M., & Griffiths, M. D. (2017b). Cognitive dissonance, personalized feedback, and online gambling behavior: An exploratory study using objective tracking data and subjective self-report. *International Journal of Mental Health and Addiction.* Epub ahead of print. doi:10.1007/s11469-017-9808-1

Auer, M., Malischnig, D., & Griffiths, M. D. (2014). Is "pop-up" messaging in online slot machine gambling effective? An empirical research note. *Journal of Gambling Issues, 29,* 1–10.

Auer, M., Schneeberger, A., & Griffiths, M. D. (2012). Theoretical loss and gambling intensity: A simulation study. *Gaming Law Review and Economics, 16,* 269–273.

Braverman, J., LaPlante, D. A., Nelson, S. E., & Shaffer, H. J. (2013). Using crossgame behavioral markers for early identification of high-risk Internet gamblers. *Psychology of Addictive Behaviors, 27,* 868–877.

Braverman, J., & Shaffer, H. J. (2012). How do gamblers start gambling: Identifying behavioral markers for high-risk Internet gambling. *European Journal of Public Health, 22,* 273–278.

Braverman, J., Tom, M. A., & Shaffer, H. J. (2014). Accuracy of self-reported versus actual online-gambling wins and losses. *Psychological Assessment, 26,* 865–877.

Broda, A., LaPlante, D. A., Nelson, S. E., LaBrie, R. A., Bosworth, L. B., & Shaffer, H. J. (2008). Virtual harm reduction efforts for Internet gambling: Effects of deposit limits on actual Internet sports gambling behaviour. *Harm Reduction Journal, 5,* 27.

Buchanan, T. (2000). Potential of the Internet for personality research. In M. H. Birnbaum (Ed.), *Psychological Experiments on the Internet* (pp. 121–140). San Diego: Academic Press.

Buchanan, T. (2007). Personality testing on the Internet: What we know, and what we do not. In A. N. Joinson, K. Y. A. McKenna, T. Postmes, & U. R. Reips (Eds.), *Oxford Handbook of Internet Psychology* (pp. 447–459). Oxford: Oxford University Press.

Delfabbro, P. H., King, D. L., & Griffiths, M. D. (2012). Behavioural profiling of problem gamblers: A critical review. *International Gambling Studies, 12,* 349–366.

Dragicevic, S., Percy, C., Kudic, A., & Parke, J. (2015). A descriptive analysis of demographic and behavioral data from internet gamblers and those who self-exclude from online gambling platforms. *Journal of Gambling Studies, 31,* 105–132.

138 Mark D. Griffiths

Forsström, D., Hesser, H., & Carlbring, P. (2016). Usage of a responsible gambling tool: A descriptive analysis of latent class analysis of user behavior. *Journal of Gambling Studies, 32,* 889–904.

Gainsbury, S. M. (2015). Online gambling addiction: The relationship between internet gambling and disordered gambling. *Current Addiction Reports, 2*(2), 185–193.

Gray, H. M., LaPlante, D. A., & Shaffer, H. J. (2012). Behavioral characteristics of Internet gamblers who trigger corporate responsible gambling interventions. *Psychology of Addictive Behaviors, 26,* 527–535.

Griffiths, M. D. (2003). Internet gambling: Issues, concerns and recommendations. *CyberPsychology and Behavior, 6,* 557–568.

Griffiths, M. D. (2009). Social responsibility in gambling: The implications of real-time behavioural tracking. *Casino and Gaming International, 5*(3), 99–104.

Griffiths, M. D. (2010). The use of online methodologies in data collection for gambling and gaming addictions. *International Journal of Mental Health and Addiction, 8,* 8–20.

Griffiths, M. D., & Auer, M. (2011). Approaches to understanding online versus offline gaming impacts. *Casino and Gaming International, 7*(3), 45–48.

Griffiths, M. D., & Parke, J. (2002). The social impact of internet gambling. *Social Science Computer Review, 20,* 312–320.

Griffiths, M. D., & Whitty, M. W. (2010). Online behavioural tracking in Internet gambling research: Ethical and methodological issues. *International Journal of Internet Research Ethics, 3,* 104–117.

Griffiths, M. D., & Wood, R. T. A. (2008a). Gambling loyalty schemes: Treading a fine line? *Casino and Gaming International, 4*(2), 105–108.

Griffiths, M. D., & Wood, R. T. A. (2008b). Responsible gaming and best practice: How can academics help? *Casino and Gaming International, 4*(1), 107–112.

Griffiths, M. D., Wood, R. T. A., & Parke, J. (2009). Social responsibility tools in online gambling: A survey of attitudes and behaviour among Internet gamblers. *CyberPsychology and Behavior, 12,* 413–421.

Griffiths, M. D., Wood, R. T. A., Parke, J., & Parke, A. (2007). Gaming research and best practice: Gaming industry, social responsibility and academia. *Casino and Gaming International, 3,* 97–103.

Harris, A., & Griffiths, M. D. (2017). A critical review of the harm-minimisation tools available for electronic gambling. *Journal of Gambling Studies, 33,* 187–221.

Joinson, A. N., Paine, C., Buchanan, T., & Reips, U.-D. (2008). Measuring self-disclosure online: Blurring and non-response to sensitive items in web-based surveys. *Computers in Human Behavior, 24,* 2158–2171.

Kuss, D. J., & Griffiths, M. D. (2012). Internet gambling behavior. In Z. Yan (Ed.), *Encyclopedia of Cyber Behavior* (pp. 735–753). Pennsylvania: IGI Global.

LaBrie, R. A., Kaplan, S., LaPlante, D. A., Nelson, S. E., & Shaffer, H. J. (2008). Inside the virtual casino: A prospective longitudinal study of Internet casino gambling. *European Journal of Public Health, 18*(4), 410–416.

LaBrie, R. A., LaPlante, D. A., Nelson, S. E., Schumann, A., & Shaffer, H. J. (2007). Assessing the playing field: A prospective longitudinal study of internet sports gambling behavior. *Journal of Gambling Studies, 23,* 347–363.

LaPlante, D. A., Kleschinsky, J. H., LaBrie, R. A., Nelson, S. E., & Shaffer, H. J. (2009). Sitting at the virtual poker table: A prospective epidemiological study of actual Internet poker gambling behavior. *Computers in Human Behavior, 25,* 711–717.

LaPlante, D. A., Schumann, A., LaBrie, R. A., & Shaffer, H. J. (2008). Population trends in Internet sports gambling. *Computers in Human Behavior, 24*(5), 2399–2414.

Leino, T., Sagoe, D., Griffiths, M. D., Mentzoni, R. A., Pallesen, S., & Molde, H. (2017). Gambling behavior in alcohol-serving and non-alcohol-serving venues: A study of electronic gaming machine players using account records. *Addiction Research and Theory, 25*, 201–207.

Leino, T., Torsheim, T., Blaszczynski, A., Griffiths, M. D., Mentzoni, R., Pallesen, S., & Molde, H. (2015). The relationship between structural characteristics and gambling behavior: A population based study. *Journal of Gambling Studies, 31*, 1297–1315.

Nelson, S. E., LaPlante, D. A., Peller, A. J., Schumann, A., LaBrie, R. A., & Shaffer, H. J. (2008). Real limits in the virtual world: Self-limiting behavior of Internet gamblers. *Journal of Gambling Studies, 24*(4), 463–477.

Wardle, H., Moody, A., Griffiths, M. D., Orford, J., & Volberg, R. (2011). Defining the online gambler and patterns of behaviour integration: Evidence from the British Gambling Prevalence Survey 2010. *International Gambling Studies, 11*, 339–356.

Wardle, H., Sproston, K., Orford, J., Erens, B., Griffiths, M. D., Constantine, R., & Pigott, S. (2007). *The British Gambling Prevalence Survey 2007.* London: The Stationery Office.

Whitty, M. T. (2004a). Cyber-flirting: An examination of men's and women's flirting behaviour both offline and on the Internet. *Behaviour Change, 21*, 115–126.

Whitty, M. T. (2004b). Peering into online bedroom windows: Considering the ethical implications of investigating Internet relationships and sexuality. In E. Buchanan (Ed.), *Readings in Virtual Research Ethics: Issues and Controversies* (pp. 203–218). Hershey, USA: Idea Group Inc.

Wohl, M. J. A., Davis, C. G., & Hollingshead, S. J. (2017). How much have you won or lost? Personalized behavioral feedback about gambling expenditures regulates play. *Computers in Human Behavior, 70*, 437–455.

Wood, R. T. A., & Griffiths, M. D. (2007). Online data collection from gamblers: Methodological issues. *International Journal of Mental Health and Addiction, 5*, 151–163.

Wood, R. T. A., & Griffiths, M. D. (2010). Social responsibility in online gambling: Voluntary limit setting. *World Online Gambling Law Report, 9*(11), 10–11.

Wood, R. T. A., Griffiths, M. D., & Eatough, V. (2004). Online data collection from videogame players: Methodological issues. *Cyberpsychology and Behavior, 7*, 511–518.

Wood, R. T. A., & Wohl, M. J. (2015). Assessing the effectiveness of a responsible gambling behavioural feedback tool for reducing the gambling expenditure of at-risk players. *International Gambling Studies, 15*(2), 1–16.

Wysocki, D. K. (1998). Let your fingers to do the talking: Sex on an adult chat-line. *Sexualities, 1*, 425–452.

Xuan, Z. M., & Shaffer, H. J. (2009). How do gamblers end gambling: Longitudinal analysis of internet gambling behaviors prior to account closure due to gambling related problems. *Journal of Gambling Studies, 25*, 239–252.

SECTION III

Challenges to evaluation and monitoring

14

A LOGICAL FRAMEWORK FOR THE EVALUATION OF A HARM REDUCTION POLICY FOR GAMBLING

Jean-Michel Costes

Introduction

Historically, since the end of the Middle Ages, gambling in France has taken place within a prohibitionist framework. This was based on the moral condemnation of the Church and of the monarchical State. It has been alternated with periods of strict prohibition and the re-installation of exceptions to this prohibitive system. This includes the implementation of legal forms of gambling such as the Royal Lottery at the end of the eighteenth century, approval of the first casinos in the early nineteenth century in certain resort or spa towns and authorisation of horse racing at the end of the same century (Inserm, 2008; Valleur, 2015). Exceptions to the general prohibitive regime increased until the beginning of the twenty-first century leading to widespread and diverse gambling opportunities. These are organised around State monopolies or quasi-monopolies (lottery games, betting on sports and horse racing) or private operators working under strong public regulation (casinos with monopolised electronic games machines). Only the supply of these games on the Internet remained illegal (except for lottery games managed by the State monopoly). This last barrier was broken in 2010 by a new law that organises the opening of a legal market for Internet-based gambling in France.

The 2010 law: A paradigm shift

Beyond the operational necessity to organise a legal offer for online gambling (which was already widely practiced despite its prohibition) this law addresses online gambling in a comprehensive legal framework, which concerns all forms of gambling. The main principles of the new approach are set out in article one of the Act: "Gambling is neither a regular trade or a regular service; in respect to the principle of subsidiarity, it is strictly supervised in relation to issues of public order,

144 Jean-Michel Costes

public safety, health protection and the protection of minors". The Act sets out four policy objectives to be implemented:

- To prevent excessive or pathological gambling and protect minors.
- To assure the integrity, trustworthiness and transparency of gambling operations.
- To prevent fraudulent or criminal activity as well as money laundering and financing of terrorism.
- To ensure the balanced and fair development of different types of games in order to avoid any economic destabilisation of the concerned sectors.

In France this is a crucial step which commits to passing from a moral approach, based on prohibition/exceptions to a pragmatic approach which organises the market and reduces the risks for a pleasurable activity, which is practiced in other countries (Kingma, 2004). Previously morally and socially devalued, gambling prohibited on principle, could be legalised in certain forms under pressure from development of the black market. The income that the community received could be used for public good and not for private profit. Today, according to a new approach to regulating the gambling market, known as risk and harm reduction, gambling is considered a leisure activity that has risks, alike to any social behaviour. We must limit the scope and thus regulate the market which can, from this perspective, be entrusted to a private initiative, controlled by the State.

Clause for review and evaluation

Since the end of the year 2000, the new French laws have been the obligatory subject of a study which has an evaluative dimension targeting the economic, financial, social and environmental consequences. The costs and expected financial benefits of gambling are also considered. In this context, the 2010 gambling law will receive an evaluation report on the conditions and effects of opening the market for online gambling and sports betting. It also created the "Monitoring Centre for Gambling" (Observatoire des Jeux; ODJ), whose mission, from this evaluative perspective, is to observe the health, social and economic impact of gambling in order to identify necessary State action. The monitoring centre has defined a matrix of indicators for this purpose, which enables a conceptual analysis of the legal framework and public policy related to gambling. It uses a method known as the "logic model", which was developed by certain theories in the programme evaluation field.

The reason for conceptualising and building a logic model

The "logic model" is a technique to "reconstruct the logic of action" of an intervention programme or public policy. It explains the mechanisms of causality supporting the interventions and shows how the programme or the combined components of a public policy meet the planned objectives in the short, medium or long-term. This analysis of the "intervention logic" is conceived as a prerequisite to better organise an approach towards evaluation. It aims to determine the critical or explanatory factors (resources, actions devices) to be taken into account and how the effects can be obtained to achieve the ultimate goals of the programme (Chen & Rossi, 1980).

Describing the logical links between resources, efforts, activities or actions, results and achievements, the logic model structures research and the definition of indicators at each level to describe in some way "the performance history of a programme or policy" (McLaughlin & Jordan, 1999).

Many studies have relied on this technique when developing specific approaches towards evaluating intervention programmes (Renger & Titcomb, 2002; Frechtling, 2007), or more generally towards the assessment of public policy as a whole (Diaz-Gomez, Milhet, & Ben Lakhdar, 2009). One advantage of this theoretical approach is that it allows us to better consider the multiple determinants for social behaviour. More specifically, it facilitates the triangulation of data necessary for documenting the antecedents and consequences of each element of the overall programme (Cooksy, Gill, & Kelly, 2001).

Development

Logic model: Definitions and concepts

The logic model is illustrated by a diagram representing the logical sequence describing the way the intervention (or more generally a public policy) transforms resources or means into activities or actions. From this process, we can measure the results, leading to an impact that is consistent with the objectives. The diagram is an overview of cause and effect links between these different elements, reading from the left to the right (Figure 14.1).

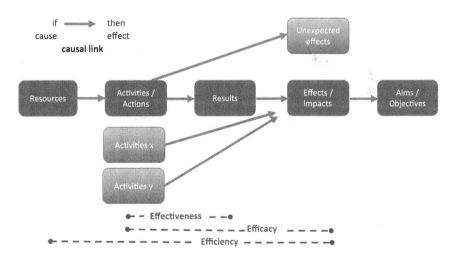

FIGURE 14.1 Logic model – causal links flow diagram

146 Jean-Michel Costes

The logical components of the model are:

- The resources: elements of a legal, human, material budgetary or scientific means.
- The activities: elements constituting an achievement.
- The results: expected following the implementation of activities. These include immediate or direct results.
- The effects: expected changes in behaviour or developments, direct consequences from the results of activities undertaken.
- The objectives: goals that are to be achieved by getting the expected effects of the activities.

Each element can then be assigned one (or more) indicator (s) to quantify it and make a value judgement (evaluation) of its performance. Several levels of performance assessment are therefore possible:

- Effectiveness: examines to what extent the activities were deployed, in comparison with the expectations e.g., have gambling operators put in place moderators for a game, that are in-line with the regulator's standards?
- Efficacy: examines to what extent, with regard to the activities deployed, the achieved effects are in line with the expected effects e.g., how much did "responsible gambling" measures deployed by an operator manage to reduce the proportion of problematic gambling practices?
- Efficiency: a judgement on the performance of achieved effects regarding the overall means that were mobilised, e.g., is the reduction in problematic gambling satisfactory if we take into account the means deployed for this purpose?

Application to the French gambling field

The logic model for French gambling policy (Figure 14.2) was constructed from legislative and parliamentary documents relating to the reform of the legal framework for gambling (Journal Officiel, 2010; Lamour, 2010; Trucy, 2006, 2011). The first task was carried out in association with the Working Group set up to analyse the social impact of online gambling development in Quebec (Nadeau et al., 2014). Several work sessions were held to construct a logic model that was specific to gambling policy for the two geographical areas. The French model then underwent a final work meeting with national policymakers and experts in the domain.

Gambling monitoring from an evaluation perspective

The operational follow-up to this conceptual analysis was to define indicators and a monitoring strategy for each element of the logic model (Figure 14.3). Monitoring can be described as a continuous process of collecting, analysing and systematically

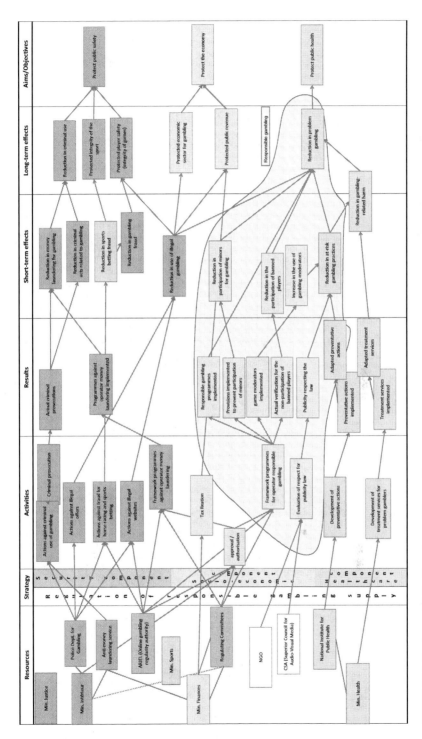

FIGURE 14.2 Logic model for French gambling policy

Results	Indicators	Short-term effects	Indicators		Long-term effects	Indicators	

Socio-Economic component

Reduction in player participation for non-regulated supply

% of players gambling on the regulated supply, by game type

Protected economic component for gambling

Part of "gross gambling product" by gambling component

Number of jobs for the economic sector

Protection of public finances

Amount of taxes received from gambling

Responsible gambling programmes implemented

% of operators having implemented a responsible gambling programme

Provisions preventing gambling by minors implemented

% of points of sale respecting the restrictions on selling to minors

Reduction in the participation of minors for gambling

% of minors practising gambling

Reduction in the participation of players banned from gambling

% of banned players practising gambling

Game moderators implemented

% of games (part of gross gambling product) offering provisions for moderation

Increase in the use of gambling moderators

% of players aware of tools for moderation

% of players using tools for moderation

Healthcare component

Preventative actions implemented

Budgets allocated to media campaigns

Budgets allocated to prevention programmes/actions

Calls treated by "players info services" phone line

People having visited the "players info services" site

Adapted preventative actions

% of budget for prevention evaluated

% of moderately at-risk players having contacted a prevention service

Treatment services implemented

Number of players seen by healthcare centres or specialised counsellors

Adapted treatment services

% of problematic players having contacted a healthcare service or specialised counsellor

% of treatment retention

Reduction in problematic gambling

Prevalence of problematic gambling in the last 12 months:

by game type, setting, age, social category, education

Reduction in at-risk gambling practices

Distribution of gamblers according to their gambling frequency over the last 12 months

Distribution of gamblers according to their spending over the last 12 months

FIGURE 14.3 Extract from the matrix of indicators linked to the logic model for French gambling policy

Evaluation of a harm reduction policy **149**

interpreting information based on the selected indicators. This is carried out in order to track the evolution of gambling and understand the impact of responses for reducing harm. Monitoring is based exclusively on evidence from four main sources:

1 Epidemiological data available from population surveys.
2 Administrative data held by government bodies and gambling operators.
3 Regulatory and legal data relating to the gambling framework.
4 Data from specific research.

This setting forth of all necessary monitoring indicators also allows us to identify (and better plan) surveys or studies necessary to fill the gaps when the desired indicator is not available in the field of existing data.

Practical applications

Such modelling has made an overall assessment of public policy possible in France, following the legal framework reform in 2010. This ambitious perspective, which would require substantial resources to produce all the indicators concerned, is not yet on the agenda of policymakers in the field. However, partial evaluation of certain components of the model are more easily produced.

This is also the case for evaluating one of the foundations for the new French strategy based on responsible gambling. Chapter 15 will consider the emergence of this concept in France by analysing its different meanings and discussing the means to evaluate its impact. Figure 14.2 represents its logic of action. This strategy covers certain measures set out in the new legislative and regulatory framework, including the obligation for operators to implement certain provisions or actions. These include information about the risks of gambling and support services for players, identification procedures for the players (preventing, in particular, gambling by minors) and the implementation of gambling moderators. The indicators which are set out in the indicator matrix, enable a comprehensive assessment, by providing answers to four basic questions, which refer to the four levels of the logic model:

- What means (actions or activities) are deployed?
- For what results? (Are the responsible gambling devices effective?)
- For what effects? (Gambling by minors, use of moderators, reduction in the intensity of factors for games that are predictive of problem gambling?)
- What impact in terms of reducing problem gambling?

Another field of partial evaluation has also been explored. This is to check if the legislator's bet (or in other words, the theory of action) when they decided to

150 Jean-Michel Costes

legalise online gambling, has paid off. In order to simplify, we can state the following reasoning: the legalisation of online gambling will enable a reduction in problem gambling (not to mention another, equally important, expected effect: to ensure more State revenue), by bringing players who practice it illegally back to a legal supply, which better protects them. To judge the success of this bet, we need to verify two things: 1) that the players predominantly use the legal offer, and 2) that practices for the legal offer are actually less problematic than for those being illegally supplied (for an equivalent activity type). These two points have been specifically analysed through questions added to the most recent population surveys. These analyses lead to the conclusion that there is at least partial success for this bet (Costes, Kairouz, Eroukmanoff, & Monson, 2015; Tovar, Costes, & Eroukmanoff, 2013).

Conclusion

The construction of such a model seems, *a priori*, to be very theoretical and far removed from operational purposes. This approach has, on the contrary, proved to be very useful and concrete in leading to the construction of an indicator matrix. The matrix is relevant to both, serving as a basis for targeted evaluation and for structured consideration of priorities for further studies or surveys. However, it is necessary to take into account the inherent subjectivity in this type of exercise. This could have been reduced if the consultation phase was more in-depth when constructing the model.

One of the side effects of this exercise, is to make explicit what is only implicit in the factual documents (laws, decrees, etc.). Thus, for example, the "protection of the public revenue" does not appear as important in these texts whilst it obviously is, in reality (as it also retraces the parliamentary debates in preparation for the Act). It also enables a judgement to be made on the consistency of the logic of action, as well as updating this. For example, the regulation of gambling advertising has an important place in the texts but only two points are regulated, whilst the basic principle remains that authorisation to publicise via popular media can affect the entire population, including minors. Therefore, we should not wait to evaluate, *a priori*, the significant contribution of this intervention axis towards the achievement of the objectives.

Finally, as stated by the European Commission (2012), the majority of European States have adopted a governance model for gambling similar to that described for France, which serves to "regulate a responsible gambling offer". It would be interesting to use the French model in order to derive a generic model applicable to other countries (Figure 14.4) which subscribe to the same logic of action. Since this model, it would be useful to produce a matrix of key indicators. Such a standardisation would also serve to make international comparisons much easier.

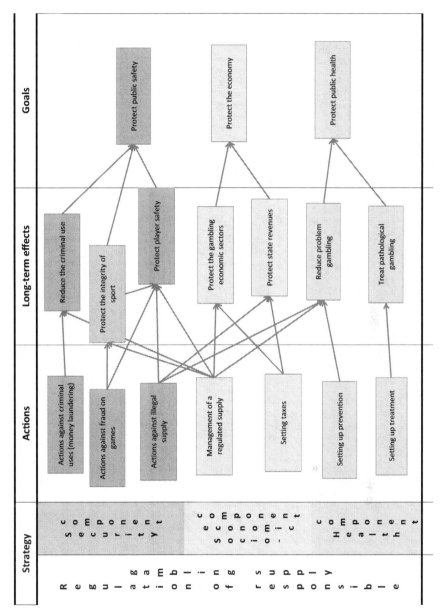

FIGURE 14.4 Logic model of a public policy on gambling which serves to "regulate a responsible gambling offer"

References

Chen, H.-T., & Rossi, P. H. (1980). The multi-goal, theory-driven approach to evaluation: A model linking basic and applied social science. *Social Forces, 59*(1), 106.

Cooksy, L. J., Gill, P., & Kelly, P. A. (2001). The program logic model as an integrative framework for a multimethod evaluation. *Evaluation and Program Planning, 24*(2), 119–128.

Costes, J.-M., Kairouz, S., Eroukmanoff, V., & Monson, E. (2015). Gambling patterns and problems of gamblers on licensed and unlicensed sites in France. *Journal of Gambling Studies, 32*(1), 79–91.

Diaz-Gomez, C., Milhet, M., & Ben Lakhdar, C. (2009). *Guide pour la mise en oeuvre de bonnes pratiques d'évaluation: évaluer les interventions de réduction des risques.* OFDT. Retrieved from www.ofdt.fr/BDD/publications/docs/epfxcdp8.pdf

European Commission. (2012). *Communication from the Commission to the European Parliament, the Council, the Economic and Social Committee and the Committee of the Regions–Toward a Comprehensive European Framework for on Line Gambling.* Retrieved from https://eur-lex.europa.eu/legal-content/EN/TXT/?uri=celex%3A52012DC0596

Frechtling, J. A. (2007). *Logic Modelling Methods in Program Evaluation* (1st ed.). San Francisco: Jossey-Bass.

Inserm. (2008). *Jeux de hasard et d'argent. Contextes et addictions.* Paris: Inserm.

Journal Officiel. (2010). *LOI relative à l'ouverture à la concurrence et à la régulation du secteur des jeux d'argent et de hasard en ligne, Pub. L.* No. 2010-476.

Kingma, S. (2004). Gambling and the risk society: The liberalisation and legitimation crisis of gambling in the Netherlands. *International Gambling Studies, 4*(1), 47–67.

Lamour, J.-F. (2010). *Rapport relatif à l'ouverture à la concurrence et à la régulation du secteur des jeux d'argent et de hasard en ligne* (No. 2386) (p. 258). Assemblée nationale. Retrieved from www.assemblee-nationale.fr/13/rapports/r1860.asp

McLaughlin, J. A., & Jordan, G. B. (1999). Logic models: A tool for telling your programs performance story. *Evaluation and Program Planning, 22*(1), 65–72.

Nadeau, L., Dufour, M., Guay, R., Kairouz, S., Ménard, J., & Paradis, C. (2014). *Le jeu en ligne: quand la réalité du virtuel nous rattrape* (Groupe de travail sur le jeu en ligne). Retrieved from www.groupes.finances.gouv.qc.ca/jeu/pub/AUTFR_Jeu_En_Ligne_FR.pdf

Renger, R., & Titcomb, A. (2002). A three-step approach to teaching logic models. *American Journal of Evaluation, 23*, 493–504.

Tovar, M.-L., Costes, J.-M., & Eroukmanoff, V. (2013). Les jeux d'argent et de hasard sur Internet en France en 2012. *OFDT*, (85), 6.

Trucy, F. (2006). *Rapport d'information sur l'évolution des jeux de hasard et d'argent* (No. 58) (p. 362). Paris: Sénat. Retrieved from www.senat.fr/rap/r06-058/r06-058.html

Trucy, F. (2011). *Rapport d'information sur l'évaluation de la loi n° 2010–476 du 12 mai 2010 relative à l'ouverture à la concurrence et à la régulation du secteur des jeux d'argent et de hasard en ligne* (No. 17) (p. 315). Paris: Sénat. Retrieved from www.senat.fr/rap/r11-017/r11-0171.pdf

Valleur, M. (2015). Gambling and gambling-related problems in France: Gambling in France. *Addiction, 110*(12), 1872–1876.

15

IS INCOME DERIVED FROM PROBLEM GAMBLING A GOOD ASSESSMENT INDICATOR OF A RESPONSIBLE GAMBLING STRATEGY?

Jean-Michel Costes

Introduction

The governance of gambling in France, as in many other countries, is gradually becoming structured around the concept of responsible gambling, a term that was even formalised in the 2010 Act, which reconstructs the legal and political framework for the implementation of legal online games (see Chapter 15).

Responsible gambling

Responsible gambling can be defined as the adoption of strategies or practices that aim to prevent or reduce the potential harm associated with gambling. It is a mode of governance that helps the player to play without risk by undertaking a "responsible behaviour" (Blaszczynski, Ladouceur, & Shaffer, 2004). The State, who organises the framework in which this responsible gambling takes place, must navigate according to two conflicting interests: to secure gambling revenue for the economic sector, which offers this to the public, and to ensure that players' practices remain controlled, in order to avoid harm to their health. From an economic point of view, this paradoxical policy can be assessed by a cost/benefit study, searching for a minimisation of the first term and a maximisation of the second (Costes, Massin, & Etiemble, 2014; Fiedler, 2016).

Responsible gambling has gradually become established and progressively spread over the past two decades. In 2004, the Global Gambling Guidance Group (G4), whose founding members are from Australia, The Netherlands, Great Britain and Sweden, took place and offered programmes for the development of responsible gambling. Other organisations such as the World Lottery Association, American Gambling Association and eCommerce Online Gaming Regulation and Assurance produce certification systems or guidelines to implement responsible gambling

154 Jean-Michel Costes

measures. In 2014, the European Lotteries wrote their third code of ethics. In addition to regulation of business practices and safety standards, this includes the concept of tackling "excessive gambling". Thus, responsible gambling is clearly part of a corporate social responsibility approach. The economic operator must make decisions, taking into account four constraints that it should take a position on: to be profitable, to obey the law, to be ethical and to demonstrate social responsibility (Carroll, 1991).

But gambling is not an ordinary subject. It is controversial because of the potential negative impact of its commerce on the common good, like other potential types of addictive disorder (tobacco, alcohol, etc.) (Palazzo & Richter, 2005). Drawing upon a current sociological approach, inspired by Foucault's theory, we can analyse the emergence of "responsible gambling" as a consequence of economic liberalism. In this case individuals who have been given their freedom are required to behave in a responsible manner, thus discharging the State and economic agents from a large part of their responsibility for gambling-related harm (Fournier, 2015; Rose, 1999). From this critical approach, responsible gambling can be seen as a "facade", imposing on everyone the image that operators and the State wish to present, inefficient in terms of protecting vulnerable players (Collins, 2006; Yani-de-Soriano, Javed, & Yousafzai, 2012).

Responsible gambling in France

In France, the State monopoly on lottery games (La Française Des Jeux; FDJ), plays a central role in the development of responsible gambling. The State can justify itself on this approach by arguing that a monopolistic regulation system is more able to protect consumers. As such, it is seen as being in agreement with European case law relating to the principle of free competition (Mangel & Trespeuch, 2009).

Thus, from 2000, the FDJ has expressed the idea of "making the general public play in a reasonable manner", funded certain research projects into problem gambling and subsidised NGOs for helping players. Then followed the development of an ethical charter setting out the principles for the integrity, security and prevention of addictive disorders in 2003 (access to minors, no targeting of minors, excessive gambling detection but few principles on reducing the addictive potential of games). In 2005, an advertising charter was developed, and a small team appeared in the organisational structure of the company, which was dedicated to the development of responsible gambling. Moreover, in 2006 a responsible gambling action plan was written. The casinos have used the notion of using a code of ethics, since 2004, by developing an ethical charter to organise staff training on responsible gambling. In 2006, Mutual Urban Betting (Pari Mutuel Urbain; PMU, who monopolise horse racing) published a document entitled "Responsible gambling and the PMU".

For its part, in 2006, the State took measures to start a transition from a protective policy to a responsible gambling policy. This concerns primarily the FDJ, by determining the objectives that it must respect, relating to games on the market. Amongst these objectives are, for the first time in an official text, the notions of channelling demand and preventing dependence. Gambling policy is, therefore, no longer a supply-related policy only, which defines products offered to the public. It is concerned with consumer protection at the same time as public order. The State implemented a regulatory commission whose role was first to examine the trade programme and "FDJ responsible gambling action plan" and then the PMU. The reviews were undertaken in order to promote reasonable gambling practices (Trucy, 2006). Finally, the 2010 Act, which permits and organises legal offers for online gambling, consecrated the term without defining it.

Assessment indicators for responsible gambling

The goal of responsible gambling is to limit the extent of harm to social and health functioning that this activity can impose on certain players. How can we evaluate its effectiveness? One of the ways to do this is to measure the prevalence of problem gambling: The proportion of players with "problematic" gambling practices according to scientifically established screening criteria. However, this indicator does not give a measure of the relative weight of problem gambling in the industry's economy. Particularly, since the activity level of problematic players, who are both highly active and extravagant, is higher than that of "ordinary" players. This is, nevertheless, essential to document as a contextual element of a public policy. Particularly as the policy sets forth the principle of responsible gambling by delegating a significant part of its implementation to the operators.

An alternative indicator, which could also be calculated from population surveys, (although this is rarely done), is the portion of spending on gambling (or gross gambling revenue) which comes from problematic players. This indicator, which can be considered by activity type, appears relevant in light of the objective. In effect, the more significant this is for a given activity, the less desirable it is in a society which seeks to maximise the well-being of the population. It therefore allows us to verify that the prosperity of an economic sector does not come at the expense of public health. A few studies, mostly in Anglo-Saxon countries, have produced such estimates. The fields of study and methodologies used are quite diverse, and the results vary widely from one country to another (Australia Productivity Commission, 2010; Volberg, Gerstein, Christiansen, & Baldridge, 2001; Williams & Wood, 2004).

However, both of these indicators are complex to produce. Large-scale investigations of the population cannot investigate players' expenditure in great detail. Moreover, from this methodological prerequisite, they do not provide this information at a very detailed level, for example in relation to game type or by operator. From this perspective, it would be useful to seek a less efficient indicator that is easier to produce at a detailed level. An indicator of concentrated spending could be such an approach. Economic studies show that gambling expenditure is more concentrated than those relating to ordinary consumption, meaning that a small minority of players undertake the large majority of spending. Other works show the crucial place that problematic players hold amongst the players that spend most extravagantly (Fiedler, Kairouz, & Costes, in press).

156 Jean-Michel Costes

The aim of this chapter is, therefore, to:

- Estimate the prevalence of problem gambling and the proportion of gambling expenditure made by problematic players, by activity type, in France.
- Study the correlation between a concentration of spending indicator and these first two indicators.
- Analyse the contribution of these indicators towards the assessment of a responsible gambling strategy based on French gambling policy.

Development

Methods

The French survey data was raised as part of the Health Barometer, a regular national health survey carried out by the French National Institute for Prevention and Health Education (Costes et al., 2015). From December 2013 to May 2014, we conducted a representative nationwide telephone survey using computer-assisted telephone interviews (CATI) amongst 15,635 French citizens aged 15–75 years. The sample was built with a two-stage random sample design approaching a selection of households using random digit dialling covering all metropolitan French regions as well as a random selection of individual members of households using the Kish method. Furthermore, the sample was composed of two sub-samples, one landline and the other mobile phone-based. The overall response rate was 56.6% (52.3% for mobile phones and 61.3% for landline).

Data was weighted by the number of telephone landlines and eligible people in the household as well as in respect to aspects of representativeness for the French population structure according to age, gender, educational level, region of residence and level of urbanisation. Participants completed a questionnaire on demographic characteristics, gambling patterns, health status, regular behaviours and self-reported problems related to gambling. Using cardinal scales, they also reported their spending on each form of gambling activity, either per session or on a weekly, monthly or yearly basis. The total spending was calculated on a yearly basis and is available for each type of game.

We used participants' total score on the Problem Gambling Severity Index (PGSI) – a quantitative sub-section of the Canadian Problem Gambling Index – to assess the severity of gambling problems (Ferris & Wynne, 2001). The PGSI consists of nine items with answers reported on a four-point Likert-type scale ("Never"; "Sometimes"; "Most of the time"; "Almost always"). Respondents were identified as either non-problem gamblers with a score of 0 on the PGSI, low-risk gamblers with a score of 1 or 2, moderate-risk gamblers with a score of 3 to 7, or problem gamblers (or probable pathological) with a score of 8 or higher. The clustering of the last two categories (score of 3 or higher) was named: at risk.

To measure the proportion of revenue derived from problem gamblers, we calculated the total expenses of those participants who fulfilled the criteria for problem

Income derived from problem gambling **157**

(or at risk) gambling and divided it by the expenses of all gamblers. To measure the concentration of revenues, we used the Gini coefficient, commonly used to describe inequality in distributions. It is normalised between 0 and 1, where 0 indicates perfect equality of a phenomenon (all gamblers have the same spending) and 1 describes perfect inequality (only one participant does all the spending).

Results

In France, in 2014, amongst those who reported having gambled over the past year, 4.7% had at risk gambling practices: 3.9% could be classified as players at moderate risk and 0.9% as problem gamblers. These proportions vary strongly depending on the nature of the activities. Thus, the proportion of at-risk players ranges from 4.7% amongst lottery game players to 19.2% for sports betters (Table 15.1).

The expenditure of problematic players is 40.3% of the total expenditures of all players (for which 23.6% is from players at moderate risk and 16.6% from excessive gamblers). In this area too, there are strong disparities, according to the nature of the activity. Indeed, the proportion varies from 24.2%, in the case of lotteries, to 76% for casino games (Table 15.1).

The average annual expenditure reported by all the players is €685; the median expenditure is €96. The distribution of players according to their spending level is very asymmetric. The majority of players spend only small amounts on their gambling activities, and a small minority spend large sums of money. This explains

TABLE 15.1 Problem and at-risk gambling prevalence and spending share for different gambling activities

Type of game	n	Indicator 1: Prevalence amongst players (%)			Indicator 2: Spending share (%)		
		Gambling behaviour			*Gambling behaviour*		
		moderate risk	*problem*	*at risk*	*moderate risk*	*problem*	*at risk*
		$3 \leq PGSI \leq 7$	$PGSI \geq 8$	$PGSI \geq 3$	$3 \leq PGSI \leq 7$	$PGSI \geq 8$	$PGSI \geq 3$
Lotteries	6228	3.8	0.9	4.7	10.8	13.4	24.2
Scratch cards	5082	4.4	0.9	5.4	19.1	7.0	26.1
Sports betting	638	14.1	5.1	19.2	38.5	20.0	58.5
Horseracing	977	8.7	3.4	12.1	22.9	17.3	40.3
Poker	421	13.8	4.8	18.6	34.0	29.3	63.3
Casino table games (w/o poker)	304	9.9	6.0	15.9	60.2	15.9	76.1
Slot machines	843	7.8	2.1	9.9	18.2	22.8	41.0
Online gambling	643	9.3	3.1	12.4	32.1	24.7	56.8
Overall	8773	3.9	0.9	4.7	23.6	16.6	40.3

158 Jean-Michel Costes

TABLE 15.2 Concentration of spending for gambling measured by the Gini coefficient

Type of game	n	Gini coefficient	PG prevalence PGSI ≥3	PG revenue share PGSI ≥ 3
Lotteries (except instant games)	5,047	0.758	3.3	8.9
Instant lottery games	868	0.796	10.7	48.4
Scratch cards-low stakes only	2,629	0.765	2.9	16.3
Scratch cards-high stakes	2,348	0.770	7.9	29.9
Sports betting	638	0.828	19.2	58.5
Horseracing	977	0.847	12.1	40.3
Poker	421	0.854	18.6	63.3
Casino table games (w/o poker)	304	0.850	15.9	76.1
Slot machines	843	0.876	9.9	41.0
Overall gambling	8,773	0.839	4.7	40.3

the large difference between the median and the average. Three-quarters of the revenue is due to the 10% of players who are more extravagant spenders; the 1% of large spenders account for 62% of the spending. This concentration varies according to the type of game. The games for which this concentration is the strongest (measured by the Gini index) are also a used by a greater proportion of problematic players (Table 15.2). The correlations between the Gini index and the prevalence of at-risk gambling, on the one hand ($r = 0.72$, p-value $= 0.03$) and the proportion of expenses attributable to at-risk players ($r = 0.73$, p-value $= 0.02$) are significant. This also applies when you consider problem gamblers ($r = 0.69$, p-value $= 0.04$) and $r = 0.67$, p-value $= 0.05$.

Discussion and conclusion

The collection of reliable information on gambling within population surveys is a complex subject. The main difficulty is that of taking into account the reinvestment of wins made during a sequence of games and the ability to differentiate the net expenditure (losses minus wins) for the total amount of bets made. Studies have shown that the information collection strategy could have a significant impact on the reported amount, with a difference of up to 60% (Blaszczynski, Ladouceur, Goulet, & Savard, 2006; Blaszczynski, Ladouceur, Goulet, & Savard, 2008). Therefore, many elements suggest that spending reported in surveys by the players themselves are underestimated. But the main question that arises here is whether this underreporting differs for problematic players compared to others. It would seem likely that this underestimation is increased for problematic players who can have a tendency to deny its real importance (Orford, Wardle, & Griffiths, 2013). In such a case, the portion of expenditures attributable to problematic players would be minimised.

In France, 40% of gambling revenue comes from at-risk players and 17% from problem gamblers. It is clear that the good health of this economic sector is dependent on the participation of players who have difficulties with their practices. Overall, responsible gambling strategy does not appear to have a deep impact. How can we explain this result?

In order to do this, we must focus on details of the problem gambling prevention measures or actions that are actually undertaken. We should consider this alongside the scientifically validated knowledge from the field of the problem gambling prevention or, more generally, prevention of addictive disorders (Anderson & Baumberg, 2006; Babor, 2003; Edwards, 1995; McNeill et al., 2004; Ősterberg, 2004; Strang et al., 2012; Williams, West, & Simpson, 2012).

Certain measures, which have proved their effectiveness are deployed (restricted availability of slot machines, a capped return rate for several types of game, etc.). However, others which are equally effective, are not implemented (restricting advertising, limiting betting or losses, etc.) and some measures with weak effectiveness or ineffectiveness are widely deployed (Figure 15.1). On this last point we should mention information and risk awareness initiatives, which for most operators are an essential part of their responsible gambling strategy.

Finally, there is a good correlation between the concentration of spending indicator and the two relevant indicators to assess responsible gambling. This opens up interesting possibilities, as the concentration of spending indicator is easier to produce, and this can be done at a very detailed level. For example, in the case of online gambling, we could easily envisage calculating such an indicator by specific

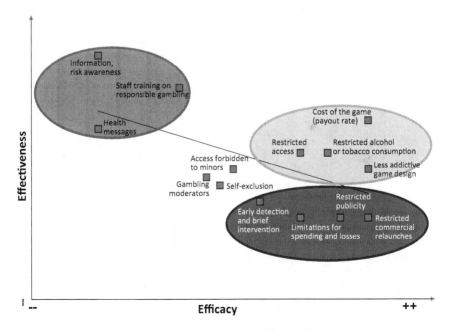

FIGURE 15.1 Effectiveness and efficiency of responsible gambling measures in France

160 Jean-Michel Costes

game or operator type in order to evaluate the "responsibility" of a particular game or operator. This paves the way for a major change in the rules of the regulation which, to be most effective, would go from an action-based obligation, on the part of the operators, to a results-based obligation. We could then agree that the notion of responsible gambling is: for players to be responsible but also for operators to offer responsible play and the State to ensure this by establishing obligations for the results.

References

Anderson, P., & Baumberg, B. (2006). *Alcohol in Europe: A Public Health Perspective: A Report for the European Commission.* Luxembourg: European Commission.

Australia Productivity Commission. (2010). *Gambling Inquiry Report.* Canberra: Productivity Commission.

Babor, T. (Éd.). (2003). *Alcohol: No Ordinary Commodity: Research and Public Policy.* Oxford and New York: Oxford University Press.

Blaszczynski, A., Ladouceur, R., Goulet, A., & Savard, C. (2006). "How much do you spend gambling?": Ambiguities in questionnaire items assessing expenditure. *International Gamblingn Studies, 6*(2), 123–128.

Blaszczynski, A., Ladouceur, R., Goulet, A., & Savard, C. (2008). Differences in monthly versus daily evaluations of money spent on gambling and calculation strategies. *Journal of Gambling Issues,* 98–105.

Blaszczynski, A., Ladouceur, R., & Shaffer, H. J. (2004). A science-based framework for responsible gambling: The Reno model. *Journal of Gambling studies, 20*(3), 301–317.

Carroll, A. B. (1991). The pyramid of corporate social responsibility: Toward the moral management of organizational stakeholders. *Business Horizons, 34*(4), 39–48.

Collins, A. (2006). The pathological gambler and the government of gambling. In J. Cosgrave (Éd.), *The Sociology of Risk and Gambling Reader* (pp. 355–390). Abingdon, UK: Routledge.

Costes, J.-M., Eroukmanoff, V., Richard, J.-B., & Tovar, M.-L. (2015). Les jeux d'argent et de hasard en France en 2014. *Observatoire des jeux,* (4), 9.

Costes, J.-M., Massin, S., & Etiemble, J. (2014). Première évaluation de l'impact socio-économique des jeux d'argent et de hasard en France. *Observatoire Des Jeux,* (5), 5.

Edwards, G., & Weltgesundheitsorganisation (Éds.). (1995). *Alcohol Policy and the Public Good.* Oxford: Oxford University Press.

European Lotteries. (2014). *European Responsible Gaming Standards.* Retrieved from www.european-lotteries.org/european-gaming-standards

Ferris, J., & Wynne, H. (2001). *The Canadian Problem Gambling Index.* Ottawa: Canadian Centre on Substance Abuse.

Fiedler, I. (2016). *Glücksspiele: eine verhaltens- und gesundheitsökonomische Analyse mit rechtspolitischen Empfehlungen.* Frankfurt am Main: PL Academic Research.

Fiedler, I., Kairouz, S., & Costes, J.-M. (in press). *Gambling Spending and its Concentration on Problem Gamblers.* Manuscript submitted for publication.

Fournier, P. (2015). La responsabilité comme mode de gouvernement néolibéral: l'exemple des programmes d'aide aux familles aux États-Unis de 1980 à nos jours. *Les ateliers de l'éthique, 10*(1), 129.

Mangel, A.-C., & Trespeuch, M. (2009). La RSE et les jeux d'argent: les nouveaux enjeux de la régulation. *Sociologies Pratiques, 18*(1), 91.

McNeill, A., Ross, H., Joossens, L., Hastings, G., & Godfrey, F. (2004). *Tobacco or Health in the European Union: Past, Present and Future*. Report for European Commission. (Office for Official Publications of the European Communities). Luxembourg: Office for Official Publications of the European Communities.

Orford, J., Wardle, H., & Griffiths, M. (2013). What proportion of gambling is problem gambling? Estimates from the 2010 British Gambling Prevalence Survey. *International Gambling Studies, 13*(1), 4–18.

Österberg, E. (2004). *What Are the Most Effective and Cost-Effective Interventions in Alcohol Control?* (p. 14). WHO Regional Office for Europe (Health Evidence Network). Copenhagen: WHO Regional Office for Europe (Health Evidence Network).

Palazzo, G., & Richter, U. (2005). CSR business as usual? The case of the tobacco industry. *Journal of Business Ethics, 61*(4), 387–401.

Rose, N. S. (1999). *Powers of Freedom: Reframing Political Thought*. Cambridge, UK and New York, NY: Cambridge University Press.

Strang, J., Babor, T., Caulkins, J., Fischer, B., Foxcroft, D., & Humphreys, K. (2012). Drug policy and the public good: Evidence for effective interventions. *The Lancet, 379*(9810), 71–83.

Trucy, F. (2006). *Rapport d'information sur l'évolution des jeux de hasard et d'argent* (No. 58) (p. 362). Assemblée nationale.

Volberg, R. A., Gerstein, D. R., Christiansen, E. M., & Baldridge, J. (2001). Assessing self-reported expenditures on gambling. *Managerial and Decision Economics, 22*(1–3), 77–96.

Williams, R. J., West, B. L., & Simpson, R. I. (2012). *Prevention of Problem Gambling: A Comprehensive Review of the Evidence and Identified Best Practices*. Ontario: Ontario Problem Gambling Research Centre and the Ontario Ministry of Health and Long-Term Care.

Williams, R. J., & Wood, R. T. (2004). The proportion of gaming revenue derived from problem gamblers: Examining the issues in a Canadian context. *Analyses of Social Issues and Public Policy, 4*(1), 33–45.

Yani-de-Soriano, M., Javed, U., & Yousafzai, S. (2012). Can an industry be socially responsible if its products harm consumers? The case of online gambling. *Journal of Business Ethics, 110*(4), 481–497.

16

CHALLENGES OF ONLINE GAMBLING FOR RISK AND HARM REDUCTION

Louise Nadeau, Magali Dufour, Richard Guay, Sylvia Kairouz, Jean-Marc Ménard and Catherine Paradis

In February 2010, the Crown Corporation Loto-Québec announced that it planned to provide Quebecers with a secure and trustworthy online gaming site. Espacejeux. com – literally Spacegames.com – would bring together in-casino and online slot machines under a single virtual banner. To this day, the site is still operational.

In the weeks that followed, there were strong negative reactions. The primary stakeholders in the field of gambling publicly opposed the decision of Loto-Québec and a resistance movement took shape. The Directors of Public Health from Quebec's 18 health regions and several researchers contended that the creation of an online gambling site would increase at-risk gambling and Internet gaming disorder (Maguire et al., 2010); the Ombudsman Raymonde Saint-Germain agreed and so advised the Minister of Finance.

Loto-Québec and the Minister of Finance disagreed. They presented Espacejeux as a solution that would thwart illegal, unsecured online gambling offers already accessible to Quebecers, keep a significant portion of this money in Quebec and return all of its profits to the community. This debate led the Minister of Finance, Raymond Bachand, to set up the Working Group on Online Gambling to closely monitor Loto-Québec's new activities in the online gambling sector.

The Working Group presented its report in 2014 (Nadeau et al., 2014). It concluded that a national programme on harm reduction for online problem gambling should include three key essential components: public health and clinical measures, controlled socioeconomic dimensions and an effective legal framework in which regulations are enforced. In its conclusion, the report made five recommendations that supported the triad of key components for a successful public health approach towards online gambling.

This chapter describes how the theoretical considerations and research processes that lead to the formulation of this model optimise the reduction of health and social dangers related to online gambling. The model can be adapted to other parts of the world and thus proves useful not only in Quebec and in Canada but also elsewhere.

The mandate

As Chair of the Working Group on Online Gambling, I accepted the following mandate to:

- Analyse the social impact of the development of online games.
- Analyse the regulatory, technical, economic and legal measures to counter illegal gambling.

Essentially, the mandate can be summed up as follows:

- Study the social impact by monitoring the prevalence of gambling and gambling-related problems (characteristics of people who gamble, gambling habits, comorbidity, e.g., gambling and drug addiction, gambling and alcohol, etc.).
- Review the evolution of online gambling.
- Review the efficacy of the prevention measures directed at online gambling.
- Consult with experts at home and abroad.
- Analyse regulatory, technical, economic and legal measures designed to counter illegal gambling.

The context

From the start, it became apparent to the five members of the Working Group that we were confronted with two competing, irreconcilable positions clashing and creating tension amongst people or institutions involved in or concerned with gambling. We began with a review of the comments from the primary stakeholders with regard to problems stemming from online gambling. They were predicated on different but incompatible assumptions about the impact of Espacejeux in Quebec. In other words, the comments included predictions on Espacejeux's impact. In scientific jargon, such predictions are hypotheses. We had to find a way to determine who was right. Thus, we needed to find a way of controlling the veracity of the competing positions. Our work plan was taking shape.

The comments of the stakeholders in the realm of online gambling can be summed up as follows:

- The **public health hypothesis** posits that the creation of a government-controlled online gambling offering would increase the availability of online gambling in Quebec and thus increase the likelihood of at-risk gambling and Internet gaming disorder.
- The **socioeconomic hypothesis** postulates that the creation of a government-sponsored online gambling site would lead to additional revenues, favour

164 Louise Nadeau et al.

responsible gambling and increase the security and integrity of online gambling offerings.

- The **legal hypothesis** posits that the creation of a government-sponsored online gambling site would thwart illegal online gambling and thus promote the regulation and control of online gambling.

The Working Group was unanimous in deciding to focus on the facts. What did the data show? Who was right? We needed hard facts derived from quantitative and qualitative data to make it possible to test the three hypotheses.

Method

To ensure neutrality and objectivity in the execution of its mandate, the Working Group decided to adopt a monitoring strategy. Monitoring is defined as a systematic, ongoing process to collect, analyse and interpret accurate, up-to-date, relevant information from various data sources with a view to describing and examining changes in a phenomenon over time (Gopichandran & Indira Krishna, 2013). Our monitoring plan centralised the available data in order to reveal general trends and changes in online gambling in Quebec since 2010, as well as document the offerings and accessibility of online gambling websites and the preventive and curative measures intended to reduce gambling-related problems. A population-based survey had been conducted amongst a representative sample of 11,888 Quebecers in the summer of 2009. We knew that 1.4% of the Quebec population had gambled online during the 12 preceding months in 2009 and that 6% of these online gamblers were probable pathological gamblers (Kairouz, Paradis, Nadeau, Hamel, & Robillard, 2015). Therefore, the baseline level, i.e., the valid data on online gambling practices prior to the introduction of Espacejeux, was known.

The survey project included a smaller follow-up study of probable pathological gamblers over two years, and our budget made it possible to increase the sample of the most recent survey (Luce, Kairouz, & Nadeau, 2016; Luce, Kairouz, Nadeau, & Monsen, 2016). Changes in online gambling amongst the population in 2012 could thus be examined with the same protocol as in 2009 (Kairouz et al., 2015). That was a great starting point. An agreement with the Minister of Finance allowed the Working Group to have access to all Loto-Québec data deemed useful to ensure the realisation of its mandate. Accordingly, for the entire duration of its mandate, the Working Group had access to the administrative data on Quebecers' gambling practices on the Espacejeux website. The data were provided to us every three months and this made it possible to analyse and quantify changes in participation and modes of gambling on the Espacejeux website over a period of three years.

The members of the Working Group and Loto-Québec signed a contract protecting the confidentiality of the data shared. Information focusing on the security and integrity of the Espacejeux website was also shared with the Working Group. The data significantly sustained the Working Group's thinking on these issues and were used to develop the five recommendations. It should be noted that the findings from the analysis of the confidential Loto-Québec data were deleted from the public report. The Working Group made sure that, despite the deletions, the reader would be able to understand the logic that prevailed in our analysis and synthesis of the facts and the formulation of our recommendations.

The three hypotheses

The sociosanitary hypothesis

The sociosanitary hypothesis postulated that the creation of Espacejeux would 1) increase the number of people gambling and 2) increase at-risk gambling and Internet gaming disorder. As a result, there was a need to put in place preventive measures and treatment services to thwart problems linked to online gambling.

The data collected between 2008 and 2012 show that whilst the public health hypothesis seemed plausible it was not substantiated empirically. The anticipated impact of government-controlled online gambling did not materialise. There was neither an increase in the number of people gambling nor an increase in at-risk gambling and Internet gaming disorder.

The Working Group did not find any prevention campaign conducted by the Health and Social Services authorities targeting specifically online gambling. The only preventive measure aimed at online gambling was developed by the foundation *Mise sur toi*. We were unable to locate the document on the website of Loto-Québec, which took over from the foundation in 2012. The only prevention programmes came in the form of dramatic messages on the deleterious effects of gambling disorder, a psychopathology that reaches less than 1% of the population. We did acknowledge a lack of data on low-risk gambling practices that might underpin constructive prevention programmes.

The Working Group questioned the validity of the government corporation's decision to take over the primary and secondary prevention mandate. Based on best practices in other jurisdictions, neither primary nor secondary prevention should fall under the mandate and the jurisdiction of a government corporation whose main vocation is commercial. The accessibility of the gambling assistance and support network, including the "Gambling: Help and Referral" line (Jeu, aide et référence, 2017) was a strong point in Quebec, particularly in comparison with other regions or countries. However, it was considered advisable to evaluate the efficacy of various programmes.

There is in Quebec a universal system providing clinical services for problem gambling. However, persons with a gambling disorder resort less extensively to services than individuals contending with a mental disorder or an alcohol- or drug-related disorders. It was considered by the Working Group that the obstacles to treatment are inseparable from stigmatisation of gambling that persists in society as well as the concealment, shame and comorbidity that characterise gambling disorder.

The socioeconomic hypothesis

The socioeconomic hypothesis contends that the establishment of a government-controlled online gambling website would have three consequences: 1) channel online gambling offers into a controlled network, 2) ensure the security and integrity of the online gambling offers available to Quebecers and 3) ensure that Quebecers have access to responsible gambling offers. Three years later, the data do not corroborate the predictions of the socioeconomic hypothesis. Loto-Québec's arrival on the Web did not fully channel illicit gambling offers in a controlled network. Moreover, although Loto-Québec's gambling offers appear to be secure and honest, limitations have been noted with respect to responsible gambling.

The Working Group questioned the structure in which Loto-Québec is called upon to regulate itself, particularly with regard to the assurance and control measures meant to safeguard the conformity of gambling from the standpoint of security, integrity and responsibility. Such a system cannot be reconciled with best control practices observed in other jurisdictions. Thus, it was hard to draw a clear conclusion as to whether the launching of a government-controlled online gambling website did make it possible to offer Quebecers a forum for responsible gambling. However, in a context where the government corporation is mandated to achieve economic profitability, the Working Group pointed out that Loto-Québec's self-regulation was (and still is) creating a conflict or the appearance of a conflict between the profitability and the social responsibility mandates. For instance, Loto-Québec had chosen to streamline the registration form by eliminating the detailed presentation of its responsible gambling tools. In so doing, it showed that the desire to register greater numbers of Quebecers on its website took precedence over the concern for offering responsible gambling tools.

This appears to come in conflict with the mission, perspective and strategic directions of the Crown Corporation as spelled out still today in its own official documents and on its website (Loto-Québec, 2018). Furthermore, were it not for our monitoring that fact would have gone totally unnoticed.

The legal hypothesis

The legal hypothesis postulates that the government corporation's website would thwart the online gambling sector that is developing and operating illegally. After three years, allegedly illegal online gambling continued to operate and be offered to Quebecers. What is more, nothing had been done to counter this. The Working Group had to concede that it is very difficult to control effectively this "illegal" market, particularly for provincial authorities in Canada. This led us to conclude that, in order to control the online gambling market, protect consumers and generate revenues for the government, the best solution would be to establish clear rules and to open up the online gambling market to private operators. In fact, from an extensive review of the international experience, the best solution would be to establish an online gambling licensing system. However, federal legislation, as it still stands, does not permit the implementation of such a system. Accordingly, the first step to take in order to set up a licensing system was to amend the Canadian *Criminal Code*, something only the federal government can do because criminal law is a federal competence.

Nevertheless, whilst acknowledging the difficulty and despite the complexity of the task, a licensing system remains the most promising avenue to control the online gambling market. For this reason, the Working Group suggested that Quebec take a leadership role in the realm of gambling, working in cooperation with the other provinces and the federal government, to secure amendments to the *Criminal Code* in order to allow the provinces to set up a licensing system if they so wish. However, in order to be effective a licensing system must be supported by a number of measures. To begin with, a licensing system must be managed by a regulatory agency with the means to enforce and ensure compliance. The agency should be given the means and the powers to engage in monitoring within appropriate parameters. The online gambling licensing solution should make it possible to compel operators to offer an honest, secure, avant-garde product and to protect consumers, notably young people and vulnerable people who gamble.

The recommendations

The 2014 report was predicated on two basic premises that were aimed at reducing the harms related to online gambling. First, we took for granted that online gambling was in use throughout the world and was here to stay. The prohibitionist option was discarded. Therefore, a set of rules and procedures needed to be developed to minimise the negative consequences. Second, a Crown or State Corporation such as Loto-Québec was a sound societal choice, one likely to promote the common good but only if public health measures were implemented. One must also bear in mind that the Internet requires adjustments since the parameters are different from those of land-based gambling.

The Working Group also agreed on the necessity of adopting an ethical approach (Massé, 2003). It was essential to protect the members of society, especially the most vulnerable. Our recommendations thus had to be designed as guiding principles that guaranteed a secure gambling environment, included measures to protect the general public and vulnerable people who gamble, and provided curative services for gambling disorder. For these reasons, we felt that the profits generated by online gambling should be deposited in the Consolidated Revenue Fund to be returned to the community.

Last, we had to take into account the fact that online gambling was developing against a backdrop of globalisation. That is in a world characterised by multiple transactions and shared knowledge, and the free circulation of individuals, capital and goods. That still remains. The five recommendations that follow are based on

168 Louise Nadeau et al.

the research, monitoring and reflections of the Working Group. They should be read as guiding principles for a successful implementation of a national programme on harm reduction for online problem gambling.

Recommendation 1

Bearing in mind that:

- A gambling operator usually pursues a general objective of profitability.
- There is a considerable risk of conflicts of interest when the same corporation pursues contradictory objectives, i.e., the promotion of gambling and the prevention of gambling-related problems.
- Primary and second prevention in the realm of online gambling is multidimensional, targets the general population, including those who do not gamble, and requires specific skills.
- Best practices observed with respect to primary and secondary prevention are to establish an independent body that can equip and support the government and the other stakeholders concerned with gambling in their prevention efforts.

The recommendations are:

1 Limit operator's social responsibility mandate to the management of online gambling offers.
2 Establish independent, autonomous, permanent foundations whose prevention mission will encompass the public health, socioeconomic and legal questions that gambling raises.

Recommendation 2

Bearing in mind that:

- Persons with gambling disorders resort less extensively to treatment and support services than persons with alcohol- or drug-related or other mental disorders.
- Persons with gambling disorders display complex clinical features in which cooccurring disorders are often present.
- Addiction therapists must know how to detect, evaluate and treat persons suffering from cooccurring disorders.

The recommendation is:

Ensure that the clinical services available to persons that have a gambling disorder take into account the other mental health needs.

Recommendation 3

Bearing in mind that:

- Gambling operators have a mandate to responsibly manage its gambling offer.
- Operators pursue a general objective of profitability.
- There is a risk of conflicts of interest when a given corporation pursues contradictory objectives, i.e., the promotion of gambling and the prevention of gambling-related problems.
- Best practices are to assign the regulation of gambling to an independent body for online gambling.

The recommendation is:

> Create or maintain an independent regulatory agency that regulates and monitors online gambling. The mandate should include regulation and monitoring of all promotion, advertising, responsible offering and security and integrity of online and other gambling activities conducted.

Recommendation 4

Bearing in mind that:

- Governments cannot control the integrity, security and responsibility of the online gambling offers of deemed illegal operators.
- Governments are depriving themselves of tax revenues by not taxing the revenues of private operators that offer online gambling.
- The reality of the Internet and online gambling goes beyond borders and makes it difficult, if not impossible, for law enforcement agencies to effectively enforce any criminal legislation.
- A government regulatory body can effectively monitor diversified online gambling offers by issuing licences and ensuring compliance with the rules that the government adopts.
- Best practices observed internationally are to allow private operators to offer responsible, honest, secure online gambling regulated by any government.

The recommendations are:

1 Take the necessary legal steps to enable jurisdictions to issue online gambling licences to private operators.
2 Establish and mandate an independent regulatory body to establish and administer a self-financing system to issue licences to private online gambling operators.
3 Implement the necessary subsidiary measures to ensure the efficacy and long-term survival of a licensing system.

Recommendation 5

Bearing in mind that:

- Online gambling and other potentially addictive behaviours are developing against a backdrop of ongoing technological innovation and change in the virtual universe.
- Monitoring is an essential tool to grasp changes in a recent phenomenon whose impact, especially amongst minors, remains little known from a sociosanitary, socioeconomic and legal standpoint.
- Monitoring must rely on reliable, valid empirical data and is necessary for decision making.

The recommendation is:

> Establish a monitoring system through an expert panel capable of ensuring follow-up to sociosanitary, socioeconomic and legal challenges.

Conclusion

In addition to these specific recommendations, the Working Group had a final message for the stakeholders concerned with all gambling activities. Our work shows that when stakeholders succeed in reaching a consensus on the broad objectives to be attained, the social climate with regard to gambling is serene. This is particularly true in Sweden and the United Kingdom. Without such a consensus, the debate over competing positions brings into play irrational elements. The opinions and choices of the stakeholders are indissociable from their conflicting interests, beliefs and perspectives. If such a consensus had existed in Quebec, the competing, irreconcilable positions clashing and creating tension would not have occupied the field.

Competition or balkanisation between the stakeholders serves neither the general public nor the most vulnerable individuals. It would, therefore, be desirable that social services, regulatory bodies, people who gamble, the government corporation, the gambling industry, public health officials and the police cooperate to develop a *modus operandi* based on empirical evidence and on the common good.

I am indebted to Hélène Le Bel for her comments on this chapter.

References

Gopichandran, V., & Indira Krishna, A. K. (2013). Monitoring "monitoring" and evaluating "evaluation": An ethical framework for monitoring and evaluation in public health. *Journal of Medical Ethics, 39*(1), 31–35.

Jeu, aide et référence. (2017, August 23). *Acceuil.* Retrieved from www.jeu-aidereference. qc.ca/www/homepage_en.asp

Kairouz, S., Paradis, C., Nadeau, L., Hamel, C., & Robillard, C. (2015). Patterns and trends in gambling the Québec population between 2009 and 2012. *Canadian Journal of Public Health*, *106*(3), 115–120.

Loto-Québec. (2018, October 23). *Responsible Gambling: Our Greatest Preoccupation*. Retrieved from https://societe.lotoquebec.com/en/corporate-responsibility/responsible-gambling

Luce, C., Kairouz, S., & Nadeau, L. (2016). Pathways and transitions of gamblers over two years. *International Gambling Studies*. Retrieved from www.tandfonline.com/doi/full/10.1080/14459795.2016.1209780

Luce, C., Kairouz, S., Nadeau, L., & Monsen, E. (2016). Life events and problem gambling severity: A prospective study of adult gamblers. *Psychology of Addictive Behaviors*, *30*(8), 922–930.

Maguire, R., Aubin, D., Desbiens, F., Grenier, G. W., Soulière, L., Lessard, R., . . . Déry, S. (2010, March 16). *Mémoire de la position des directeurs régionaux de santé publique sur l'étatisation des jeux d'argent par Internet au Québec*. Retrieved from www.dspq.qc.ca/documents/Memoirepositiondes DSP2010031.pdf

Massé, R. (2003). *Éthique et santé publique: Enjeux, valeurs et normativité*. Québec: Presses de l'Université Laval.

Nadeau, L., Dufour, M., Guay, R., Kairouz, S., Ménard, J. M., & Paradis, C. (2014, June 11). *Le jeu en ligne: Quand la réalité du virtuel nous rattrape/Online gambling: When reality catches up with us*. Montréal: Groupe de travail sur le jeu en ligne. Retrieved from www.groupes.finances.gouv.qc.ca/jeu/index_en.asp

CONCLUSION

*Cheryl Dickson, Caroline Dunand, Olivier Simon
and Henrietta Bowden-Jones*

In a society that now offers wide and diverse opportunities for gambling, governments, local entrepreneurs with an interest in commercial growth, corporations and community organisations are believed to increasingly benefit from the growing revenue (see Chapter 1). In many jurisdictions, legal and regulatory changes have limited previous restraints on gambling, and gambling has become a normalised practice (see Chapter 4). Nevertheless, problematic gambling practices can have profound effects for certain individuals and those close to them and can lead to multiple harms (see Chapter 2). Moreover, gambling-related problems often co-exist with other disorders, which can give rise to a complex array of overlapping issues (see Chapter 3). From a neuroscience perspective, individual emotion regulation strategies, and gambling-related cognitive distortions, have been linked to self-deceptive thinking in some people who gamble (see Chapter 6). The impact of the consequent gambling behaviour can extend to family members and represent a serious health burden for close relations (see Chapter 5). At a societal level, the impact appears to be significant and the costs extensive (see Chapter 3).

In order to reduce the impact of gambling, risk and harm-reduction approaches are currently evolving, which are often informed by approaches for other addictive disorders. Whilst a consensual, scientifically and legally grounded definition for this has not yet been adopted, the laws, programmes and practices that are put in place in accordance with human rights requirements, are recognised as its central features (see Chapter 7). Currently, prevention efforts, commonly termed "player protection" are argued to involve predominantly post-hoc gambling harm minimisation strategies (see Chapter 9) and the development of a comprehensive public health-oriented approach towards prevention and minimisation is felt to be a priority. The development of a matrix of indicators (see Chapter 14) suggests that certain effective measures, such as restricting the availability of slot machines and capping the return rate for certain games, are already deployed. However, other equally effective

Conclusion **173**

measures (limiting advertising, spending on betting or losses) are not currently used and, conversely, some weak or ineffective approaches (risk awareness initiatives) are practiced (see Chapter 15), leading to the conclusion that, presently, "responsible gambling" strategies do not appear, overall, to have a deep impact.

Within this book, we have considered how a successful public health approach towards harm reduction would include prevention, consumer protection and a range of possible interventions for addressing mild to severe gambling problems. A useful overview of the effectiveness of current initiatives is presented (see Chapter 8), and a stepped care model has been included as a helpful conceptualisation for services (see Chapter 10). Support systems should also take into account wider mental health needs (see Chapter 16), harm to others, particularly family members (see Chapter 5) and to society (see Chapter 3). Specific tools to identify harms (see Chapter 2), and neurocognitive models of gambling disorder (see Chapter 6) are a good starting point for understanding the impact of gambling, both on individuals and their concerned significant others. Similarly, cost analysis tools have also been presented (see Chapter 3), and the need for a more sensitive instruments has been highlighted. The importance of standardised and validated procedures in the early detection of problem gambling (see Chapter 12) and the potential approaches towards intervention have also been considered (see Chapters 11 and 13).

Further steps forwards

The work presented here reflects the growing momentum of a public health approach towards gambling. The main issues discussed imply further steps that could be taken, in order continue along this path. In particular, the conflict of interest that exists between various actors in the field has been recognised but remains to be placed the forefront of public debate. In order to encourage the development of a body of knowledge which is independent and unbiased, research projects and interventions which are funded by other means than gambling industry profits, appear particularly important. Where such independence is not possible, researchers could bring transparency to their work by documenting funding sources and highlighting any conflicts of interest arising.

A second theme that has been discussed is the need to rigorously evaluate interventions that are made as part of a harm reduction framework. Research projects designed specifically for this purpose would enable the identification and dissemination of best practice to ensure the effectiveness of framework components. The transfer of interventions to other jurisdictions would also be facilitated by this work.

Similarly, the need to identify a clear set of indicators to enable the monitoring and evaluation of public policies has been emphasised. Such an approach is important in order to build a framework, which is both clear and effective. The role of an independent body, or group, appears key to the success of this work, and several examples have been included in this book (see Chapters 14 and 16), which could be used to inform future efforts.

174 Cheryl Dickson et al.

Finally, with the development of higher-risk games, and easier access to gambling through mobile phones and the Internet, there is an ever-increasing risk to public health. This presents an important role for public policy in assuring that health promotion provisions are made. In particular, legislators will need to consider policy that is adapted to the current gambling environment and remain responsive to future developments.

Within this book we have touched on many core issues related to a public health approach for problem gambling. We hope that this work will encourage further consideration in the field and contribute towards the future evolution of respectful practices that are grounded upon the principles of human rights.

INDEX

Note: Page numbers in *italics* indicate a figure and page numbers in **bold** indicate a table on the corresponding page.

anxiety 19, 48, 50 63, 102, 105; public anxiety 8

biological vulnerability 56
blame 50, 51

chains of influence 8–10
Cognitive Behavioural Therapy (CBT) 108–9
comorbidity 31, 102, 105, 163, 165
compromised: knowledge 9–10; politics 10; public good 8–9
conflicts of interest 7, 153, 166; regulation of 10, 76, 170, 173; risk of 168, 169

deep democratization 6
depression: and gambling 25, 30, 48, 60, 117; in relatives 23, 49; as a risk factor 32; and treatment 102, 105
DSM-5 1, 33n1

educational initiatives 78–82
EGM 37–39, 95–96; and data collection 122; density 5, 41; market context 7; pokies 83, 95; structural features, 79–82 87, 95, 96, 106, 115, 132
emotion regulation 54; mechanisms 57–8; *see also* Gambling Space Model
European Union xviii, 73
expanded stepped care model 102, 106–9

gambling disorder 1, 165; and neurocognition 54–64; and pathological gambling terminology *33*; and social cost 24–33 *see also* comorbidity, pathological gambling, problematic gambling
Gambling Space Model 54, 58–62
game characteristics *see* EGM structural features

harm reduction: definition 71–6; historical context 71–2; *see also* public health approach
Harm Reduction International 73, 74
help-seeking 80, 97, 102, 103–6, 108, 109

incentive salience 55
incentive sensitisation 54–56, **59**, 62
Influence Market corruption 7, 10, 11
Internet *see* online gambling

legislation *see policy*
logic model 144–152
Loto-Québec 162, 164–6, 167

Monitoring Centre for Gambling (Observatoire de Jeux) 144
monitoring indicators 76, 118, 155–160, 163, *see also* logic model
Motivational Interviewing 109

176 Index

neuroscience 55, 61–62
nudge approach 112–13; applied to
    gambling 114–18

online gambling 40–41, 170; and
    behavioural tracking 123, 125, 128–136;
    interventions 86, 96, 102, 106, 108;
    opening of the market 121, 128, 162;
    promotion 39

pathological gambling 16, 103, 124, 144, *151*
policy xviii, 49, 64, 78; Australian 96;
    Canadian 162, 166–167; Finnish xviii;
    French xviii, 143–144, 153, *see also* logic
    model; gambling policy initiatives 82–84,
    87; and harm reduction 72, 73, 74; and
    influences 8–10, 94; involving family
    members 51; and minors 84, 144, *147–8*,
    149, 150; 154, 159, 170; New Zealand
    96; and *nudge* approach 118; Norwegian
    96; policymakers 42, 51, 125; and
    responsible gambling 154–5, 160; Swiss
    xviii, 120–1, 125, WHO xviii
pre-commitment 85–86, 96, 97
prevalence rate: of comorbidities 32, 105; of
    gambling disorder 5, 45, 112, 114, 118,
    118n1, 164; as a monitoring indicator
    148, 155–8, 163
prevention paradox xviii, 14–18
problematic gambling: and adolescents
    40–41, 170; distribution of gambling
    related harm 18–20, 41, 91–2, 94; and
    family 23, 45–48, 49–51; general impact
    5, 23; impact on children *16*, 49–50, 51,
    91; levels of prevention xvii–xviii, 103
Problem Gambling Severity Index 19, 86,
    103, 156
profits *see revenue*
psychobiology 62–3
public health approach: for alcohol and
    tobacco xvii–xix, 91, 96–7; barriers 9,

10, 11; burden 63, 112; evolution of 1,
    11; monitoring *162–170*, *see also* logic
    model; potential components 50, 78 87,
    102, 173, *see also* expanded stepped care
    model, *nudge* approach; stakeholders
    114, 170;
punishment sensitivity 56–7

research funding 9–10, 93–94
responsible gambling 153–155, 172–3:
    the discourse of 92–93; and individual
    responsibility 8–9, 80, 91, 92; and
    monitoring 159–160, 163–4, 166, *see also*
    logic model; from responsible gambling
    to harm reduction 1, 76, 97; strategies
    80–82, 86, 87, 93, 94, 121
revenue 95; derived from problematic
    players 155, 156–9; protecting state
    revenue 150, *151*; return-to-player 37–8
reward sensitivity 56, 58, 59

sawtooth oscillation 123
self-exclusion: evaluation of 133; initiatives
    8, 84, 94, 96, 108, 114; prediction of
    123–4
social determinants xvii, xviii
stress-strain-coping-support 50
substance use disorder xviii, 33, 55, 103, 105
suicide 23, 91, 117

theoretical model of gambling related harm
    14–18
treatment: involving family members 51;
    versus non-treatment assisted change
    103–6; *see also* Cognitive Behavioural
    Therapy (CBT)
treatment uptake *see* help-seeking

United Nations 73, 74

World Health Organisation xviii, 71, 73, 74